Don't you know there's a War on?

Voices from the Home Front

JONATHAN CROALL

SUTTON PUBLISHING

First published in the United Kingdom by Hutchinson in 1988 as
Don't you know there's a War on?
The People's Voice 1939–45

Copyright © Jonathan Croall, 1988, 2005

British Library Cataloguing in Publication Data
A catalogue record for this book is available from the British Library.

ISBN 0-7509-3698-3

Typeset in 11/13.5pt Sabon.
Typesetting and origination by
Sutton Publishing Limited.
Printed and bound in England by
J.H. Haynes & Co. Ltd, Sparkford.

For Lesley,
with great love

Contents

List of Documents

Acknowledgements

The stories which appear in this book are drawn from interviews with people who responded to my requests in the national and regional press for information and memories of life on the Home Front. I made it clear to them that I was especially interested in the experience of schooling of both adults and children, the working lives of women and the issue of opposition to the war, especially conscientious objection.

I'd like to thank wholeheartedly the hundred or so men and women who talked to me. It is their book much more than it is mine. With some interviews, I have been able to use most or all of the material. With others, it has only been possible to use a sentence or a paragraph in the section headings. I'd like to say an extra word of thanks to those who were kind enough to give me hospitality as I travelled around the country. I'm also grateful to Laura Kamel at the Imperial War Museum for helping me to trace some of my interviewees, and to Dieter Pevsner for making constructive and helpful comments on my first draft.

For permission to reproduce original documents I am grateful to Jack Murrell, Olive Markham, Jean Drew-Edwards, David Hopkinson, Ethel Weeks, Mary Davies, Kay Ekevall, E.A. Penny, Frank Mayes, Doreen Weeks, Alex Bryan, John Emburton, Arthur Lockwood, Betty Watts, Prudence Wendt and Pat Kettle. For permission to use illustrations I must thank – in addition to the interviewees – Nick McCarty, Arthur Lockwood, Helen Briggs, Godfrey Stott, Alan Staley and Douglas Beavor.

Introduction

We lived at last in a community with a noble common purpose, and the experience was not only novel but exhilarating. We had a glimpse then of what life might be if men and women freely dedicated themselves, not to their appetites and prejudices, their vanities and fears, but to some great communal task. . . . We were, you see, better people than we had thought.

J.B. PRIESTLEY, BBC Radio, 17 May 1945

'Don't you know there's a war on?' was a familiar catchphrase. . . . The tobacconist retorted with it when customers complained about the shortage of cigarettes. 'Doesn't she know there's a war on?' asked the clippie when a well-dressed woman fussed about the lack of seats in the bus. 'Don't you know there's a war on?' asked the irate Churchillian householder when an Independent candidate appeared to solicit his vote.

ANGUS CALDER, *The People's War*

War was a permanent feature of the twentieth century. Today, after the events in the United States of 11 September 2001, and the subsequent alarming increase in terrorism worldwide, a new fear has entered our daily lives. Yet for most of us war exists only as a phenomenon played out on our television screens. It's an experience at once vividly immediate and curiously distanced, made more so by the battery of maps, statistics and computer graphics by which reporters and presenters attempt to explain the ebb and flow of the conflict.

Looking back to the Second World War, we find a very different experience. Between 1939 and 1945 the British people were exposed to the realities of war to an unprecedented degree. Virtually every man, woman and child was in the firing line at some point during that traumatic time. Never was this more obvious than during the months of persistent German bombing of London and other cities, the period of the Blitz. The casualties were of course enormous: indeed, until halfway through the war, more women and children had been killed than soldiers. The effect on family life was often devastating. This was a people's war with a vengeance.

In the late 1980s, fifty years after the outbreak of the Second World War, I talked to over a hundred men and women who survived those years of living dangerously on the Home Front. In selecting thirty-five of their stories for inclusion in this book, I wanted to provide as wide a range of experiences as possible, with a particular emphasis on home life during the Blitz, evacuation, the problems of schooling, women at work, survival techniques, conscientious objection, and other forms of opposition to the war.

To my surprise, many of these men and women claimed that the war was the most meaningful period of their lives. It brought fulfilment, a sense of adventure, even excitement; the common danger gave a shape and a purpose to their lives that they have rarely been able to recapture since. It was, one man suggested, 'the last time we were all happy'. Yet in other cases the recollections I was offered were distinctly downbeat. For some, it was essentially a time of nothing more valiant than endurance, of 'making do', of deprivation, restrictions and boredom. For others, while there was certainly intensity, it was to be found in the frustrations and dis-appointments they experienced, perhaps through an ambition being thwarted, a relationship abruptly severed, an education cut short, a childhood missed.

Human memory is a complex mechanism, and often a profoundly unreliable one. The recollections of observers of the wartime Blitz have provided some striking examples of the problem of long-term recall. During the early 1970s the Mass Observation organization resumed contact with some of its volunteer wartime observers. It asked them to re-write their experiences from memory, so that they could be compared with their original accounts of the bombing, usually written down the morning after. Not only were there substantial differences between the two versions, but one observer could not even remember having been in Coventry during that momentous time in the city's history. He was amazed to read his own detailed account of a lengthy visit he paid during the worst of the bombing, and the conversations he recorded at the time.

From this kind of comparison, Tom Harrison, Mass Observation's wartime director, concluded that 'the only valid information for this sort of social history of war is that recorded at the time on the spot'. If this argument is accepted, it would clearly reduce drastically the range of sources on which historians could draw. I believe, however, that the argument is a flawed one. It fails to take into account a different set of 'contaminations' affecting the contemporary observer. The Mass Observation reports were not simply private notes, but written for a specific purpose, often at moments of great danger. Being 'on the spot', while often enabling the observer to provide accurate detail and plenty of colour, has its own drawbacks when one is trying to catch 'the truth' of a situation.

Yet how can we be confident about the authenticity of personal reminiscences offered by people looking back across the span of nearly half a century? I think it depends what you mean – as one member of the wartime radio programme *The Brains Trust* famously put it – by authenticity. There is evidence to show that the greatest loss in the ability to recall accurately experiences or information comes in the early stages of the process. It seems, for example, that we may remember almost as much about the facts of an incident forty years later as we did one year after it took place. Yet personal reminiscence is not just about verifiable facts, though these play an important part in enabling us to test authenticity. It is also about people's values and opinions, and how they see their past experiences in relation to the present. Part of our culture consists of what people make of their own past, what they choose to find of value and significance. The existence of a shared view of the war years as some kind of Golden Age provides its own comment on our times.

While personal recollections may indeed be flawed in certain respects, they are certainly no more so than other kinds of record used by historians to interpret the past. As A.J.P. Taylor has rightly put it, 'All sources are suspect.' Those which emanate from official historians, civil servants, politicians, academics and journalists – in the form of reports, memoranda, memoirs, surveys, journal or newspaper articles – each have their particular bias and omission, depending on the explicit or implicit purpose of the individual record. Curiously, this problem is rarely acknowledged by conventional historians.

Another particular value of the personal recollections of ordinary people is that they provide us with a different perspective on the past. Instead of the broad sweep of events, the analysis of changes in policy, and the generalized discussion about the behaviour of nations used in conventional histories, we can find out what effect the actions of the famous and powerful had on the fabric and quality of people's everyday lives. In particular, we get glimpses of the changing patterns of personal relationships – between men and women, adults and children, employers and employed – that can reinforce or call into question conclusions reached in works using the more traditional sources.

There is a specific benefit to be gained from using oral evidence, as I have done in this book, and as many others are now doing for other periods and groups. It's a method which enables the historian to, as it were, argue with his or her documents. Under questioning, people will often modify their original statement, come up with a telling detail that they themselves had forgotten until that moment, or shift into a more confessional mode. I recall a moment in an interview with one woman who had been a child during the war. We had been proceeding for an hour or so, steadily though not spectacularly. I put a fairly routine question to her, after which there was a significant pause. She then told me that her father had been killed by a bomb while she was in bed at home. From that moment the interview took on a different colour; but it had taken an hour.

Oral recollection also enables the individual to tell a story in a manner very different from that which he or she might use if they were writing down their experience. Stories really demand a live audience. In any case, for most people writing is a much less natural means of expression. Our print-based culture and education system tend to downgrade the verbal arts, of which story-telling is one of the most potent. Oral recollection puts the story back into history.

Few general books published about the Second World War have used this method of gathering evidence. There have been several local history or oral reminiscence projects that have focused on the period, which have resulted in a booklet or pamphlet that encapsulates the memories of a group or community. Pete Grafton's book *You, You and You!: The People Out of Step with World War Two* uses this method to capture in particular the mood of resistance to the war effort, while Studs Terkel's panoramic oral history *'The Good War'* includes a few interviews with people who were in Britain during the war. The best-known social histories of the war, such as those by Angus Calder, Norman Longmate, Arthur Marwick and Tom Harrison (see Further Reading), have also focused on the experiences of ordinary people, but have relied almost entirely on written documents. There is of course no inherent superiority in either kind of book, but it seems to me worthwhile to try and restore the balance.

The people whose lives feature in this book are not a representative sample of the wartime civilian population, nor were they ever intended to be. For one thing, they were self-selected. For another, I wanted to look at distinct areas of experience, such as home life, schooling, women at work. I also wanted to explore in parallel to all this the notion of resistance to the war effort, especially as expressed by conscientious objectors, some of whom went to prison for their beliefs. My project therefore drew in those who felt they had something specific to offer under one or more of these headings.

I believe that these thirty-five accounts of wartime life, selected from a much greater number, all have something special to offer: everyone's life is interesting in some way, as is their ability to re-create it and reflect on it. Each account can of course be read for itself, but I have put them in a particular sequence, which I hope will enable the reader gradually to build up a detailed picture of how ordinary people survived those extraordinary years.

Home Front

My father was killed in an air raid in our house one evening in 1940.
The Council said my mother could have assistance with the burial
provided it was in the borough cemetery. But that was a long way
away, and she preferred to have him buried in the local churchyard.
So they said, sorry, we can't help you.

LONDON GIRL

Before the war my mother used to go to tea parties where the ladies
would gather with their hats on, and sip tea and play hands of bridge,
and have maids around. That sort of thing never happened again. For
one thing, all the maids disappeared.

MANCHESTER BOY

Make do and mend was my star turn. I got great tufts of below-
standard sheetings and made them into little jackets for all the
children I knew. Every blessed scrap of anything was sewn on to
them, and padded with all sorts of nonsense.

DERBYSHIRE WOMAN

I have a vivid memory of standing at our front door one evening
after a Blitz the previous night. The whole street was deserted,
everyone had gone in buses to outlying areas to sleep, in village
halls or in the fields. It was the most eerie feeling, and I remember
being very frightened.

HULL GIRL

We each had a butter dish, and my mother divided the butter out at
the beginning of the week. She had to do this because my grandmother thought that butter was there to be spread liberally, and no
one else would have had a chance.

MONMOUTHSHIRE GIRL

The Second World War was the first truly civilian war to be experienced by the British people. As a Mass Observation publication of the time put it, *War Begins at Home*. The dislocation of daily life brought about by the bombing, together with the problems of the blackout, shortages, rationing, travel restrictions and general austerity, placed an often intolerable strain on people. For women especially, with their men often away serving in the armed forces, and their children needing to be evacuated as many as three or four times during the war years, it required extraordinary courage and resilience to keep the home going.

The bombs of course proved the greatest threat, psychologically as well as materially. It was estimated at the end of the war that the average interval between air-raid warnings for the whole of the previous five years was only thirty-six hours. The physical damage was frequently devastating, noticeably in London, Coventry, Southampton, Plymouth, Liverpool, Hull, Bristol and Glasgow. Between September and November 1940, 3 million London homes were damaged or destroyed. By the time the main Blitz ended in May 1941, one Londoner in six had been made temporarily homeless. In all the major urban centres affected, those who had nowhere else to go had to wait in improvised rest centres, often with only a few possessions retrieved from the wreckage of their homes and the clothes they were wearing at the time. Yet the wait for new accommodation was often a long one: the repairs to damaged houses did not begin seriously until 1943.

Those whose homes remained intact had plenty of other pressures to contend with. Food rationing was gradually increased on basic items such as ham, bacon, sugar, butter, tea, margarine, fat, cheese, sweets, chocolates and other commodities. On the radio programme *The Kitchen Front*, and in numerous posters, leaflets and advertisements, women were exhorted to find a hundred and one ways to use dried egg or carrot, to experiment with patriotic pudding, parsnip wine and all-clear sandwiches. The government also encouraged people to 'dig for victory', in order to lessen the country's dependence on food from other countries. So vegetable growing suddenly became a majority pastime, with flower-beds, lawns, allotments, even bomb sites being harnessed to the drive for self-sufficiency. Another campaign, this time for salvage, pressed householders to give up their garden railings and their unwanted pots and pans for the war effort. Housewives were also asked to save paper, metal, tin, rubber, string, rags, bones and scraps of all kinds, which were then collected regularly by members of the Women's Voluntary Service (WVS), the Scouts and Guides, schoolchildren and others 'doing their bit'.

Restrictions were also placed on clothing, which was rationed from June 1941 onwards, to halt the steep rise in prices. The 'points' system introduced allowed people to buy the equivalent of one complete new outfit a year. However, the 'utility' clothing that soon appeared in the shops cut down choice even further, and people turned to second-hand shops and jumble sales to try and beat the all-pervading drabness and uniformity. Similarly, and in response to the government's plea to 'make do and mend', clothes were unpicked, dyed or recycled in a variety of ingenious ways, with imaginative use being made of material such as parachute silk and blackout curtain.

Petrol too was rationed at the start of the war, so that even those who owned a car – only one in ten families in 1940 – could travel neither far nor frequently. Those without their own transport were even more restricted. Seaside holidays mostly became a fond memory, as resorts in many areas were closed and train travel officially discouraged. If your journey really *was* necessary it all too often meant several hours in a cramped compartment in virtual darkness, with constant stoppages for air raids or alerts. Not surprisingly, there was something of a boom in walking and cycling, and hitch-hiking was suddenly considered respectable.

Inevitably, though, people's lives tended to revolve around the home much more than usual. Interest in reading and literature quickened, fuelled by the serialization of some of the classics by the BBC. Radio programmes such as Tommy Handley's *ITMA*, Richard Murdoch's *Much Binding in the Marsh* and Arthur Askey's *Band Waggon* kept people entertained through the bombing and the boredom, while *The Brains Trust*, J.B. Priestley's famous *Postscripts* and, of course, the news bulletins provided a regular link with the grim reality of life outside the home.

Despite the upheaval of war – and in some cases because of it – women went on having babies. The conditions in which they had to give birth, however, were often appalling. Even before the bombing started, the standard of maternity services in the voluntary and municipal hospitals was at best patchy, and in some cases prehistoric. Anaesthetics were rarely used for births. Nursing mothers would often find themselves in the same ward as sick children or elderly patients. During the months of the Blitz the luckier mothers were able to have their children in country houses specially converted into maternity homes for the occasion. The less fortunate gave birth to their children to the sounds of air-raid sirens and screaming bombs. Many hospitals suffered direct hits; expectant mothers frequently had to go down into the shelters, while nurses and doctors tried to maintain a basic service as the bombs fell around them. It was not, to say the least, an auspicious time to bring a new life into the world.

The City Mother

The health visitor came round, and she took one look at him and said, 'If I was looking after that baby at home, I'd be put in prison for that.'

Ethel Robinson

I lived in Liverpool during the war, and had two children. There was no National Health Service then, no free medical care. When I had Keith in Walton Hospital in 1942, it was a nightmare. They'd commandeered most of the hospital for the wounded servicemen, so we were put in a room that they'd just opened up. It wasn't properly equipped like the rest of the hospital. There were hardly any nurses, and the food was absolutely dreadful. Every morning you got porridge, but it was like Polyfilla. You got a glass of milk which was sour, always, and a piece of bread curled up at the edges.

But that wasn't the worst of it. They'd no clothes for the babies, no napkins or anything like that. So half the time they had old pieces of khaki round them, sometimes for a whole day. Half the babies got sore bottoms, and our Keith was in a dreadful state when I brought him out. Being my first baby I was terrified, I didn't know anything at all. They couldn't look after you or the baby, and they kept you in for two weeks, though there was no real need to stay that long. When he came out he was in such a dreadful mess, he had diarrhoea, there was no skin on him at all, he was just like a piece of liver underneath. His nails were septic, his mouth was covered with thrush. I won't forget all that in a hurry. The health visitor came round – we used to call them the blue ladies – and she took one look at him and said, 'If I was looking after that baby at home, I'd be put in prison for that.' I didn't say anything, except that they were short staffed, which they were.

It wasn't too difficult bringing up young children because we made a lot of things ourselves. You couldn't buy clothes because we had no coupons. But we used to go to rummage sales and buy old shirts and skirts, and then wash them out and cut them, and make their clothes ourselves. There were no sewing machines, you had to do it all by hand. We used to buy knitted things and unpick them and wash the wool, and re-knit them up for the children. Everybody did that. Things used to get handed round when people had finished with their clothes.

When Keith was born he had one of those gas masks made for babies, and we used to have to go down underground in one of those Anderson shelters. Sometimes you were down there for hours, listening to the drone of the planes. And then you'd come out and you'd see the whole sky lit up. It was really terrifying; you'd think, 'I wonder who's gone now?' I think that's why there were so many quick marriages, people thought there wasn't going to be any tomorrow. Lots of girls got married after they'd only known the man for a week. And then they wouldn't see him for four years, and they'd meet again as strangers. That's why there were so many divorces.

I got married in 1940: my husband was the manager of the pub opposite where I worked. We had our wedding breakfast in what is now the Odeon in Liverpool, but was then the Paramount. There were no wedding cars then, so we had to get taxis all the time. First of all we took one to the registry office in Broom Street. Then we took another to the photographer's in Lime Street, and while we were there the air-raid sirens went and the taxi disappeared, so we couldn't come out. Eventually we got to the Paramount. We were just sitting down in the restaurant and the siren went again, and everyone disappeared and left us sitting there, waiting for the meal. We had to sit there until the All-Clear went. After the meal we got into taxis again. It was chaos from beginning to end.

At that time I was working in Littlewoods during the day, on the ice-cream bar there. All the French sailors used to come in. We had a horrible manager, so when I got married I didn't tell him. You see, you weren't allowed to work if you were married, you had to leave. But I got hauled up on Monday and I was out. Before that I'd been on the football pools side, but when war broke out we were all fired – everything like football where there were crowds stopped, you see. I did various jobs then. I worked in the Dunlop factory for three weeks, and hated every minute; it was an awful spell. Then I went for a job with my sister, who was a power machinist. I had never seen a power machine, and I just hadn't a clue, you know. They put me on battledress, making epaulettes. Have you ever seen a power machine? Well, as soon as you do it, the machine just runs away with you. I didn't know what to do at all. I was only there three days.

Before I got married I was living with my mum in her herbalist's shop in Walton Road, and I used to work there six nights a week, while working in the day as well. We never thought anything about that, it never entered our heads that we should get paid; it was our mum's shop and we were helping her. It was open until twelve o'clock at night, but she had a hotel licence, so she used to shut at twelve and open again at five past. We used to have tables in and chairs round, and we used to sell draught 'sas' – that's sasparilla – and draught dandelion and burdock, in barrels. We had a big soda fountain downstairs and we used to pump it up. We used to have cordials, but it was in gallon jars, and really thick, like syrup. Also Oxo, Horlicks, all that sort of thing.

When we first worked there it was all civvies. But within a very short while all those young lads that used to come in were all in uniform. They used to come in from Burton's Dance Hall when it closed and sit round and buy pints of half and half, like a pub, and if you didn't get a top on, they wouldn't have it. There were a few fights, we had some windows smashed now and then, but they were lovely lads most of them. It was like a little community there. Even when the shop closed at twelve we all used to sit there talking. We used to have the ukelele, and the special customers would just sit there and sing. We had a lot of laughs in there, it was a great time for the people then. But a lot of the boys never came back.

My husband had wanted to go in the Navy, but he had spondylitis in the spine, which is a form of arthritis, so they wouldn't take him. He was shattered really, because he'd set his heart on getting into the Navy. When they found he had spondylitis, they couldn't give him any treatment, so he had to just get on with it. He had to give the pub up and go and work on the docks, repairing ships. It was horrible, he'd never done anything like that in his life, you see, and it nearly killed him. He had to climb rigging and climb over the ships' sides and things like that. Then, after the children were born, he had to go and work in the Royal Ordnance Factory, making guns on shift work, and he hated that as well. But he wouldn't go on the disabled list, not with the sort of jobs they offered you then. So he stuck it out.

Although he couldn't go to the war, he'd get a lot of women saying, 'Why aren't you fighting for us? My husband's out fighting for you.' Well, you just don't bother to answer; and these were the same women who were carrying on with all kinds. This was the abuse they used to get, men that were working during the war, a *lot* of abuse from women and other men.

There was a lot of thieving going on down on the docks, I suppose because they were desperate for food. As you know, we had to carry gas masks everywhere we went. My husband told me that one day on one ship there were some frozen hearts, and this chap had put a couple in his gas mask case, having left the mask itself at home, and they'd been in there all day, frozen. And the policeman stopped him at the gate of the docks and said, 'What have you got in there?' He said, 'My gas mask.' And the policeman said, 'Well, the gas mask's nose is bleeding.' The thing had started to thaw out, and all the blood was dripping out. That was typical of what went on. There was lots of good humour around.

There was quite a lot of black market going on – in eggs, butter, meat, bacon, and that sort of thing – for those that could afford it. I don't blame them, if they had the money. Of course the rationing was a bit of a bug really, but on reflection it was good for us. They do say it was a very healthy time. I used to cook a lot of my own stuff. You only got meat once a week, and I used to use a lot of dried egg and spam, a lot of stuff that came over from America, and was horrible. We used to have a lot of chips, but then potatoes were rationed, so you couldn't have a lot of that. But we didn't starve, and we used to improvise a lot, making pies and things, much more than you do now.

Of course we used to listen to the radio, to programmes like *The Man in Black*, with Valentine Dyall, every Saturday night. I used to love that, and also the plays. We also went to the cinema, although a lot of the films weren't very good really. But they were an escape: people queued for hours, and every picture house in Liverpool was full every night of the week. It was Betty Grable and a lot of war films and detective films and *This Happy Breed*. I used to sit there entranced and fascinated by all this glamour, with Jack Hulbert and Cicely Courtneidge and all those. My husband was in and out of work, and with the children we couldn't really afford to go to the pictures. But my mum used to have the adverts for the Victory and Queen's cinemas up in her shop, so she used to get a free pass, which we took in turns to use. I used to go out done up to death in my Woolies' earrings, with my bar of Cadbury's chocolate and five Woodbines for my husband. That was our night out, and we enjoyed it.

We also used to go to the theatre, mostly variety: there was the Rotunda, the Lyric, the Pavilion, the Shakespeare, the Empire and the Playhouse. I used to love variety: I suppose they were awful, but at the time it was all you'd got. Betty Turpin of *Coronation Street* – she was Betty Driver at the time – was a big star then. She used to come on at the Empire with this big white fur coat and two white poodles, on the same bill as Leslie Hutchinson – 'Hutch'. She used to sing Gracie Fields-type songs. She was very good, dripping with diamonds and very blonde and glamorous. I saw a lot of the stars there, we used to love going.

We used to live in just a little room, because there weren't a lot of houses around anyway. We went to live with his mum, but the house we were in got bombed in one of the raids. I remember that day there was a big crater right in the city centre, where there was a men's public toilet. Lots of servicemen had come home on leave and were down there when the siren started. All that was left was a hole. I remember going home to my mum's that morning, and all along Walton Road and County Road all I could see was windows smashed in, and police and ambulances. It was awful. Of course I was frantic by this time, until I got to my mum's. Her window had blown in, but fortunately they had been in the shelter and everybody was OK. But lots of other people in the street had died. Those were awful times, when people that you'd known, one night they'd be standing there having laughs and jokes, and the next day you'd be told by their friends that they'd been blown up. I think you try to block these horrible things out, but they are there.

My two youngest sisters were evacuated to Shrewsbury. It was just horrific for them. They were a little bit spoilt, and the woman they went to stay with wasn't nice at all, she treated them as strangers. Some of the evacuees really did well for themselves, but ours didn't. She was very strict and Victorian, this lady, and her husband was terrified of her. My sisters had to wash outside in the freezing rain water and that sort of thing. When we visited them they looked completely defeated and miserable and really unhappy. They *pleaded* with us to take them home, it was awful. So my mother did take them home. A lot of the evacuees touched lucky, you see, and got into good homes. Don't forget they were getting paid, these people, and that's all they did it for, lots of them. They wanted the money, but they didn't want the children.

But even though all these awful things were going on all around us, we always had this feeling that we were never going to give in, that we'd survive somehow. I think Churchill did that for us: he bluffed us, but still, he did it, he kept us going. He gave us all these yarns about what we had and what we didn't have – and we didn't have anything. He told us in his speeches that we were great, and that's all you need, isn't it? We used to laugh at things that we wouldn't normally laugh at: you had to, or you would have just gone mad otherwise.

Everybody kept saying the war would be over by Christmas – but they didn't say *which* Christmas. We just couldn't believe it on VE Day, we were all out in the street, you know, running around in circles. We just didn't know what to do. We couldn't believe it was all over.

The Soldier's Daughter

I had a terrible fear that when my father came home I wouldn't recognize him. I kept a photograph of him by my bed, and every night I studied it closely, kissed it good night, and put it to bed in a cardboard box with a blanket.

Jane Barham

I can just remember the day my father went into the Army. He left my mother holding the baby and myself standing at the front gate, and he kissed me and said, 'Be a brave girl, and help mummy.' And I remember my mother and the baby crying like anything, and me biting my lip and trying very hard not to cry, so that I should be a brave girl. I missed him terribly, but at least I understood he had to go, and that he didn't know when he was coming back. My baby sister didn't understand this, and she kept walking round the house asking for him all the time.

I was at the infants' school then. The headmistress would sometimes get all the children in our class to draw pictures or write little letters to the soldiers, and then she'd send them off to our fathers, and my dad used to write back to every child in the class. He kept one letter which a little boy sent him, which said, 'I hope the Germans don't shoot you!'

Once I went to the junior school I had to go 3 miles each day into Cambridge. The buses were very crowded, because very few ordinary people had cars, and you couldn't get petrol for them anyway. Sometimes I had to sit on somebody's lap, and I didn't like that. When I got off I had to walk about a quarter of a mile. Walking down Jesus Lane I went past one of the big houses the military police had taken over, and each morning I saw some of them sitting round their breakfast table in the semi-basement, and they used to wave to me. I'd been told not to speak to strange men, but I hadn't been told not to wave to them, so I used to wave quite gaily as I skipped past. One morning I was carrying a bunch of roses for my teacher, and there was one of the soldiers outside, cultivating the tiny strip of garden. And he said to me, 'I wish I'd got some lovely roses like that. Perhaps if I dig this well enough I can get something to grow?' I was too shy to answer him, but I took one of the roses and threw it over the railing at him. I was delighted when I went past the following morning and saw my rose in a milk bottle on the breakfast table.

The school in Cambridge was an old building. The teachers were elderly ladies, some of them past retiring age, but staying on because there was a shortage – there were no men on the staff, of course. We had lots of chanting tables, chanting spellings, it was Victorian-type teaching, but it was a very happy place. Sometimes we went out for nature walks on Jesus Green, but we did no geography, and very little history. Although I knew eventually that my father had gone to France and Belgium, I had a very hazy idea of where they were – just that they were across the sea. Books and paper and pencils were in very short supply and we had to paint on newspapers. I remember I learned to sew by doing cross-stitch on squared paper, which would tear every time you put a needle near it. It made me hate sewing.

On some occasions we had to file down the road to the shelters on Jesus Green. We had to keep a rug or a blanket in school to wrap round us in the shelter, because it was pretty cold in there. We also had to keep a dessert spoon with our name tied on the handle, so that we could be given a spoonful of malt or cod-liver oil. We also had little brown vitamin pills. Occasionally we had to bring a screw-top jar and it would be filled with chocolate powder from America. I remember we loved to dip our fingers in it and lick them clean.

We had school lunches in the British Restaurant in Jesus Lane. They were *dreadful*, macaroni cheese or mince with parsnips or carrots nearly all the time. One lunch-time we heard that Mrs Roosevelt was going to be coming along Jesus Lane. I stood at the side of the road to watch her. She came past in an open-top car, and the lady who was standing next to me said, 'Go on, wave, she likes to see little girls wave.' But I didn't want to wave to her, I just wanted to see what she looked like.

We had big open fires in the classrooms, and sometimes there was a shortage of coal or coke, so there was no fire, and we all had to sit with coats on or rugs round us and try desperately to keep warm. Because of the shortage of books, I remember having to read and re-read those Beacon readers, until I knew some of them by heart. The teachers were reduced to reading us some of their old school stories. We had *John Halifax, Gentleman* and *A Peep Behind the Scenes* – some really old ones.

There were a few bad memories. I remember broken nights with gunfire in the distance, being hauled out of bed and hurrying downstairs to huddle under the table shelter, and then waking up in the morning forgetting that you were under it, and sitting up and hitting your head on the roof. I also hated the blackout. Sometimes after school I would go to a music lesson on the way home, and then have to walk home in pitch darkness. I remember one night I ran into a Negro soldier, and all I could see were the whites of his eyes and his white teeth. And I dropped my music and ran for home, really scared. He was probably as scared as I was. I also remember seeing a white US soldier – there was an Army camp just behind our home – and I saw a Negro soldier ask a white one for a light for his cigarette, and the white one refused the light and spat at him. That was the first time I had seen racial prejudice, and it really shocked me.

I also remember on my tenth birthday my father had sent me a present from Belgium. It was still wrapped up in a parcel, and of course you had to declare everything in the parcel, and he had put 'fountain pen' on the outside. When I opened the parcel there was nothing inside – the pen had been stolen. I was bitterly disappointed. There was a happy outcome, though, because the person next door gave me a fountain pen when he heard how upset I was, which was very kind.

A happier memory was when my grandparents were going to take me to the seaside, and in the morning they heard that the railway line had been bombed, so we couldn't go. 'Well,' my grandad said, 'don't be disappointed, we shall go to the seaside anyway.' And he went along the road to where some building work had been done and came back with a bucket full of sand. He filled an old tin bath with water outside in the yard, and he taught me how to make little paper boats to float on the water and let me make sandcastles in the sand with an old cup. And he cut bread and butter into tiny little sandwiches, and labelled them Paste and Jam, and we pretended that we were at the seaside. I've never forgotten that day – although I'm sure that if I'd gone to the *real* seaside, I'd have probably forgotten all about it.

I have happy memories of going into the countryside and gleaning corn for our chickens, or blackberrying or picking rose-hips for rose-hip syrup, or going out for bike rides and visiting little country churches. Sometimes we went to the Botanic Gardens, where we walked down the five 'wishing steps' in the rock garden. I remember my first four wishes were always the same – 'I wish Dad would come home', 'I wish Uncle Robert would come home', 'I wish Uncle Sid would come home' and 'I wish the war would end.'

I remember one day at school my father walked in and asked the teacher whether I would be allowed to go home for the afternoon. He'd come home for forty-eight hours' leave unexpectedly, with a driver and a jeep. They took me outside and put me in the jeep, and because they weren't supposed to take civilians, I was told to bob down and not show my head above the window. It was very exciting going in the jeep and having my father there for the weekend.

Uncle Robert was my favourite uncle. He used to read to me and tell me stories and play with me. And then he went abroad to North Africa with the Eighth Army, and I didn't see him for about four years. I was staying with my grandparents when at last he came home on leave. And when he walked into the room I didn't recognize him; this tall, brown soldier was a total stranger to me. Everybody else was rejoicing, and I sat in the corner, realizing that this *must* be Uncle Robert, but not knowing him. After a moment he came and spoke to me, and all was well. But from that moment on I had a terrible fear that when my father came home I wouldn't recognize *him*. I don't think I ever told anybody that, but I kept a photograph of Dad by my bed, and every night I studied it closely, kissed it good night, and put it to bed in a cardboard box with a blanket.

Another happy memory is the end of the war, on VE Day, when my mother took my sister and me on the bus and walked us across Parker's Piece to hear the bells of the Catholic church ringing out after six years of silence. Later we went into King's College Chapel to see the stained-glass windows, which had been put back in their rightful place, and were letting in the sunlight. And on VJ Day I was at Clacton, seeing the sea for almost the first time with my young aunt, who had decided it was safe enough to take a holiday. They had a display of fireworks and rockets which we watched from the end of the pier, and it was so exciting to see all the bright colours, and to realize that the war was over, at last.

Letter from a soldier with the BEF in France to his brother-in-law

26 November 1939

Dear Jack,

I am very pleased to hear from you and to know that you, Doris and your baby are quite well. I must make it my duty to see the baby when I get on leave, which starts on the 17th Dec, of course that does not say that I will get leave then, the 17th is when it starts. I might not get away for a week or two after that, but I would like nothing better than to spend Xmas with the whole of the family, even for a day.

Well Jack I thought of you it must be hard for you being on your own. I expect it is worse for you when you get home at night from work and I do hope that Doris will soon improve and return home.

Well Jack I have seen no fighting yet and do not wish to, the only thing I want is peace like us all. This France is nothing like I thought it was, the roads are like nothing on earth, the fields are like ponds, the weather, well I leave that to you. I am none the worse off for being called up but we get digging every day sometimes coming back wet through. The trenches we have dug have to be pumped out every day sometimes 2 per day.

I have just received a letter from your mum and I thank you for leaving the 2/6 for me, when we are out here there is nothing better than receiving letters from those one thinks a lot of and to know that you are all well.

I think this is all for this time so I will close trusting that when this letter reaches you that you, Doris and the baby are quite well and happy.

With the best of luck to you all.

Your brother-in-law

Syd

The Country Mother

We lived very well, we were very fortunate, we hardly suffered at all. But life could be very lonely.

Gwendolen Potter

My husband was a clerk on the Great Western Railway, and we were living in Hayes. When war came the staff were evacuated to Aldermaston, and we heard of a lock house going on the Kennet and Avon Canal, between Savernake and Wootton Rivers station. The GWR owned the canal in those days, so we went to live there. It was called the Brimslade Lock House.

Coming from an all-electric house in London to lamps, candles and no laid-on water supply made for a hard life. My sons were six and eight when we arrived. They had to go to school in Wootton Rivers, and walk along the canal path in all weathers, which was slightly different from going to school on the estate in London. At first the village children hated them, and treated them rather badly at times. They had new macs that winter of 1940, to go on that long walk, and I think the local children were a little bit jealous, and they put them in the ditch. Another time one of the boys got a broken finger from having his fingers trodden on.

When the London evacuees first arrived, they were met on the station by the minister, and he stood there and said, 'Welcome to Wootton Rivers', and one of the London kids said, 'Cor, what a name, Rotten Rivers!' The children kept coming and coming, especially after the heavy bombing. As more and more came we had some sleeping not only in the house but in a tent on the lawn, which was lent to us by the WVS, and camp beds. Some of them soon went back, they didn't like it at all.

But my children soon grew to love the country, and by the end of the war they were quite hooked on it, and so was I. It was a marvellous life for boys. There was a spinney at the side of the house, a stream, and of course they made dams, and had bonfires at night. We used to go and collect moorhens' eggs along the canal. In the winter when it froze over and the oil man couldn't get down the hill with the van, the boys took an old chair up to Burbage Wharf bridge with the cans, and the vans waited for them and filled them up, and then they brought them back on the ice. They loved everything about the country really. They loved the flowers in the local copse – they couldn't get over the snowdrops when they came, and then the celandine and the bluebells and the other wild flowers. They would make a flower show on the sideboard in cocoa tins and jam jars.

The village school consisted of two rooms, the Big Room and the Little Room, with just the two teachers and outside loos. There were no school dinners then, and the children who lived outside the village would bring their own. The teacher used to have a kettle on and make the children mugs of cocoa, or they could take soup and she would put the saucepan on the big iron stove in the centre. She also used to dry the children's clothes if they got wet. She was very good like that. But I remember her being cross if your exercise book was full up too soon, as there was such a shortage of materials. They had to scribble on everything, and use up all sorts of odd bits of paper. My children were quite bright, and every time the teacher asked questions they were the ones who answered. In the end they had to stand outside the door sometimes; she would put them there to give the others a chance.

Once I called them in for dinner and there was no reply. I found them in the copse by our garden, looking into a field where a cow was calving. We all watched and they were very excited, and I thought what a lovely way to learn about birth. Not long after I met them one day from school, and they came rushing up to me and said, 'Mummy, Mummy, can we have a baby sister? Bryan Ponting has got one.' So I laughed and said, 'Well, I can't do that by myself,' and they said, 'Oh, we know that, you want daddy, he's your buck and you're his doe.' I asked them how they knew about this and they said that Mr Nutting the local vicar had told them on a visit to the school.

We became almost self-sufficient in the lock house. The garden was already cultivated when we got there, there were fruit trees and fruit bushes and a strawberry patch and all sorts of things. We used to give a lot of the food away to friends. We did get people coming round and asking us if they could have some beetroots or onions. These were people who had come down from London to get away from the raids, walking by and seeing us busy in the garden. We were generally lucky because tradesmen came out to the lock house: we had a butcher and an oilman who came, and a grocery lady from Burbage who drove a rickety old van; she came about three days a week and brought us bread. We had chickens and all our own vegetables and later on a goat for milk. So we lived very well, we were very fortunate, we hardly suffered at all. But of course there were some shortages, and we did have ration books. I remember going to the food office in Marlborough and reporting the greengrocer for not letting me have any tomatoes because he said I wasn't a regular, which I couldn't be when I was so far away. Of course he then had to let us have one tomato each.

I also got very annoyed once because boys from Marlborough College would come down and skate on the ice when the canal was frozen over. Petrol of course was very short, and they would come down in a huge car and this young madam who used to drive would park right in front of our house, so that we couldn't get in or out. In the end I wrote a letter to the *Marlborough Times*, which was published, complaining that they could get petrol to bring these boys out to skate when other people couldn't get it at all. There was a bit of an upset about it: one or two people wrote nasty letters to me, but other people applauded me for doing it.

The Women's Institute was the focal point of the village; you could always get ideas there about what to make out of what. Most of the women were walking about without stockings on, you just couldn't get them. But we also used to get together in each other's houses. I remember one Christmas time we made the children quite a lot of toys out of knitting wool – most of my youngest child's toys were knitted clowns, policemen and soldiers that the ladies of the village had knitted. I was quite an expert myself on making do and mend. People used to bring things to me from the village and say, 'What can we do with this?' – an old coat, perhaps, from which you could make a lumber jacket for a boy or a skirt for a girl.

We used to get up concert parties in the school. We would dress up as cowboys with all the hats and sing Country and Western songs. There were dances too, although the blackout stopped quite a lot of social life. It was mostly women dancing together, of course, although there were more men around there than in some other places because it was a farming area, and farm workers didn't get called up.

There were all sorts of upsets over the evacuees. They used to say that they wet their beds, and there were complaints about this when the village people met up. They would complain about their behaviour. Most of them were good to the evacuees, but one or two were quite cruel to them, and a lot of the children were very upset.

I remember also there were some conscientious objectors living on the edge of Savernake Forest, and they were not liked at all. They used to come down fishing on the canal sometimes, and there was a great furore. They had a very bad time with the local people. There was one family of COs, they were living in a very isolated place – most of them worked for the Forestry Commission – and nobody would ever speak to them. People just said, 'Oh, they're conchies', and if they appeared in the village they didn't seem to want to mix with them. I felt sorry for the wives really; I don't remember ever seeing them come to any of the social occasions.

We had some German prisoners of war working in the fields, and I had a bit of a brush with one of them. I felt a bit sad for him really. He came across my garden and opened the chicken house door, and obviously took an egg and put it in his pocket. I felt terrible really, but I thought, 'Well, my children after all . . .' So the second day I saw him coming across I went and told the foreman, and of course he called him up and he had two eggs in his pocket, and he made him give them back. I felt a bit mean about it, because when the prisoners came to get water they showed us photographs of their children. I felt sorry for them because they didn't want the war any more than we did. In fact they were very kind, and they made us all slippers with plaited string. They measured our feet on newspapers and took the patterns away and made them at the camp.

Life could be very lonely, especially during the day when the boys were at school and my husband out at work. We listened to the radio ever such a lot, we were great ones for *Friday Night is Music Night* and *Saturday Night Theatre*, we were mad keen on that. But often the battery used to run out in the middle, and we hadn't got any electricity. The only heating we had was the old kitchen range in the main room, but later we moved that to the outhouse and made it into a kitchen and had a big open fire. And we had an engine to make our own electricity and a pump for the water. But when we first arrived you had to take a bucket into the garden and put it under this drip, which came out of the side of the bank into the stream – this turned out to be a land drain. Washing day was terrible, because you had to go to the canal to get all the water. You can imagine bath night. In fact we used to bath the boys in the canal if the weather was good.

We only had one enemy aircraft come over, and it dropped its bombs in the fields past Marlborough. The only real fright we had was when the railway bank caught fire from the engine sparks. We would rush out with buckets and fill them in the canal, and form a human chain to put the fires out, as they would have been a landmark for enemy planes to bomb the railway. We also had a big explosion on the railway siding at Savernake. I remember I was at a meeting in the chapel at Wootton Rivers and the door blew open. We all rushed out to see this huge column of smoke, and heard further explosions – it was the ammunition dump in the forest. When I got home I found most of the ceiling flaked off in the house, and the light down on the table. Some of the local fishermen came and helped me clear up.

When you look back you seem to remember all the nice parts, but there were quite a few times when you were really fed up with it all and wished you could get away. My mother and father had a shop in Strand on the Green in Chiswick, and I went back to London once. But we had a dreadful night, about fifty bombs came down around the area, so I was glad to get back to the country again.

POEM WRITTEN BY A YOUNG MOTHER

Battle of Words

There's too much talk of war,
Too many fighting words;
There's no peace anywhere
Neither in bed nor chair
Nor down green lanes.
Let us be quiet, or
We'll lose the joy of birds,
The swallow will swoop
And kestrel wheel and loop
Like enemy 'planes';
Window and open door
Will speak the fear of flight
And guns will sound again
In April drops of rain
That spit at night.
Let's curb our tongues before
Our panic-stricken sight
Makes each wall a shield
And every mustard-field
A death-bed bright.

The Shopkeeper's Son

Having been brought up in a depressed area, we never had much, so we didn't miss a great deal when the war started. In fact many children, though not myself, were slightly better off.

John Howell

I was brought up in a typical Welsh valley mining community. I was only eight when the war broke out. One thing I recall quite vividly is going on holiday with my parents and grandparents to Paignton in the summer of 1940, and on the sea front set back from our hotel there was a big green area, and there were soldiers parading up and down. It was the first time I realized there were soldiers involved. Not long after we came back from holiday my father was called up – which is of course why we took that holiday then.

Although my father had to go into the Army early on, I was never short of men in the house, being a very close community in the valleys, as you can imagine. In a way it was an exciting period. You've got to remember that we'd gone through the Depression, and then suddenly work started to come to the Welsh valleys. It wasn't just coal; all my family were in the steel works, and both of these were reserved occupations. So not many men left the district.

There was an air of excitement about it all. I didn't understand it at the time, it was just another fight. I remember on the local rugby field we had a platoon of Indian soldiers, and they did an exhibition on horseback with their lances, galloping at speed and spearing blocks of wood. Also – and this was much more laughable – I can remember a couple of exhibitions of the Home Guard when it was in its infancy.

Things became much clearer from the time I went to the local grammar school. In the valleys every village, every town had its grammar school, and mine was very close to where I lived. It was a very deprived school, though we didn't see it that way then. Looking back I realize that all the teachers were old; there were very few men, and a lot of people who had retired were called back to teach. There were some very odd characters. Some of the teaching was appalling, quite abysmal. But what they did was bring in teachers from the elementary schools to take over, and some of them were very good and well-qualified teachers, some of the best we had. Of course, the Welsh valleys have always been a breeding-ground of teachers, and in order to get back into the valleys teachers would be prepared to take any sort of job. The elementary schools had some very good staff in them, so it wasn't a great hardship for them to move into grammar schools.

I remember the black market during the war very vividly. You used to be able to kill one pig, and you would have your rations deducted accordingly, but people always used to kill two and hide one. The local butcher would come and kill the pig, and the food inspector would come to check up on how many you'd killed. We used to hide one side of bacon under the shop window, all wrapped in muslin; there was a false floor there. It was the best bacon I've ever tasted.

Having been brought up in a depressed area, we never had much, so we didn't miss a great deal when the war started. In fact many children, though not myself, were slightly better off, because everyone had their fair share of butter; there was a fixed price, and children who'd never known what butter was suddenly started to acquire a taste for it, because it was part of the rations.

In 1938 we'd bought a hardware and ironmongery business. So when my father was called up I had to help with the business. Hardware stuff used to be delivered in great crates to the railway station. They were very big crates, and they used to be brought down on a dray. It was double summer time then, and I can remember being up until ten or half past ten at night – I was only ten or so – helping my mother unpack these great big straw crates. I was working very hard, having just started at the grammar school during the day, and helping my mother run the business at night and at weekends. I didn't know what a social life was as such, although I was very well looked after. I was fortunate to have very good grandparents. I had a younger brother who was only four, so my mother had to look after him, but I had an uncle in the steel works.

I recall a feeling that people in reserved occupations were getting the best of it, when a lot of men had to go away to the war. There was a lot of ill feeling at the time, I remember that even at a young age. I also remember that my Sunday School teacher was a conscientious objector, and I think he was incarcerated for a short while, but then released. He was a bit of an oddball in many ways. On the whole I don't think people worried too much about him, there was no question of tarring and feathering or anything like that. I can't say he was victimized in any way, because he'd made his views very clear from the outset. There was one man who certainly was put in prison for his views. I learnt afterwards that he was an avowed communist and he spent quite a bit of time in and out of prison. He used to speak against the war at public meetings, and I think he caused a lot of resentment. I can recall that after the war, when they were starting up the urban district council again in what is now the parliamentary seat of Islwyn, this man stood as a communist for the council, and took a pasting. I can remember that his attitude to the war was thrown in his face during the election. He got very few votes.

As boys we used to play a lot in the street, and some of the games were quite dangerous ones. We used to throw stones at each other in gangs, and we had a game called 'Catty', where you shaped a stick with two sharp ends and hit it with a bigger stick to see how far it would go. We also used to play marbles, but never with real marbles; instead we used ball bearings which we got from the steel works. We were very near the river, though there was never any fish there, because it was filthy dirty with all the effluents and coal dust. So another thing we used to do was collect coal dust that used to come down the river and congregate on the side – it was known as 'duff'. We used to collect this in buckets and make it into bricks to burn, because although we were in a mining community there was a shortage of coal, it was all needed. There was also a cinema, the Palace, and we used to pay tuppence to go in on Saturday morning. But as I got older I had to work in the shop with my mother on Saturday morning.

My mother had only worked as a housewife before the war, and yet she turned out to be a very good businesswoman. My grandmother lived not very far away – no one lives very far away in the valleys – and she used to come down and do a lot of the cooking and cleaning. I remember one thing I had to do was clean the old black-lead grate. One of my jobs was to get the polish and cleaning brushes and get the lead dust off. I also had to light fires. It was very primitive. Monday was wash day. I used to have to help light the fire and do the boiler – an old copper, as we used to call it. It was damned hard. We did have electricity, but only just – it was only in one room. Initially the electricity board came round and put one light in everybody's house free. Otherwise it was gas, if you were lucky. But we had nothing upstairs in our rooms. I remember the floors being very cold, because the only thing we had on them was lino. It was always cold in the winter, we used to use the old linen sheets, and they were like bloody icebergs to get in – we used to jump in and kick around to get warm.

But there was an element of luxury as a result of certain things that came in during the war. One thing was the British Restaurant. We had one up the valley, and I used to go there on Wednesdays when my mother had to go in to the warehouse in Cardiff. It was excellent, the food was good, the cleanliness was amazing. All right, it was solid stuff, but as a young boy that was what I needed. So I used to look forward to Wednesdays. And then they opened a canteen at the school, and those meals were excellent too, they were the one good meal we had a day, spotted dick and a lot of shepherd's pie.

We walked everywhere in those days, because there was no public transport, and a car was quite an event. I remember the doctor had one to do his rounds, but few other people had one. The local tradesman might have a van or a lorry, but on the whole we tended to walk everywhere. An outing for us was to pick a nice day in the summer and go up on the mountain and have a picnic. People who could afford it actually built huts on the mountainside, and that became their holiday resort. Or we might go out picking wimberries. We used to make our own amusements. The local hall used to hold dances, old-time dances mostly. I can also remember in school one very old thespian coming, a sort of Bransby Williams character who did monologues.

I remember prior to D-Day the road was lined with tanks and Army trucks, over a mile long both sides, full of convoys ready to go to Newport Docks and Cardiff Docks. The Americans had been there for a year or so, waiting for the invasion, I suppose. They had a billet on a very old piece of scrap ground on the main road. They were living under tents. They mixed very little with the local people: most of them were coloured, and there was strong discrimination against them, people tended to shun them. Of course we had never really seen any coloured people in the valleys before.

I can recall the VE celebration, that was a bean feast, we had a marvellous celebration down at the Salvation Army hall. Food suddenly appeared that we'd never even seen. I think a lot of it had been hoarded, and was suddenly unearthed; some of the tins were rusty by the look of them. I can remember that night walking up to Cross Keys, which was the next village, and celebrating on the bandstand. For some reason everybody congregated up there, and an impromptu dance started.

I don't think I resented having lost out on my childhood, because everyone was in the same boat. In a community like ours everyone was very much on the same level. Class distinction in a mining community is very, very narrow. In the valleys you know just about everyone. OK, some people might earn a little bit more than you did, but basically it was a one-class system, up to and during the war. You see, everybody helped each other. Since the war the class distinction has grown, I think. When I go home I see rather more of it than I did before.

I don't think my generation has an accurate view of the war. I can remember certain sad occasions, when families lost children because of the bombing – we were fairly near to Cardiff, which had a lot of bombs. I remember we used to hide under the stairs when the sirens went. But on the whole we tend to remember the good parts. I think it's like pain: while you're enduring it, it's terrible, but in retrospect you tend to forget it, the mind tends to close things out because they're uncomfortable. So the things I remember were the things I enjoyed. I think you become very selective in that respect.

Two Nations

During the evacuation, when all these children who were sewn into their vests in September or October and didn't take them off till the spring came from Newcastle and Manchester, a woman wrote to *The Times* saying, 'The evacuation has caused us to lift the stone and see what is crawling around underneath. Let's make a promise that at the end of the war we won't just put the stone back.' That represented very much a feeling people had.

HERTFORDSHIRE MAN

The country boys had never seen London children. You'd have expected great polarization, persecution, jealousy. But none of this happened. My particular friends were very often the local fellows. We weren't treated as outsiders.

LONDON BOY

One of the things that most impressed itself on the London evacuees was all the talk of the locals after just this one bomb had dropped on the town. They themselves were battle-hardened veterans of London's East End during the September 1940 Blitz.

ESSEX BOY

I would never, never, never countenance having a lot of children away from their homes like that. It was very difficult indeed, your lap was never big enough. If you picked up a child that had fallen down, you had six others climb on you straight away. You couldn't give them enough love, you just couldn't.

LONDON WOMAN

Some 4 million people, the majority of them children, were involved in evacuation away from their homes at some point during the war. This sudden, enforced mingling of the population caused a massive cultural shock to all concerned. It revealed the enormous differences in social behaviour and attitudes between the classes. It also dramatically highlighted the disparity in living conditions endured by many families in the cities and large towns, compared with those of the more prosperous rural communities.

Before war was declared the government had divided the country into three categories: evacuation areas, reception areas and neutral areas, the latter having neither to receive nor send evacuees. The first evacuation took place in September 1939, with a further wave in the summer of 1940, when invasion threatened, and another during the period of the V1s and V2s towards the end of the war. The scheme essentially aimed to move children away from the urban centres most vulnerable to the German bombing, to the comparative safety of the small towns and villages in rural areas. Children under five, who made up the bulk of the evacuees, were normally accompanied by their mothers. School-age children were evacuated en masse with their schools, under the supervision of teachers.

While it soon became compulsory to receive evacuees, evacuation itself remained voluntary throughout the war. This posed an agonizing dilemma for many mothers. Firstly, should they go at all? Secondly, if it was best for the child or children to go, should she go with them, or stay behind and try to keep the home running until their return? Their problems were exacerbated by the very small amount of bombing that occurred during the first few months of the war, a period which was nicknamed the 'Phoney War'. This fact, together with homesickness or a dislike of their new surroundings, drove a large proportion of the evacuees back to their homes by January 1940. Many then refused to leave again, even at the height of the Blitz: as one mother put it, 'We'd rather be bombed in our own homes than live this awful country life.'

The evacuation also failed for other reasons. Firstly, while all the transport arrangements had been well worked out, and on the whole operated smoothly, the government seriously underestimated the ability of the authorities in the reception areas to cope with the influx of newcomers. While many did the best they could in the circumstances, it was only because of the prodigious efforts of such organizations as the Women's Voluntary Service that the results were not more chaotic than they were. Secondly, there was a disastrous lack of understanding of the evacuees' human needs. All too often the reception committee that met them treated the occasion like an auction or a cattle market, with the less personable or attractive children invariably being the last to be found a home. Thirdly, too little thought was given to placing many evacuee families in appropriate homes, even though this would clearly be a difficult task. The result was a huge number of chronic mismatches, which in turn led to further problems.

For many middle-class homes in the reception areas the wretched condition of so many of the evacuee children came as a tremendous shock. Those from the poorer families were often unwashed, infested with lice, and dressed in shabby, threadbare or dirty clothes. A few were still sewn into their undergarments during the winter months. Their appearance, together with the way in which they talked, ate and behaved in general, provoked strong adverse reactions among the local people. Some complained outright about the imposition; others mistreated their 'guests' cruelly in subtle and not-so-subtle ways; and there were plenty of examples of householders finding ways of not taking any evacuees at all. The billeting officer's lot was not a happy one, and he often became a highly unpopular figure. Among other problems, he had to face the very justifiable resentment that arose when some of the gentry with larger houses initially managed to avoid taking evacuees in.

While many evacuees found a warm and sympathetic reception awaiting them, there was a substantial number whose lives were made a misery. Not only were they often separated from their parents, they were having to live in a household run to very different rules and with very different expectations and standards from their own. Bed wetting became a widespread phenomenon, which in turn led to further complaint among the host community. In general, though, the children adapted better than their mothers to the strange surroundings. Mothers found it particularly difficult to carry on their normal maternal and nurturing role under someone else's roof. Life indeed seemed to be more problematic for everyone if the mothers remained with their children, and many soon returned to their own homes, leaving the children to the not always tender mercies of their 'foster mothers'.

The evacuation seems to have brought out the best and the worst in the British character: tolerance, sympathy and generosity on the one hand, selfishness, rigidity and snobbery on the other. Yet there was at least one happy consequence. The exposure of the conditions in which so many of the urban poor lived provoked a widespread feeling that something had to be done to reduce such inequalities. It was a feeling that was soon to be translated into practical action and reform.

The Scholarship Girl

*She was a very sadistic woman, she used to hold my sister's
head under the water, that sort of thing. So one day we ran
away.*

Cynthia Gillett

During the war I went from junior school to the grammar school; I was
the first one in my family to do so. The whole scheme was to better
yourself. Fortunately, when I did eventually pass the illustrious scholarship
my mother was having an affair with her boss, who of course provided the
finance. You see, even if you passed the scholarship, if you couldn't afford
the uniform, well, it was just not on. So I did very well out of that
situation, because it enabled me to have quite a different sort of life to what
other members of the family did.

In the 1930s my family came out from inner London to one of those new
Wates places in the suburbs. My maternal grandmother had been a parlour
maid in London, she used to come up from the country in Kent. She had a
very large family, she had thirteen children, and my mother was one of the
oldest. She had me when she was in her teens, so there were always all
these aunts who were only six or seven years older than me.

I always lived with my grandmother, who was a very strong influence.
She looked after a lot of children. She took in lodgers, and did the doctor's
washing so that she didn't have to pay the doctor's fees. She ruled everyone
with a rod of iron. She was a great one with a copper stick. She used to

have a big rota for washing up, and she used to bash people with the stick if they didn't do their turn. She was a real good working-class Tory, and Mr Churchill was absolutely *the* one. She was also very anti-communist, and she always stood up when they had the national anthem on the wireless. I remember her also saying, 'Don't talk when the King's on the wireless, the poor man stutters, and you'll put him off.'

All this was very much the attitude at school as well as home, at least in my junior school, which was in Woolwich. The headmaster was into the war in a big way. His son was in the Air Force, and he was *tremendously* patriotic, and we all had to sing 'Land of Hope and Glory', and 'Jerusalem', which was his favourite. He had a wind-up gramophone and records of patriotic marches, which he used to take out into the field. I can see him now winding it up, and we would march off smartly to the music. I think he liked to see his little private army marching round.

I remember one teacher at the school whose husband was killed in the fighting. There was a great to-do, and we were told not to speak to her when she came back, because she'd cry. One of the other teachers was called up into the Auxiliary Territorial Service, and I remember she came and stood in assembly, and we all went over her uniform. And when the headmaster's son won a medal he came into school, the citation was read, and everybody had a day's holiday. There was a little wooden stand with a book on it for assembly, and if you got the scholarship to the grammar school your name was inscribed in this book. Each page would take twelve names, and the headmaster aimed to fill a page a year. That was quite heavy going, of course, so the pressure to get your name in the book was extensive. So when his son came in for the medal, I remember the head saying, 'You all could do great things if only you would get your name in this book. So learn your tables, only speak when you're spoken to, fold your arms and stand up straight.'

On Fridays you wore uniform, Brownies and Guides, and you saluted the flag as you walked round the field. Guides and Brownies played ever such a big part in the war, you know. You got a war service badge – I've still got mine. What I did was mix up cocoa for the air-raid warden and fill sandbags. You had to notch up so many hours to get this badge to sew on your uniform. I remember also there was something called the British–Polish Guide and Scout Friends, which was very, very strong because there were so many Poles here. They were very into scouting before the war in Poland, so you got tales of the Polish Guides, who were killing rats with their bare hands to feed their little brothers and sisters, while we were mixing up cocoa. The contrast!

I remember that if the siren went at home *before* midnight, you had to be at school at quarter to nine, but if it went *after* midnight you didn't have to be there until dinner time. The school shelters were on the playing fields in two lines, the first marked Mixed Infants, the second marked Juniors. I can remember that very vividly. It was very dark during the lessons we had in the shelters; I can still smell the horrid smell, very musty and damp. You sat in lines, and as soon as the siren went you lined off, 'Tallest at the back, shortest at the front, hands on head, single lines, no talking, lead off' – that sort of thing. The teacher went first into the shelter with a torch, and then once you were in you numbered off. As it was dark, lessons consisted of tables, and spelling was a great one. Also the teacher used to read by torchlight, she used to read stories and ask us questions about them. We also worked with bean-bags, passing them round, feeling them and estimating the number of beans. And you couldn't come out until the clock monitor had counted up to three hundred – that was five minutes.

We were evacuated twice during the war. The first time was to Edworth, a village in Bedfordshire, where we stayed for eight months. We were billeted in a manor house on a dairy farm. The parlour maid, who was the one designated to actually look after us, used to beat you for reading in the morning. I can remember getting really severely beaten for reading *Anne of Green Gables*. She didn't approve of working-class people reading, and anyway morning was for work, not reading. She was a very sadistic woman. I had this younger sister who was almost mentally deranged, a funny little girl. I had to look after her all the time, I was always hemmed in. My mother used to say, 'Promise me you'll never leave her.' The parlour maid didn't want to look after us, so she used to get at me through my sister if I didn't do what she wanted. She used to hold her head under the water, that sort of thing. So one day we ran away; there was a nice lady on the evacuation panel, and I can remember trying to find her in the village. The woman at the manor sent her son after us, so after that he had to follow us on the bus to make sure we went to school.

School there was quite different from London, because no one talked about the war as such. The only thing I can remember there is the rivalry between the kids from East Ham as against those from the Woolwich area, who were on different sides of the Thames. It was all, 'We've had more bombs than you' type of effort. I remember that we used to get two large pieces of bread spread with stewed rhubarb for lunch every single day. As there was only one room in the school, the door was closed at lunch time, so that those who lived too far away had nowhere to go. We lived a good mile's walk away, so if it rained we used to sit under these great enormous hollyhocks just outside the school.

The teacher was also very different. She had a bun and a long skirt almost to the ground, and a man's tie and a cane. She was ever so pleased that the war had come because it meant she had got some bright children. She kept saying 'Sharp as pins you are, bright as buttons you are.' I remember when we said that twelve people got the scholarship from our school one year, she nearly hit the roof. She had never had anybody go to the grammar school from her village.

One day the lady of the manor rang up my mother and asked her to come and collect us, as she was going to hold a ball and she needed the bedrooms. So we went back to London, and after I passed the scholarship I got to Dartford Grammar School in Kent. Only two people from our area went there. The headmistress was a Quaker, and so of course to her there wasn't any war. She ignored it completely, there were no such things as wars in her book. Her thing was the honour of the school, not the country, like old Mr Watts in the junior school. She never read the news at assembly or anything like that, as he did.

We were evacuated a second time to St Neots, which was then in Huntingdonshire. The reason was home background as much as anything else. It was a very haphazard life at my grandmother's. My mother was always rowing with her, and my grandmother was always having times when she wouldn't look after us, and we had to be taken to one of the aunties. Another time my mother was in hospital, and for a while we didn't go to school at all, but just stayed with my grandmother's younger sister.

The lady we were evacuated to at St Neots had been a parlour maid before she married. She was a pantry girl, and so everything ran just so. I owe a lot to her, she was a lovely lady, with rules, which had been missing in my life up to then – house rules, you know. At first she didn't want me as I was rather large, she wanted my sister, who was a pretty little thing with a snub nose and who hung on to me. It was like a slave market, that evacuation. I remember one man coming in to the village hall and saying, 'The missus has just had a new baby, we'll have a good strong girl to help her.' This lady only wanted my sister, but I was hanging on to my sister and saying, 'If you have her you'll have to have me, because I have promised mummy I won't let her go.' So she said, 'All right, but you'll have to sleep in one bed.' As we were used to being seven or eight in a bed, that was no problem.

When we were there we got a transfer to the grammar school in Huntingdon, which was quite a long bus ride. There were lots of evacuees there from all parts of London. It was very much Them and Us, because we stayed together in the playground, swapping war horror stories with the other Londoners. This was a mixed secondary school, which was very unusual at the time, and very frowned upon; at Dartford it had all been notes from boys up your knickers, that sort of thing. We also had showers, which was unusual. I can remember vividly seeing another girl in the nude for the first time; at my grandmother's you didn't get to be in the nude, or even mention things like that. I can remember seeing the girl's pubic hair, and it was red, and it was such a shock. It's funny what sticks in your mind.

There were two prisoner-of-war camps at St Neots. We were told not to speak to those in the German one. I can remember they had patches sewn on their grey uniforms, and how they would walk away if anybody came near them. It was quite different in the Italian one, where they wore brown uniforms; we were all encouraged to talk to them. I can remember they used to shout and stamp and clap and say to us, 'Come-along-da-fance.' They were ever so friendly, and we would watch them playing football. My aunt said it was perfectly all right to speak to the Italians because they didn't want to be in the war, and anyway they liked children, whereas the Germans ate them for breakfast, of course. The Italians were in great demand for joining choirs, so they used to go to the local churches and church halls, whereas the Germans I only remember walking away.

There was also an American camp there, and that made a tremendous impression on us, even though we were little, because of the films; we loved all the accents. I think nowadays people forget what a big part films played in our lives. We used to go to the pictures every day in London; my grandmother used to go every afternoon. They used to flash up messages on the screen, 'Telegram for Mrs So-and-so, please come out', and you used to get a free cup of tea and biscuits, they used to come round with a tray. The manager used to walk across the stage when the sirens went and tell us we could come back afterwards. It was all very casual.

You told stories a lot. We used to tell film stories to each other. I remember particularly I made *Spellbound* with Gregory Peck and Ingrid Bergman last a whole fortnight's lunch times. We used to take it in turn round the table to tell these stories. Music also played a very large part in people's lives. My sister sings very well, and we used to run concerts. At my aunt's we used to get up early and sing Handel's *Largo* as a duet, as a special treat for her. My sister was also a very good mimic and used to do impersonations. One of my many uncles played the accordion. He used to play Joe Loss things, and he would dress up as the Sheikh of Araby. He was a real showman. We also used to play a tremendous lot of party games just as a family group. Battleships was *the* thing, Tossing in the Blanket was another. Then there was Winking, Postman's Knock, and Fan the Kipper – that was a great game then.

The diet was good during the war, it was very high in fibre and very low in animal fat. I remember how my grandma used to let us choose how to have our egg – singular – boiled or fried. You could only have two slices of bread, although bread was not rationed. My grandmother, who was known as Old Mother Ding-Dong, because she was Mrs Bell, bashed the hell out of my mother once because she gave us a piece of cheese. You either had bread with marge or bread with jam, but not bread with both, and my mother broke the rules. I remember another time when one of my aunts wanted to go off with a married man, my grandmother locked her up with no food. We used to have to secrete food for her up our knicker leg.

If anybody got married of course you got extra ration points. Having all these aunts, we were always in the queue with the extra points. I particularly remember getting a tin of peaches, which was a real luxury. As my aunts all married quickly because the men were going off to the war, we were always having extra points for ham and things like that.

My grandmother had a tin bath by the back door which everybody threw any little scraps of bread in. Imagine, there were about fourteen people coming in and out of the house – she had lorry drivers as lodgers, who slept in the beds in the day-time; and we had them at night – when we weren't under the stairs or in the shelters during the raids. So you can imagine the dirt. At the end of the week my grandmother used to take out all the bread bits and make them into the most delicious bread pudding, on the theory that you have to eat a peck of dirt before you die.

We were always very sickly though, especially children from our kind of background. You can see in the photos we always have great sticking plasters where we had boils on our knees, and sties in our eyes, which of course is related to vitamin deficiency. You were always having to have these wretched sties lanced. I remember when we first moved to the country my mother said that the doctor said that it had made us – the walk to the school, being out in the air, and all those big thick slices of bread.

There was this tremendous feeling that somehow the war was changing your life absolutely, completely. And at the end I remember one of my aunts explaining to me how a National Health Service would work. My aunts all had boyfriends in the services, and of course they were all very keen to vote Labour after the war. Mr Churchill was OK during the war, but Mr Attlee was the one who was going to actually change things afterwards.

Extracts from the diary of a provincial woman, 1939

20 October. When I arrived in London it was a wonderful day with blue sky and sunshine. The balloon barrage looked magnificent glistening in the sunlight – just the day for a raid, as W remarked nonchalantly as he left the train. I wanted to go to Oxford Circus by tube, but that station was closed, and so I must travel by bus. As I went along I noticed the various directions showing people the way to air-raid shelters, with the number the shelter was capable of holding: room for 400 people, room for 800, and most terrifying of all, room for 1,600 people. I hoped it would not be my fate to dive into this particular shelter. Shopping in London seemed fairly normal, not quite such large crowds and everybody carrying a gas mask, but once inside the shops it was the same as of old.

Kensington Gardens seemed to be horribly mutilated by the mounds of earth thrown up by human moles busy with the very necessary precaution of erecting shelters. As I did not venture out at night, being unwilling to test the difficulties of finding my way in the blackout, London seemed to me to be a pleasant place to be in for a time, a place where one could bask in the light of a 200-watt electric light indoors, and turn a bath tap for boiling hot water, and sleep between smooth, freshly laundered sheets – an enjoyment due mainly to a contrast with my usual surroundings, and no bearing on the war. True, I heard occasional noises which made me wonder if an air-raid siren was about to sound, but really I had no fear, and the balloons floating like sentinels of the sky gave me an additional feeling of security.

17 November. Today I passed through London on my way to Oxford. London streets are strangely deserted, but the shops seem just as usual. On the way up I travelled with an RAF pilot. He had been out to France with the first detachment, had a smash, and come back to recover. He said that during the last war he had got medals for killing Germans, but that now he just felt sorry for them because they seem so lifeless and dispirited. This may of course simply reflect his own maturity, and not be completely indicative of the German nation. While he was in France he said he often flew over the Siegfried Line, and there was never a shot fired. They just took photographs of what they wanted.

On all the stations it is heart-rending to see young things in uniform looking very handsome and courageous, accompanied by parents and sisters and sweethearts who have come to see them off. On the return journey I travelled with five soldiers of ordinary rank, who were returning from 72 hours' leave, and were being shipped to France on Sunday. They were amazingly cheerful, in spite of being fed up and wanting this sickening war to end. It was dark when we left London, and the compulsory blue light was little consolation. However, they made jokes most of the way, such as: 'We have two shillings a day and all found – the trouble is we can't find it.' One of them had some very sticky sweets which he handed to us all. Another one had an awful hacking cough, and when they left the train and disappeared into the darkness, only this persistent coughing told me of their whereabouts as the train moved out of the station.

When I changed trains I had to wait three-quarters of an hour. The waiting room was practically dark, only a shaded night light at one end, at the other a small fire, and outside searchlights passing smoothly and silently across the sky. Such is life in the twentieth century, when all our energies are directed towards self-preservation.

The Town Kid

We were living four in a room, with just a mattress on the floor, no real bed. There were tin baths too, as the houses didn't have baths.

David Card

When war was actually declared, me and my brother and a whole crowd of us were outside Betteshanger Colliery just outside Deal, on the marshes. The sirens started up, and my brother said, 'Let's go.' I remember I lost a shoe in the bog, and we all hared for our new home. And there were our new foster parents digging this shelter.

We had only left London the day before. At the time I was at Middle Park Infants' School in Eltham, in south-east London. We had to muster there daily, and being only eight I had no clear idea what the hell was going on. On that Saturday as usual we had our little suitcases packed, and our little tabs tied on with string. Mine had a square on, while some had crosses and others had nothing; I never did find out what this meant. We were all given a large brown carrier bag, a tin of condensed milk, a tin of bully beef, a packet of biscuits and what seemed to me an enormous bar of chocolate. Things weren't very clever financially at home and we never saw anything like that.

We took off in coaches and eventually arrived in Deal, just round the coast from Dover. We were then packed off with the butcher's assistant with a little family in Deal. We were living four in a room, with just a mattress on the floor, no real bed. There were tin baths too, as the houses didn't have baths, which was not unusual for that kind of area at that time. We went to the school; it was a tiny one-classroom school, the old village school, which was crammed with kids. I remember the desks were all carved to hell.

But what really sticks in my memory was that my father came down to see us at the beginning of December. We went out on to the beach with the guy who was looking after us. I well recall my father pointing across the sea and saying to this fellow, 'What's that?' And the bloke said, 'That's the French coast.' And my father said, 'Oh, is it? Right, you lot, pack your bags, we're going back to London.' My father's view was that the Germans were coming, like it or not.

So we went back to London. I gathered later that whole lorry loads of kids came back to London almost immediately because of the problem of where they were put; housing conditions weren't all that clever. But in London most of the schools were closed and turned over for use as all kinds of headquarters. After a while we were given half-day schooling in people's houses. We were all mixed up in the age groups, and we would have one week in the afternoons and the next in the mornings.

Then in July 1940, after France had fallen, we were off again. This time the organization was better, we didn't seem to be hanging round much. The coach came and took us to Paddington station, which was absolutely swarming with kids, I can see the sea of faces now. We eventually arrived at Totnes in Devon. We were then taken to a school which was much plusher than I was used to, and all farmed out. We just sat and waited while rather busy local people in hats sent us off. About twenty or thirty of us were put into a small bus which took us off to Staverton, a village just beyond Dartington Hall. Then started what can only be called a bartering system. People who were in the know in the village would come and say, 'I'll have him and him and him.' My brother and I – he was four years my senior – were just left to wait and wait, and dusk was coming. Eventually we were put into a car and taken to the Luxons, a farm labourer and his wife.

The following day the village squire said he didn't want the girls who had been dumped on him, he wanted two boys. They came down to us and said did we want to move? We said no, and all this bartering continued. Brothers and sisters found themselves separated, all this sort of thing, although they did try to keep them together. We stayed with the Luxons and learnt a lot about the countryside, mostly from Mr Luxon, who was very kind to us. He used to take us out ferreting and things like that. My brother is still in touch with him.

The trouble started when we were put in the school at Staverton. It was another of these one-room schools. There were only two teachers, a lady teacher and her much younger assistant. She taught from the middle both ways, so to speak. She had two classes going on in the one hall, and her and the other girl would teach both ways. The place was virtually dictated to by the local vicar. Our head, Mr Goldsmith, came into conflict with him. There was this shout-up between the two men on the village green. It was mainly about who was going to use what, and all of us kids witnessed it. Mr Goldsmith had come down with his children, and as he saw it they were entitled to what was there. The village hall had been requisitioned, and he should be able to run it as he wanted. He obviously wanted to set up a proper school in the village. Looking back now it's easy to see why the vicar reacted like that, with the village suddenly inundated with all these children, and having the problem of where they were going to sit.

Mr Goldsmith was quite determined that his children wouldn't rot in the village. So people like my brother, who was comparatively clever, he tutored them for what was then the old junior technical scholarship. I myself had not learnt to read at that time. I was given very little tuition, and no one discovered until quite late that I couldn't read, because I had hidden behind this mate of mine who did my written work for me. It was my brother who knew I couldn't read and who used the newspaper to teach me. We had no reading book whatsoever. I was introduced to *Hiawatha*, for instance, by Mr Goldsmith reading it to us from cover to cover. This was his way of using the time up, because he had very little in the way of resources. We didn't have any books; what we were given was always *a* sheet of paper – it was always *a* thing. I remember our pencils were always collected afterwards, and because of overcrowding we never had the same desk. I don't remember doing any arithmetic. For music we went up to the village hall and had it with other kids, and that was when divisions arose, as the London kids were kept together. I don't recall any problems with the local kids, any problems were between kids who had come from different areas of south-east London.

I enjoyed being a town kid on a proper farm. We didn't have much contact with the war. I do remember the bombing of Plymouth, when we climbed the hill to look across, and we could see it being attacked. Also when there was an Army exercise, we kids got chased because we gave away some Army emplacements. And then my mother came down in a dreadful state from being in the Blitz, she must have been near to a nervous breakdown. She was an apprentice dressmaker, an exceptionally gifted but untutored woman. She was a real toughie, she looked after her own grand-parents. Later in the war she went and trained and became a very skilled detail fitter on bridge blocks in the Woolwich Arsenal. My father sent her down to visit us because she was in a terrible state, but she did go back.

My father was already working in some administrative job in the Woolwich Arsenal. He had been badly gassed in the First World War, and when he came out of the trenches he was blind for eighteen months. He suffered from chronic bronchitis and had TB. He was given ten years to live, but survived until 1962, but it had the effect of his being out of work for a very long time.

When my brother moved to Exeter my mother didn't like the idea of my being by myself in Devon, so I came back to London in 1941. But that's when the real problem started, as there weren't *any* schools by that time, and no children. We lived on this estate in south-east London, and there was nobody else around. Gradually the authorities started to pick up various children, and I then went to Cooper's Lane School, which was much farther away than you would normally go to school. The lower school was bricked up as shelters and the gym was a store room, so all we had was classrooms on the upper floor. To do woodwork we had to walk a couple of miles to another school. And as part of the school day we used to dig for victory. We had a big plot, though God knows who got the produce, because we never did, although we did most of the labour.

Singing, we were always singing; our assemblies seemed to go on for ever. Mr Daley, the headmaster, would talk at length about the war. He used to have a big map in the hall, and we would plot the progress of the British in the Middle East. I remember we adopted a freighter, and the captain and one of the crew came and gave us a long talk on it, and brought us things. We collected for them, we sent them comforts, so to speak. My mother used to knit socks and we'd take them in. That was done with great relish. We had lots of pictures of the ship, and I seem to remember there was a model of it.

The Blitz was over, but they started the daylight hit and run raids. The school was attacked two or three times. One lunch hour I remember the Yellow Nose Squadron attacked the school, and then went and bombed the next school in Hither Green and killed a lot of kids. Herbert Morrison did a broadcast telling the German people what a cowardly run it was. Our school was machine-gunned, and I well remember Mrs Jackson, who taught music, being under the table with a spoonful of spuds while I'm still standing there wondering what the hell she was doing.

We used to collect salvage and do a bit of fire-watching. One night my father and I were out the front of the house with our tin helmets on. He was standing on the concrete path in front of me, and some oil bombs started to drop. They came down in a kind of stick, and for some reason they seemed to be curling round our road – bonk, bonk, bonk. I was looking up for the next stick, thinking they were coming towards us, and my tin helmet fell off on to the concrete path. My father turned round and gave me such a blinking mouthful, because it made him jump out of his skin. He thought a bomb had fallen behind him. You can imagine the tension of those bombs coming towards us – they were very cheap and nasty incendiary devices they'd concocted.

When the night raids were reactivated we spent a lot of time in the shelters, and I did a lot of my reading at night, sleeping on the top bunk in the shelter, with my mother and father in another one down the road. They were quite nicely done up. But when my older brother came home on leave I was allowed to sleep in the house, because he wouldn't sleep down the shelter. But we went to school during this time, it still kept going even though we were raided.

As the war went on I did all the shopping and a lot of the housework, as my mother used to work very long hours; sometimes I didn't see her until late at night. I remember in one shop in Woolwich I was asked if my mother would like some ham. I said, 'Yes of course she would.' The woman in the shop said, 'How much?' Things like that just didn't exist, so I said, 'As much as you can give me.' So I walked home with a whole ham on my shoulder. How I wasn't arrested I don't know. My mother nearly had a fit when she saw it; it had cost a bomb apart from anything else. But she managed to resell a lot of it in the Woolwich Arsenal.

My mother was much more communicative than my father about what went on in the Arsenal. The black market was rife, and the women had the money (my mother was earning twice as much as my father) so they were always the target. She told me that once she and a friend were asked to meet a man in a wood. It was dark when she went there, and this guy passed over a box which purported to be 1lb tea – except that it was green China tea, which was utterly useless. My mother paid an enormous amount for it.

For a while we went down to Eton, to get away from the doodlebugs. I remember we went to the cinema there, to see *Gone with the Wind*. But when it came to the famous scene with Scarlett O'Hara walking across the dead and wounded, my mother says, 'I've seen enough of all this here in

London, come on' – and we walked out. The cinema only cost ninepence then, and it was even cheaper for children. But then we had a lot more cinemas; immediately around us we had the Palace, the two Odeons and the Gaumont in Lewisham, which was always the favourite. It was there that we used to see the Russian films that were sent over to boost our feelings about the Russians. *In the Rear of the Enemy* was one, and *The Kharkhov Trial* was another. They were propaganda films that were shown in ordinary cinemas.

I remember on D-Day my mother saying, 'They've landed.' But prior to that we kids had been involved with the convoys. We used to stand there for hours, being pelted with sweets. 'Give us some gum, chum', originated with us, though it wasn't just Americans, they came from all over. Once D-Day came the euphoria really built up. And even when the doodlebugs were falling later, the spirit was tremendous. I can remember sitting on top of the Anderson shelter Sunday lunch time. The doodlebugs always used to follow the same paths: one used to come up our road and the other used to come up to the bottom of the garden. So my brother would sit eating his Sunday lunch on the shelter, keeping watch, while we sat in the house. People say, 'Weren't you frightened of the doodlebugs?' But we weren't, that's the funny thing. Once we were scrumping in an orchard and one came out of the clouds; there it was looming large, and it hit the farmhouse. And all we were interested in were the chicken feathers coming down out of the sky for ages and ages afterwards. That was far more significant.

For us the war was over the day before VE Day. We had gone to Scouts that night and it was an incredible sunset, I can see it now. We came home and the whole place was euphoric. My sister was beside herself, her husband was safe. She got my brother's photographic light and hung it outside the window at the front of the house. She just wanted to do something. People were having bonfires, playing pianos in the backs of lorries. The crowds went potty. It wasn't organized, it was a purely spontaneous thing.

Extract from a letter to a friend from a railway worker in Cambridge, July 1939

In your letter you detract from the Chamberlain policy at a time when national unity is essential for the well-being of the country, I am told. Will you please stop doing that sort of thing at once. The crime of sedition ought to be extended to cover the spreading of doubt and dissension among His Majesty's subjects by persons intent on relieving their own feelings. It is well known that the people of Great Britain and Northern Ireland are at this time of one mind. If you ask any sensible person what he thinks (and everyone is deemed to be reasonable in England until he is shown to be otherwise), he will reply without hesitation, although despondently, 'I don't know.' And just when everyone at last is thinking the same way in this country, you set up as Propaganda Minister. What I want to know is, if war is a disease, why can't we bellicate ourselves with a Little war, and be immune from another Great one?

The Airman's Daughter

It didn't matter what I told them, I was still an evacuee. We were regarded in Stranraer as dirty Londoners. We did feel very, very ostracized and very different.

Jean Stafford

I was five when war broke out. I was going to St Mary's Church School in Ladywell, in south London. As soon as war was declared half-time schooling started – or rather, hardly-any-time schooling. I was just learning to read and had the reading cards, and I was most upset that nobody would help me. They were too busy rushing round deciding what to do with the blackout, or what to wear in the shelters. This apparently was very important, in case you had to go down in the middle of the night and the neighbours saw you.

The very sad thing that upset me was having all the dogs and cats put down. The vets had queues and queues during the first few weeks, and people brought the animals home in little brown sacks because there was nowhere to bury them. I didn't understand why this was, but this was the general panic at the beginning. But people were concerned about their animals throughout the war. One of my grandmothers looked after our cat in Beckenham. You couldn't get cat food or liver, so she used to queue for hours at the fish shop. The poor old cat actually died of old age, and on the exact time and day that my grandmother would have been queuing for this food, a doodlebug dropped, and both the fish shop and the queue were wiped out. So poor pussy's death saved my grandmother.

My other grandmother, who lived in Kentish Town, had a very big house with a large basement. She had made a little room under the stairs for the cat. It was covered in carpet to stop the sound, with an armchair and a little bowl of food, and every time the siren went they used to rush and put the cat into this little place. They told all the neighbours, so that if they were killed they'd know where to look for the cat. This was a mood that was very strong, you did *think* you were going to be killed, you did put your valuables in tin chests so they wouldn't get burnt. Some of the very elderly didn't want to leave their beds; they'd rather be killed in bed, so they didn't go down the shelters. The safest place, we thought, was under the stairs. We had special tables that were specially strengthened that you could lie underneath. But towards the end of the war nobody used them, we just thought, 'We haven't been hit, and if we are, that's it.'

I can remember going by underground train – my aunt lived in Kentish Town – and walking over everybody who had gone down there to sleep. No one took any notice of us, and we felt very embarrassed, as though we were in somebody's bedroom, with all the children asleep, and little tiny babies too. Everybody carried their gas masks, and some of us had posher ones; we had little rexine covers on them, which was rather good.

We all had shortages. I was quite pleased about the shortage of soap. I can remember my cousin, who was the same age as me, was learning housewifery at school, and used the whole week's fat ration in one swoop to make a cake or something, which upset everybody. Soap flakes and soap were very precious, but then we just didn't wash so much. My clothes were unpicked woollies knitted up again, which ended up with a very crinkly look. I never bothered, I was never very fashion conscious. All the wool used to be different colours. You almost had a fight to get anything like that. But it got to be so that it didn't matter, as long as you were warm. It was very cold, not having so much heating. I remember somebody pinched our coal supply, we saw their footprints in the snow. We were very upset about that.

I can remember the ARP, the Air Raid Precaution wardens, being particularly bloody-minded as regards putting lights out, especially with families where the husbands were away. When he knocked on the door and said, 'You've got a light showing', my mother used to shout up the stairs, 'Go and fetch Bill', and the warden used to flee, he thought we'd actually got a man in the house. They got very important and officious in the uniform. Nobody liked them, they were always regarded as the lowest form of life.

My father was in the RAF reserve, so he was posted straight away, and we went up to Blackpool. I was transferred to an ordinary class in the school, and was just treated normally. Then my father was posted to Stranraer in Scotland, and that was entirely different. The Scottish people are very much higher than us academically – they have academies, not schools – and I was regarded and treated as an evacuee. It didn't matter what I told them, that my father and mother were there with me, I was still an evacuee, we were regarded as dirty Londoners. We were put in one room and just given a book to read, and that was our sole education. I was only seven, but for our homework we had to learn parts of books, and of the Bible I remember having to learn the twenty-third psalm by heart. I sat up very late, my parents helped me, and I had it word perfect. I stood up in class to say it, and I started off. 'The Lord is my shepherd, I shall not want . . .' and I was told to sit down: the teacher said, 'That's the *English* version.' We did feel very, very ostracized and very different.

I then went to St Albans where my aunt lived; she was a nurse. I was taken to the usual school and everything was just normal again, except for the fact that we never had any heating, there was never any coal; we sat in our coats blue with cold, I remember. There were rules, very strict rules for anyone playing near the enormous square tanks they had for the emergency water supplies, and I can remember being caned for going near the tanks.

At the grammar school I went to later in St Albans we adopted a mine-sweeper, and the older girls knitted balaclavas and gloves and wrote to the sailors. The letters, the replies that came, were read out on Friday mornings in assembly. I can remember once a rather embarrassed captain or naval officer appeared, very red-faced and tongue-tied among hundreds of girls. He tried to thank us very much, but we all just stared at this officer. Also in assembly we always had to sing 'For Those in Peril on the Sea'; I always remember this, and feeling very affected by it, especially as at the time the convoys were being continually decimated. I can remember one of my school friends standing in the playground rather quiet, and the other children said, 'Oh well, his father was on the *Hood*.' We never gave much sympathy, we just accepted it, that was it, your father's dead.

In Blackpool we were in a boarding house. During the summer we were put in the attic, because the holiday-makers had the best rooms. One day, I was about six, I remember coming into the parlour, which was the best room (in Lancashire they had these beautiful parlours, with the chairs laid out), all the chairs were round the room, completely to the back of the room, forming a large square, and on them were soldiers, privates in battledress, very dirty, very grubby, very tired. And they just sat there with their hands on their knees, just looking down at the floor, and the landlady was rushing round with great mugs of tea. Nobody said anything, it was very quiet, and I was told to get out of the way and not annoy anybody. I eventually slithered in and danced round to the soldiers, and they half-heartedly talked to me. One gave me a handkerchief embroidered in France, which was very good, I thought, but none of them really wished to talk to me. They were all extremely tired, and this was a great puzzle to me. My mother afterwards confessed that she didn't want me near these men because they were probably carrying disease. They had of course come up the coast from Dunkirk and they'd just marched through Blackpool, and at every boarding house they stopped and so many were put in, and they sat there for about twenty-four hours, just waiting to be taken off somewhere.

All the little lads at Blackpool used to go on the beach and play war on the sand dunes. I always had to be the nurse; I always had to stay behind. One day I remember they went and made a huge harbour in the sand, and bombed it with bottles and bricks and shrieks of 'We're Pearl Harbour'. We always used to play the war games about whatever was in the news. We didn't know what it was all about, but we *did* enjoy ourselves, and the names we loved to hear were Timoshenko and all the Russian leaders, and de Gaulle. We knew all the names – our cat was called Timoshenko, I remember. Of course we listened to the programmes on the wireless, Tommy Handley and so on, and we loved the propaganda films, although we didn't know they were propaganda: *The Squanderbug* and *Don't Tell Anybody 'Cos Somebody's Listening*. It went to the extreme where nobody spoke to anybody in case you were a fifth columnist. Anybody who looked slightly odd was immediately almost arrested by the children. We played these games all the time about the war.

For me the best moment of the war was lying on the playing fields at school on a very warm June day and watching the planes go over, for hours and hours, it seemed. We knew something was in the air, and then we heard that the invasion had started. The worst moment was two of my friends coming up to me and saying, 'Our daddy's come home.' So we said, 'Where's he been, where's he been?' And one of them said, 'He's been in Burma, and he's a bit thin.' And we danced up the garden path and knocked on the door, and all stood round waiting to see their daddy. And then this *thing* appeared at the door, dressed in khaki. He was a living skeleton, with heavy trousers like a clown. He had a belt and braces and a thick army shirt, which gave the illusion that he was fairly solid, but he had stick-like wrists and the most terrible skull. We stood there, we just didn't know what to do, and then, worst of all, he smiled. And I think that smile will haunt me for the rest of my life, that terrible smile in that skull. And we backed away and went away, and we didn't say anything. And our friends never forgot that.

We met lots of soldiers during the war. There was a Polish flyer staying with us and his face was so sad all the time because of the family he'd left behind after the fall of Warsaw. Even as a child, the sadness on his face, I can still remember it. At the end of the war the Americans arrived in St Albans. They were very, very popular with the children, of course, because they gave us sweets, but not only that, they were such friendly people. They had time to talk to us, they had time to take us for walks and talk to us as *people*; they didn't seem to regard us as nuisances, which everyone else did. Their uniforms were always so clean, the two-tone with the jacket and trousers to us was far superior to the khaki and serge battledress that everyone else wore. The officers particularly, with their beautiful cream uniform and the darker brown jackets, appealed to us. Of course I was only a child, but the women, it knocked them off their feet. The Americans were so much more charming, they always wanted to please the ladies, always brought little gifts, chocolate – and stockings, which you couldn't get normally; I remember my mother painting her legs, and it used to run if it rained. At St Albans they were disliked intensely by the male population, quite understandably, I suppose. My aunt was a district nurse and a midwife, and she came back and told us some funny stories about delivering children. She delivered a black child once; one woman who got in that position was heard to remark, 'Well, I must have been frightened by a black man.'

There wasn't just the animosity towards the Americans, there seemed to be rivalry between the English soldiers, sailors and airmen. My father took me to the pictures at the end of the war – I can remember the film was *Bluebird* with Shirley Temple. There was an enormous queue outside the cinema, including a couple of dozen soldiers in uniform. My father wouldn't stand in the queue, we had to wait across the road. Being in the RAF, he felt so embarrassed and awkward with the soldiers, who started making comments about the boys in blue, Brylcreem, and all that sort of thing. It seemed to be extraordinary that grown men should be so petty, I didn't understand that at all. There were several instances of this rivalry; the pubs often had fights going on, especially between the RAF and the Army.

But during most of the war everyone was friendly, everybody cooperated, and there was a definite spirit that we weren't going to be beaten, that Hitler wasn't going to come across and kill us all. We were fighting for our lives, we knew that if Hitler got over we would be finished. When we saw the film of the concentration camps we knew that if we hadn't fought, if we hadn't sacrificed, if we hadn't stuck together, we would have been annihilated. My father took me to the newsreels of Belsen, Auschwitz and so on; he made me sit and watch them. I remember he said, 'You're never going to forget what they've done, never in your life.' And I don't think my attitude to the Germans will ever change.

Letters from a Lancashire school to the parents of an evacuated boy

The Grammar School
Stretford, Lancashire
11 July 1941

Dear Parent,
I believe your boy is very comfortable in Blackpool, and I hope you will realize the importance of keeping him there. May I also urge you to keep him there during the holiday period, for two reasons:

1. His personal safety
2. In order to retain the billet.

Billets are very difficult to find in Blackpool, and if a boy is taken away for a week the billet automatically becomes vacant, and the billeting authorities may find it necessary to put someone in his place. It also adds to the difficulties of the householders if boys go home and become unsettled.

May I urge you therefore to leave your boy in his billet during the holiday. If at any time circumstances make it desirable that he should be with you for one or more nights, a written statement to this effect should be sent to Mr Whitaker at Blackpool some days in advance.

Yours sincerely,
A. Dakin, Headmaster

Stretford Grammar School
At Palatine Central School
Blackpool
18 December 1941

Dear Mr Weeks,

Thanks for your letter. I'm glad you agree with my remarks.

I didn't see Norman until Tuesday and I had a talk with him. He seems to be, quite naturally, anxious to be home again – we should all like things normal again. He says he is very happy at school and likes his work (his report shows that he has benefited).

He is quite happy in his billet where Mrs Hedges seems pleased to have him.

I have really nothing more to add to my last letter, and knowing that you agree with its purport, the final decision must rest with you, and I suggest that you consider it from all points of view and let me know what your conclusions are.

We shall be sorry to lose him if you decide to keep him, and glad to welcome him back should he return.

Kindest regards,

Yours sincerely,
T.J. Whitaker

The Scholarship Boy

I was trying to balance these two worlds – going off at eight in the morning to my Hotspur-type day, and coming back at night to sit by the oil lamp and listen to the fifteen-year-old plumbing apprentice who had been out all day on his bike.

Dennis Briggs

We had been living in a Victorian terrace in Leyton during the Depression. My father was handicapped by the First World War: he was deaf, and had been unemployed for quite a long part of the Depression. There was a gradual process during the 1930s of things getting better. First of all my father got a job, though not a very good job. My mother, who was a tailor by trade, got some outdoor work and then some indoor work. And that spring of 1939 I think was a high point, when I was about to go to the grammar school. It was a feeling of joy that I can't recall experiencing since.

But then this awful decision had to be made. In the evacuation you had to decide whether you were going with your new school with staff you'd never met, or with the old school, which theoretically you'd just left. Because I was the only one from my junior class going to this particular school, I just didn't fancy going on my own, and I certainly didn't want to go with the old junior school. I remember a feeling of isolation, but the kids I would normally meet I somehow couldn't find at the right time. In the end it was agreed that I would go to the friend of a friend of a friend who had a place in the country.

As it turned out it was in this village called Daylesford, near Adlestrop, in the Cotswolds. So on 1 September, when the national evacuation was under way, I went off with my mother to Paddington station, and then to the country. We had to spend the night on Oxford station, and I slept in the ladies' waiting room, a fact which I talked about with inverted pride for some while afterwards, until I got my leg pulled about it, when I stopped. The following morning we picked up the slow train to Adlestrop, and then walked to Daylesford. There I met my foster-mother, and there I stayed for the next fifteen months. My mother stayed with me during the negotiations about where I should go to school, and it was agreed that I should have my scholarship transferred to the school for grammar school kids, which was Chipping Camden, 20 miles away. There was a Dr Barnardo's boy who was going there, who was fostered in a temporary way, but I was the only other child to go there from the village; all the others were going to the village school.

This hamlet was dominated by the self-sufficiency of the allotment – nobody ever *bought* a vegetable, for example, you found everything for yourself, and if you hadn't got it you went without. I think the only thing that was delivered was bread and meat, though once rationing started there was very little meat. The Co-op van also brought things on approval, so that if you wanted a new pair of shoes you told the man, who was really the baker, and the next week he would bring four or five out for you to choose from. The other thing that dominated the village was the church. Daylesford was a community of about ten houses at the most, with no shop; the only thing it had was a pillar-box and a church – not that people were particularly religious, but it was the only place where people could gather. If you went on Sunday, it was simply to say, 'Oh, so and so isn't there, she must still be ill, I better go across and see her.' It was a new experience for me to go regularly, and when I came back my foster-mother would want to know who was there and who wasn't. There was also a village hall, and in those early days of the war I went to it once to a Christmas party organized by the vicar. He stands out in my memory as somebody who I think recognized me as some sort of alien force with whom he could identify. He took me a couple of times in his car to see a film in Cheltenham, and this was quite a treat. I remember my foster-mother being a bit uneasy about this, though I didn't know why then. But he was quite a delight, and it was a tremendous change to go out with him.

Chipping Camden School was then very much a grammar school for local kids under sufferance. It was based on a very old foundation, and the whole approach was that of a boarding school. For me, brought up on boys' comics like *Wizard* and *Hotspur*, I could recognize this sort of thing coming through very strongly. To have local kids coming in for free who had just passed the scholarship, and were probably anxious to leave as soon as possible, wasn't welcomed by the head or the older members of staff, who I think shared the head's view. Within the school there were two sorts of boys: the boarders, who were clearly well known to the head, and then all these irritating kids, some of them, dare I say it, sons of farm labourers, who were very much first-generation grammar school kids, who clearly didn't like the school and whose one aim was to get out as soon as possible at fourteen or fifteen. So there was a lot of tension. That, combined with the fact that nobody in Daylesford had any idea where I'd been except that I'd got on a train to Chipping Camden, made for a very weird existence. The only reason I didn't worry overmuch about the place I'd left, and that my homesickness, when it occurred, wasn't all that persistent, was that I was trying to balance these two worlds – going off at eight in the morning to my *Hotspur*-type day, and coming back at night to sit by the oil lamp, and listen to Ernie, the fifteen-year-old plumbing apprentice, who had been out all day on his bike. Nobody knew about the sort of homework I was doing, there was no support of that sort. I knew that I wasn't happy, but I knew that my parents were very worried and wouldn't want me to be unhappy, and I was very conscious of not wanting to offend my foster-mother. I didn't say anything to her, though there was a week during the summer of 1940 when my parents came to stay, when I was very much tempted to say, 'I want to go back with you.' It was at this point that the daylight bombing of London started. But there was also the constant pressure of the view that I was in the best place, the stiff upper lip, you had to be glad about things if you weren't actually suffering. You had to grin and bear it, keep smiling.

I was very much aware of wanting the war to end. The strong ties I had with my peers in London had gone. Yet I couldn't lock in to the kids in the village, who were intrigued by this kid who brought home this case with French books in it. They were smashing kids, but I never really established a very strong friendship with them. The ones with whom I felt I might share certain things, I really couldn't get very involved with them, because they lived in odd villages and there was no access to them. So my friendships were really non-existent, and I hankered to know what my London friends were doing. I still feel that, I've never met them since, never caught up with them.

Then the Blitz became very bad, and my mother's sister appeared. From then on, with some frequency, various members of the family would appear. My aunt was the first, and she was in a terrible state from the bombing. She got temporary accommodation in the village. Then my mother and father had a bad time, the London house was blasted, and my mother came down for a short while, and then went back. There was this to-ing and fro-ing. Clearly it was very worrying and something of a risk to have my father on his own, as he was completely deaf. So there was an attempt to get him a job locally. This was the boom time when aerodromes were being built, and he got a job as a storeman in the local aerodromes. At this point we moved into a house as a family in the next village, which was Adlestrop. This house was even more primitive, because there was no sanitation, and although it had electric light it had no water.

In Daylesford the village had been opened up; we had a group of kids come from Dagenham in spring 1940. They were all laughed at because of the way they spoke, because of the things they did or didn't say, because of their clothes, by both the other kids and some of the grown-ups. I had this feeling of wondering how they'd looked at me when I came as an evacuee six months earlier.

I think the village, probably as a result of the war, became a little wider in its horizons. For example, when I first went the basic occupation was always within cycling distance, if you didn't work on one of the local farms. In Daylesford almost everybody did; they lived in tied cottages; the carter always had this house, the cowman always had this one. The only other thing which was possible was to actually get on your bike and become something fairly traditional, like a plumber's or carpenter's mate, and go through the process of an apprenticeship. Or in the case of the girls, like the daughter of the house to which I was first evacuated, you went into service. She would cycle home every Sunday morning to have her gear changed and her lace caps pressed by my foster-mother.

The war allowed people to have jobs further away, and many went off to the local aerodrome. The local lads of seventeen or eighteen would get some of these jobs and go off and make a lot of money. Some wide boys appeared and took digs in the village; presumably they were trying to avoid being called up. I remember one man, who had digs with us, who was working at the aerodrome, and quite a rogue he proved to be. He always treated me quite well, but I don't think he was very popular with my foster-mother, who thought he was a bit of a drunkard.

Daylesford House was taken over by the War Office and soon filled up with troops and Nissen huts in the grounds. The same happened in Adlestrop, so that in both cases there was an enormous population of soldiers just 'up the drive', and they influenced the village in lots of ways. First of all, from my point of view, it was, 'Have you got a cap badge, mister?' I'd moved on from cigarette cards to cap badges, which we used to put round our belts. Then, when the camps had a social event, they sometimes would need female talent, and so they would advertise a film or a dance – and even if it wasn't advertised, the word would get round. It wasn't very long before Adlestrop Camp, as the House was now called, became known for its social opportunities. They even had boxing matches, which my father used to go and watch. When you realize how isolated we were, for him to be able to go up the road to a boxing tournament, and then come back and laugh his head off at some of the things he had seen, was a very big change.

There were liaisons with local girls, and all the gossip and the rumour-mongering that this generated. Certainly in my house there was a feeling that the soldiers that people rubbed shoulders with were OK. I don't think there was any general resentment. It surfaced where an illegitimate child appeared, and then there would be a lot of gossip about that particular girl. In general the feeling was that it was a good thing that the soldiers were here, and that we all ought to feel sorry for them. When the Americans arrived the social events got grander, so that a dance put on by them, with all their facilities, was quite an outstanding event. Free coffee or ice-cream or cakes would come round to everyone – the generosity was quite extraordinary considering the privations people were suffering through rationing.

Rationing was quite tough. I remember the way in which things were counted out, and tins gloated over: if you had one tin of spam, the question was, when should you eat it? One of the things that marked our house out a little differently from the rest of the village was that we had relations in London, who kept appearing. My mother's uncles had been caught in a bombing raid and had suffered quite badly in a nervous sense from having to be dug out. When they came down they would be pleased to find that we could get eggs from the woman next door. So there would be a constant exchange of parcels: we actually used to wrap eggs up in newspaper, and then wrap that up in some box, and post a dozen eggs to my uncle in Bermondsey, and we'd get a letter back four days later, saying, 'That was lovely, only five were smashed.' This was considered some sort of treat, that seven eggs got through out of the twelve. The reciprocal arrangement was

e account holder

account

on form

ation. Please complete and ensure the cheque is

wn on a bank or building society account held by
e, or by a building society branch cheque or

a new cheque.

andhelp and we'll be happy to help. We're here
se. We may record your call to help us give you

that they would go round to shops in London and find odd things that weren't on the ration, such as Symington's soup tablets. Some very weird items would come through the post, but they were cherished.

As far as school went, there was a feeling that we were okay, that we were out of it. When important things were happening in the war, then at least one member of staff would draw our attention to it. The senior mistress rather fancied Churchill's oratorical style, and would say, making quite a meal of it, 'Did you hear Churchill last night?' I remember our being told about Pearl Harbour and that things were very bad. But I don't think the kids' morale was low, or that we felt threatened in those early days. I remember actually celebrating when France fell. I was on the field eating my sandwiches with another two kids, and someone rushed up and said, 'France has given in.' We thought this would mean not having to learn French any more, so we went round the field laughing our heads off.

We were very conscious of the men on our staff, and why they weren't fighting. We had one man join the forces who we loved very much. We thought he was a great teacher, very kind and gentle, and we knew that he was going into the Army. We had another man come to the school who was labelled a CO – I don't know if he really was, this was never verified. He went through hell, and eventually left. He was really pilloried by the kids, because we thought he should be fighting. It was very vindictive, a very nasty campaign, and I was part of it. He had a terrible time. The head took it very seriously and we were given a lecture about it. The other person who had a rough time was a French lady, middle-aged, with a very bad limp, whose command of English was very poor. She idealized Charles de Gaulle and could never stop talking about him. So as soon as she came in it was, 'Who's going to start on Madame?' Someone would have a picture of de Gaulle and would take it out to her, and she'd be off, going on about what a marvellous man he was, and we'd have no lesson at all. And if she didn't do this she'd get a barracking, someone would be planted somewhere to create a disturbance and she didn't have the command of language to control it.

At the ages of eleven and twelve we very much identified with the hero side of the war. When we wrote our names in our school exercise books, we would actually put things like Squadron Leader or Group Captain, and then start adding DSO and the two bars. This was a characteristic of 1940 and 1941, that we saw all these 'good' things about the war. If someone had an older brother who had gone, we were full of admiration for him. It wasn't until some of them that I knew as schoolboys went and never came back that the whole thing turned upside down for me.

I remember that of the three sixteen-year-olds that travelled with me on the train to school, two were dead before the end of the war. This I found very distressing indeed, that this could happen to kids who were almost my peer group. It became very disturbing. The atmosphere was very noticeable after Dunkirk. Adlestrop was on the main Worcester to Paddington line, and we travelled on the ordinary trains to go to school. So we met people daily who were either coming from London or going there. I recall one train which had a ghost-like quality, it was packed with troops who were quite ashen and didn't smile. They were like dead soldiers, and someone said that they had come from France. The whole train gave out this quality of lifelessness.

Blackout was an extraordinary thing to cope with for four or five years, never being able to go out without this tiny light from a torch. My father always kept a poker behind the door, because one didn't expect anyone to knock after dark, and if they did it might be a parachuted German. So the door was never opened without a poker in the other hand.

I left school at fifteen and went back to London for a while, and suffered some bombing there. I found that very, very frightening, a terrible feeling of helplessness. I hadn't been in an air raid in daylight, but the feeling of complete helplessness in the darkness in the house where I was staying with my aunt and uncle, I didn't like that at all. I would get a knock and they would say, 'It's started, I'm not sure if it's worth getting up yet, but if it's bad we'll go down the cellar.' Then there was this concern the next morning to find out where the bombing had been, if it was close, and then to go past and see the desolation and the stunned, expressionless people.

Since the war I have felt much closer to suppressed minorities, like Jews often are. I have great difficulty in coping with programmes about, for example, Belsen, or anything of that sort. I think this is partly because I went to school with quite a lot of Jews. I say to myself, I grumble about what happened to me, I think it was a tremendous disappointment which dashed all my aspiration at a stroke, but my God, fancy being a Jew in Poland, or wherever. And I think of the Jews at school who were smashing kids and big mates, and it makes me think what a terrible thing persecution is. And it's not a very big step for me to transfer back and say, I wonder what happened to the Jews with whom I went to school? Supposing instead of London I'd been in Berlin or Prague?

I think most kids who grew up during the war feel they missed out. I also have a feeling of displacement, of not belonging, of wondering where my roots should be, of missing a period of time.

Women's Work

My mother was a conventional woman, all her time was spent washing and rolling out the pastry. She never would have dreamt of wearing trousers before the war. Then suddenly she came in dressed in this serge uniform, for working as an ambulance driver.

CHESHIRE GIRL

I don't think people had time to be prejudiced against us. Also we did add a little light relief, a little decorative touch; flowers on our table and things like that, and such scent as there was, which wasn't much.

HAMPSHIRE WOMAN

A female mechanic was a revolutionary concept. All our instructors on the course had been men, who subjected us to a constant tirade of mockery. At the workshop eyebrows were raised so high and the scorn was so weighty that all but two of our group were at once intimidated into withdrawing into the calibration office, thus completely wasting their arduous training.

SOUTHAMPTON WOMAN

The attitudes of the women to work in the factory were very bad indeed. They had tried to strike, but they had been told that they would have to be compulsorily redirected away from their homes. So there was a lot of simmering discontent.

LIVERPOOL WOMAN

I saw a side of life I would never have seen. I met a man in a factory who was doubled up as he worked. I asked him if it was arthritis that made him like that. He said it was now, but that he'd been a miner all his life, and had been doubled up all his working hours. And I thought, this is something that ought not to be. It was contact with people like that which changed my views.

LONDON WOMAN

By 1943, around 90 per cent of single women and 80 per cent of married women were engaged in some kind of war work. This represented a remarkable change from the pre-war situation, both numerically and in the kind of jobs open to women. It also prompted a radical, if temporary, shift in male attitudes, both to the principle of women working outside the home and to the kind of jobs they were capable of undertaking.

Women had, of course, played a key role in the economy during the First World War, providing personnel in industry, agriculture and transport after conscription was introduced. But once the war was over and the men had returned from France, they had been compelled to give up these jobs. During the 1930s opportunities for work outside the home had been severely limited. More than a third of British women at work were in domestic service. Most of the rest were employed in the textile industry, the service and distributive trades, and on the assembly lines turning out cars, electrical goods and cigarettes. Women were excluded altogether from the steel, engineering and shipbuilding industries, either by legislation supposedly designed to protect them, or by traditional male attitudes. While the professions and the civil service were technically open to them, in practice they remained on the lower rungs and grades. For most women the pay was low, often less than half the male rate for the job. In addition, there was widespread prejudice against married women being allowed to work, even in areas such as teaching.

The needs of a wartime economy transformed this situation. The government encouraged, exhorted and, eventually, with some reluctance, compelled women to sign up to 'do their bit'. In December 1941 the National Service (No. 2) Act became law. Single women between the ages of twenty and thirty now had to make themselves available for vital war work by registering. A failure to do so resulted in being 'directed' into work not of their own choosing. Those who registered could choose to work in a munitions, tank or aircraft factory, civil defence, the transport industry, the Women's Land Army, nursing and other key occupations; or opt for one of the women's services such as the Women's Auxiliary Air Force (WAAF) or the Auxiliary Territorial Service (ATS). Women with children under fourteen were exempt, as were married women not living apart from their husbands – though plenty of women in both categories chose to take work anyway.

Thousands of women undoubtedly relished their changed lives, especially for the new horizons that were opened up for them. For many the chief attraction lay in the opportunity to earn additional money.

Others welcomed the independence the work gave them, or the chance to prove themselves in jobs that tested both their skills and their endurance. For many there was a desire to see new parts of the country, to escape from a humdrum life, or to meet people from different backgrounds. Most women entered their new workplaces for a variety of reasons, no doubt in the majority of cases impelled by an underlying desire to serve their country's cause.

Yet the work they undertook in their millions, while absolutely crucial to the war effort, was never a quarter as glamorous or exciting as the ubiquitous recruiting posters implied. In the factories the work was monotonous and repetitive, the conditions characterized by a lot of dirt, little air and even less light. On the land the physical demands were considerable, the conditions tough, especially in winter, the isolation sometimes extreme. In these, and most of the jobs now undertaken by women, the hours were long and wearisome: at one stage the average working week was fifty-seven to sixty hours.

A further bugbear was pay. Though women were often doing the same jobs as men, they were technically employed only as semi-skilled workers, and therefore paid at much lower rates. Thousands of women joined unions in order to battle for equal pay. Although they had some isolated successes, notably in the Royal Ordnance factories, in most occupations their claims were successfully resisted. Arrayed against them were the combined forces of the traditionally minded trade unions, the experienced male shop stewards and, not least, Churchill himself, who was violently opposed to such a notion of equality. This resistance led to widespread resentment and frustration and, occasionally, strikes.

Men were the problem in other spheres too. Some husbands retained their dislike of women being employed outside the home and said so, thus posing a dilemma for many women. Those married women who did opt for war work had an especially hard time of it, having effectively to cope with two full-time jobs in the time normally allowed for one. Those with children had further problems, since the factory crèches and nursery schools belatedly set up by the government after protests by women were not sufficient to cope with the demand.

Male prejudice at the workplace was certainly in evidence, though it would appear that in general there was a surprising readiness among men to accept the principle of women working outside the home in the special circumstances created by the war. Peacetime, of course, would prove to be a different matter.

The Railway Inspector

*I went along to a union branch meeting, and they didn't quite
know what to do with me, so they decided to call me 'sister'.*

Mary Wolfard

My father was B.M. Yates, who wrote *Winged Victory*, which was
published in 1934. It was his only book; it was about the life of a pilot
in the First World War, which is what he was. During the Second World
War pilots had nothing to read that would give them any insight into the
feelings of a pilot. I gather the book was changing hands at about £5 a
copy, which was quite expensive then, as it was out of print. It's called a
classic, it's been reissued and reissued.

My mother came from a comfortable middle-class background. Her
family were brewers, with maids and all that kind of thing. I remember that
my grandmother called all her maids Ethel, all her cats Tibby, and all her
dogs Matty – the lower orders were a kind of collective, and she couldn't
distinguish between them.

During the war I was working on the railways, which was quite unusual
for women. My first job was at head office in Newbury, where I was a clerk
in the claims department. Then I moved to the station-master's office at
Cirencester, which was quite interesting. If anyone claimed they had lost a
Spitfire or an engine – that was the sort of thing that happened, they were
packaged in crates – or if people claimed that anything had been damaged

or mislaid, it had to be inspected. I was the inspector, and I went along and made notes about it. One of the things I was always chasing was stolen cigarettes. I never got them of course. There was a tremendous amount of theft on the railways, though I don't think anybody actually stole aircraft engines. I presume it was partly railway staff, partly that it would be loaded out of trains on to sidings, and people would just come along and help themselves. You got very few cartons of cigarettes that didn't have a little hole in them – a hand had gone in and perhaps a package or two had been extracted. Quite a lot of clothes were stolen too.

Being one of the only women on the railways in the early stages of the war, I joined the union. They had the clerical workers' union, which was a bit 'upper', and then the workers 'what was in the NUR'. I wasn't in the manual grades but I joined the NUR because I thought it would be more interesting. I went along to a branch meeting, and they didn't quite know what to do with me, so they decided to call me 'sister'. Then I became a delegate to the local trades council, a group of unions in the area. So I came into contact with an awful lot of people who were doing war work. We even had some titled ladies who came along to some of the meetings. I remember one of them picked on me as being a bit more civilized than the layabouts that actually worked: 'Oh well, you don't usually do this sort of thing, do you?' In pre-war days people spoke with very different accents. You could tell from the way they spoke what class they came from, or even by just looking at their clothes. You could certainly tell about their educational background. It was much more marked.

One day the union had a letter from the BBC, saying that if any of their members spoke French they would be very interested in having them help in the foreign broadcasts to Occupied France, to give a picture of what workers in Britain were doing to help the war effort. They were just about to put it on one side, not expecting anyone to speak French, when I said that I did. So they put my name forward and the BBC sent down a chap to interview me. 'You look very young', he said, which I was, and very naïve.

I used to go up to London to Bush House, where the overseas service was, and do some recordings. In those days you were on record, and if you made a mistake you had to do it all again, all the technicians looking angrily at you. I based the broadcasts partly on my observations of the locality which I knew. They were always something to do with women and the war effort. Women on the railways was an obvious topic, another was women in factories. I used to go round on my bike to factories to see what women were doing. I also did stuff based on talking to people and reading the newspapers – for instance, what the attitude was of female workers to the Soviet Union, who were our allies then, and quite respectable?

It was very dangerous for the French to listen to the broadcasts, because the Germans were in occupation, and if they were caught they could be shot. A lot of the broadcasts were very valuable to the Resistance, and women would listen to them in great secrecy. The purpose was to tell the French people that British women were behind them and their sufferings, and that they were contributing. As far as I was aware, I was the only woman doing this. It was just propaganda, but it was true; propaganda doesn't have to be lies.

One event I covered for the BBC was a big meeting at the Albert Hall of women workers from all over the country. I was selected by the NUR to go, which was a bit extraordinary as I wasn't even a manual worker. I think every minister in the government attended, to speak to the women about the war effort, and to pat them on the back and say, 'Thank you, duckies, we shan't need you later, but at the moment we do, so come in and get on with it.' They depended on women to get production up. But I was absolutely astonished that in the middle of London, with the bombs all falling round, so many ministers attended. It was quite a risk. But the government's attitude to the unions was very pally then: we all loved each other.

On the railways they had women shunters, going along the tracks and pushing the rails around, and that kind of thing – permanent way staff they were called. I don't think there was a lot of prejudice against women. Some of them got sarcastic remarks from chaps about the jobs they were doing, though I never got any personally, but then I wasn't really competing with them. Today there's sometimes still a fight about having women bus drivers. Men don't want them, and so they adopt certain attitudes. During the war it was *war*, women had to work, and if women were sent by the Labour Exchange to work on buses, that's where they worked, there was no argument. The trade unions were very reactionary about this, but they could say what they liked, the women still got the jobs. There weren't many bus drivers, but there were a few, and there were masses of conductresses. I think a benevolent despotism can be quite a good thing for some things.

I remember before the war I was working in one place where a secretary got married, and as she needed the money she had to keep it quiet, but one of the bosses found out and the poor thing was just flung out. That was typical: women who were married, their place was in the home and they got on with it. During the war that disappeared entirely. If you had children, whether you were married or not, you were expected to work –

indeed you *had* to work when registration came in. I think one of the great spurs to women's changing attitudes was the fact that they mainly earned equal money. Women for the first time had enough income to keep themselves – for instance, if their marriage didn't work, they could push off.

I think a lot of the Women's Lib movement came from the war. The women who were growing up then are the mothers of today, and I'm sure they've been affected by the fact that their mothers worked then. For my age group you felt very inhibited about wanting to work. Before the war, if you heard people talking about education, it was always, 'Oh, of course, the boy must go', and 'The girl, well, she's only going to be a housewife anyway, so she's no time for that'. I myself was at the stage when I wanted to be an explorer, an adventurer, a discoverer, go to Africa. I didn't know women had done it in Victorian times, it wasn't talked about in my family. I thought the only way to have any life was to be a male. So when I was ten or so I dressed as a boy, had my hair Eton cropped, went round in short trousers and called myself Bill. I thought the only people who got a decent deal, from the point of view of education and what the future held for them, were boys. I don't think you get that today, because girls know that they can do things too.

The war wasn't fun. A lot of people think nostalgically back to those days, and think that everybody was friendly and so on. But there were quite a lot of problems. One terrible one was the breaking-up of families, not just husbands and wives, but also mothers and children, many of them being sent overseas. It's very difficult in a situation where you don't know whether you're going to be alive tomorrow, to think about, well, to put it crudely, being faithful to your husband if he's away – and you don't know what *he*'s up to anyway. There was a lot of that, and it really broke up families: the divorce rate was very high after the war.

Food and clothing were also a problem. You only had a minimal ration, so it was quite difficult to feed a family and get clothing. The food situation was very different between the city and country. In the cities you had the British Restaurants where you got your bowl of slop, which wasn't particularly appetizing. There was also a good selection of restaurants in London, for example, which kept open. There was a price limit; you couldn't pay more than five shillings for a meal. Of course they got round that by charging a lot for the wine. So you could extend your rations by eating out at restaurants; you didn't have to give up coupons or anything there. In the country, on the other hand, you might have a neighbour who had a pig, and you might get a bit off there. But of course it was easier to grow your own vegetables, you had much more space.

There were pubs, of course, but there was a great shortage of beer and fags. There was also a lack of entertainment, and a shortage of general goods, even books. One did get them, and I remember being very grateful for poetry, because it was another dimension from the physical coping with life. There was a great deal of poetry published then, and a lot of people turned to it.

There was a lot of prejudice, which was fear really. In Cirencester I helped run a war workers' club. There was absolutely nothing going on, so we set up this club and had interest groups. I ran a music circle with records, and we also used to hold dances in the town hall for war workers. Naturally soldiers used to come. We had an approach from an American officer, who came to me and said, 'We understand you're holding dances; our men will be attending, but we cannot have black and white together.' I was furious. So I said, 'OK, we'll have black.' And we did. Of course the English people at the dance were quite all right with the black Americans. They politely asked them to dance, and it all went off very well.

I remember there were a couple of Indians in the town. The poor things, they were lonely and lost. As part of my war work I befriended them and discovered they played tennis. I took them up to the tennis club, and my God, the reaction – fancy bringing *coloured* people to the tennis club. I did it, and I didn't give a damn. But it was horrid.

My *bête noire* of the war – and I'm in a minority – was Churchill. I just could not stand that man, he was such a bloody jingoist. Obviously I didn't go out into the street and say, 'Churchill's a bastard'; that would have been silly anyway, and he did contribute to the war effort. Most people liked him very much; not everybody did is all I want to say. There was a minority, of course, that felt as I did, and who didn't think it was all great fun. There's a tendency among certain British people – it's the Knees Up Mother Brown syndrome – when things get awful they just slop the beer and have a knees up. I think it was very difficult to look at things clearly.

I also couldn't stand the jingoism that saw all Germans as bad, the folklore that the only good German was a dead one. It was rather horrible; even normally quite decent people felt that way. One of the things I did, which sounds a bit daft, was to study German – not that I in any way approved of what the Germans were doing, but I just hated all the jingoism.

Of course I was living in the country, so it wasn't as bad as London and other cities. It was really quite extraordinary to see the peace of the countryside and to grasp that there was a dreadful war going on. And yet even in isolated spots you weren't entirely safe. I was bombed myself once, when I was out walking along the canal one lunch time. This German plane came down and I could actually see the pilot shooting at me. It was quite extraordinary.

I've lived in Germany since the war, and it's quite remarkable to find people who didn't know anything about it. In one house I was living in I had a picture by John Piper of the bomb-damaged Coventry Cathedral. I remember my housekeeper coming and saying, 'Oh, who bombed Britain?' So I said, 'Who do you think?' And she said, 'Was it the Russians?' And I said, 'No, it was your lot, the Germans.' But the older German people didn't care to talk about the war very much, they don't want to be reminded of it. They think it was a bad deal for Germany, but if Germany had won they wouldn't have found anything wrong with Hitler, I don't think. They say they never knew about the concentration camps, but they did. I remember after the war talking to a member of the Berlin Symphony Orchestra, and he had played in the concentration camps. Oh yes. The Germans are very sentimental about it, the tears flow down their cheeks as they listen to the Ninth Symphony, and then they go and gas the Jews. I don't much like Germans in general; of course there are exceptions.

I think at the end of the war the important issues for women were social equality, questions of education and the health service. These were what brought the Labour government into power in 1945. I think for certain wooden heads the result was a great surprise, but for ordinary people it was not. Pre-war life was a different life. People can't really imagine what the class distinctions were like, the misery for instance of being ill and not being able to afford a doctor, or having a child and not being able to afford it. These were great problems. Also of course there was tremendous unemployment, people didn't have money, they couldn't buy food. So, even with wartime restrictions, people were better fed than they had been before. But after the war I think there were a lot of women who were not particularly what you might call Women's Libbers, they'd been without their menfolk for years, and they were quite glad to get back to producing children.

The Pilot

The editor of the Aeroplane *magazine wrote about women being a menace thinking they could cope with piloting a high-speed bomber, when some of them weren't intelligent enough to scrub a hospital floor decently.*

Lettice Curtis

Everyone said, 'You'll never get a job as a woman pilot.' I was born and brought up in the depths of Devon. I was one of a large family, and I wanted to stand on my own two feet once I'd finished my education; I didn't want to be a drag on family finances any more. In the pre-war world it was quite difficult for a woman to get a job, even with an Oxford degree. There was a field quite near where we lived which had been turned into an aerodrome. Only light aircraft could have landed there, but then there weren't many large aircraft in those days. It was probably this that put aviation into my mind.

There were lots of pre-war women pilots, they were flying all over the place. I'd decided that I'd like to have a go at getting a commercial flying licence. I couldn't afford to fly for fun, so I'd have to earn money at it. I had £100 that my grandmother had left me, so I put this towards my licence, which I eventually got after passing the necessary ground and air tests in 1938. Much to everyone's surprise I managed to get a job flying for an air survey company, which was taking aerial photographs for the Ordnance Survey.

them. The editor of the magazine wrote about women being a menace thinking they could cope with piloting a high-speed bomber, when some of them weren't intelligent enough to scrub a hospital floor decently. But I personally didn't come across any prejudice against women. We were soon treated equally and there was very little bias against us; eventually we got equal pay with men. After all, when there's a war on, you get on with your job; I don't think you look over your shoulder and criticize what anyone else is doing. You hadn't time when you were doing a job of national importance.

We took the planes all over the UK. In the early days we came back by train, but when you learnt to fly several types of plane then you could bring one back on your return journey. The Tiger Moths, which were the smallest, were the ones that women started on. But in 1941 we were allowed to take on operational aircraft, such as Spitfires, Hurricanes and Oxfords. For some reason they wanted to store a lot of Tiger Moths up in Scotland, which was a ghastly journey in winter in those little, light planes. It was about four hops up there. When you arrived you got straight on a night train, and sometimes when you got back there was another one waiting for you, and off you'd go again for a whole night and a day. It took all your thought and energy, you didn't have much time for anything else. I think some of the older ones did have a social life, they perhaps knew a chap at an RAF station. There was a big gap between those who were slightly older and married and the others.

You flew by yourself most of the time, except on the four-engined aircraft, where you had a flight engineer. I think the attraction was the challenge, like anything else. People do rave about flying, and it certainly has its moments, there's a lot of adrenalin in it. On lovely days when there were no war worries, it could be fabulous. Things got much better towards the end of the war, there weren't so many balloons, and they weren't so strict about danger areas and what you were doing. So you did have some fabulous flights, taking a Spit up to Prestwick or something. But it was still worrying in winter because of the weather.

In the early part of the war we had no weekends, no Christmas Days, nothing. We worked theoretically ten days on and two off, but if the weather was bad and there was a hold-up, you very often lost your two days off. It was only at the end of the war that we started getting weekends off. We went to the cinema an enormous amount; when you got a wet afternoon it was about the only thing you could do.

After the war there were no jobs for women pilots; there were too many ex-RAF pilots looking for jobs. In the war a force had been formed to ferry aircraft built in Canada across the Atlantic. Some of the ATA men went over to this, but the women weren't eligible. But I suppose the war did alter the course of women's careers to some extent. Girls where I came from, who would have just lived in one small village all their lives, were called up and went into the world to join the forces.

You knew little about the background of the people you worked with during the war, you didn't stop to ask. But there was certainly a very strong community spirit. You had to get on with one another, and it was much better that way. Now, everybody criticizes everything, and the world has become practically ungovernable. Everybody has their say about everything, and whatever anybody does, somebody gets up and says it's wrong. We're no longer all aiming in the same direction. In the war you were: the object was to win, and you just got on with your job.

Extracts from the diary of an 81-year-old woman living in Norwich, 1942

28 January. Nasty snowy day. I went to Hopper's and took gas mask to ARP shelter near church. Men came and took B. Stove as old iron salvage.

21 February. Snow falling all day! Did not go out – sorted and tore up old letters for munitions.

29 April. Guns in early a.m. Went to city and saw much broken glass and Collers' smashed roofs. Bad raid at midnight, Restrevor bombed to bits. H and W took refuge here with bandages and bleeding and slept in drawing room.

30 April. Bright cold day. Tried to find Dr Aitken, his house roofless. Mrs Eaton's house still burning, all the houses damaged. Helped to fetch things from Restrevor and arrange beds, etc. in Edie's old bedroom. Again looked for things in the ruins of number 125.

1 May. Siren and some bombing late. At Restrevor nearly all day finding and bringing back small things among the plaster and broken marble, etc. Warmer day – a peaceful night after bombing stopped.

2 May. Went to try for things in city – an awful ruin. Mrs Edwards and Miss Clarkson called to ask how we were. More salvage from number 125.

9 May. Raid in early a.m. before H and I had gone to bed. House shaken and great noise but no windows broken. I was still too lame to go beyond garden.

15 June. Rainy and cold. Went to city in a.m. and had lunch there. Mrs E.M. called about bombed-out lady. Boy Scouts came for waste paper.

27 June. Raid in early a.m. Hospital and shops burnt. I went to ask after Hilda at 4.45 a.m., as not worth going to bed again.

23 July. E went to City Hall and got her new ration card. No one called. Chilly and windy. Siren at 11.30, no all-clear till 1.30.

29 July. Sat up knitting till 1.30, and then as siren sounded and guns were heard sat in hall till nearly 4 a.m. when all-clear sounded.

3 August. Fog in a.m. rain in evening. Five sirens and all-clears through the day. Soldier beggar came to door, I gave him a shilling. A quiet night.

The Civil Servant

*He had worked his way up from office boy practically, and
here was this little pipsqueak of a woman coming in, who
he thought couldn't possibly cope.*

Mary Davies

I went to university in Oxford just as war broke out. My parents were very
humble people, so I was very lucky because I got what was then an
enormous scholarship, something like £300. I actually passed for Westfield
College in London, but it was evacuated to a theological college in Oxford,
St Peter's Hall.

I went up to Oxford with all kinds of wonderful ideas. I thought, 'Oh
yes, this is the beginning of a wonderful new life for me.' But we didn't
have a lot of chance to play, because we were encouraged, or rather forced,
to work very hard. It was a women's college and I was brought into contact
with rather high-class girls, whom I had never dreamt of meeting before.
The working-class people like me – and there weren't many – worked hard,
but the upper crust didn't work at all at first. But then they realized that it
might be better to do so in order to have a job after the war.

There was one girl from my sort of class who was a rebel. We were
supposed to dress for dinner at college. Sometimes we had to sit at the top
table. I had been told this before I went up, so I had provided myself with a
home-made long skirt and top. Well, this girl said, 'I can't afford to have a

long dress. The only thing I've got long is my dressing-gown, and if they want something long, they'll get that.' This was considered enormously rebellious. I can still see her marching through the college and up to the high table in a long, woolly dressing-gown. She revolutionized the rule about long dresses. I don't think that could have happened before the war.

The women mixed much more with each other in Oxford, because there were so few men. They were all called 'weeds', because there was something wrong with all of them. When you went out with a man you swapped stories: 'What was wrong with your one, was it his heart or his eyes or his kidneys?' It wasn't always obvious what it was. So the question of men hardly cropped up at all.

Anyway, I managed to blunder my way through Oxford. But I gradually broke from my roots, although this would probably have happened anyway. I was brought up in Norwich, and at school we had a very ambitious headmistress who used to teach all the girls in speech so that we would get rid of our East Anglian accents. She used to say, 'You'll never go anywhere with that accent', and in those days you didn't. So we were made to practise not having a glottal stop: 'The woman in the woolly hood pushed the pudding with her foot' – sentences like that.

I used to go back to Norwich for the holidays. We were near the coast, so there were raids; we used to have odd planes drop bombs. There was a great deal more of this camaraderie you hear about. But then at that time our road was still like a village, there was still an atmosphere of mutual help. My mother used to look after babies for neighbours. But some attitudes were very narrow. Before the war, because we had very little money coming in and my mother wanted me to go to university, she went out to work. This was *unthought* of, and some of her friends wouldn't talk to her. Before that she had been a dressmaker, and when I was much smaller she used to make clothes at home. That was allowed, that was considered a suitable thing. But when she became an assistant in a fur shop, I remember people not only not talking to her, but stopping me and saying, 'Why don't *you* go out to work?' I felt very guilty about this. I was an only child, and my mother was determined that I should get on. She was rather an early, nice Women's Libber. I was quite staggered even then by the fact that these people would send her to Coventry and would try and persuade *me* to go out to work – I should be helping to keep the family at home, they felt.

So there was a great gulf between that, which was my sort of life, and the sort of life of most girls who went to university, with their expensive clothes and things like that. Up until the war the universities had been very select places. Funnily enough, the social side didn't really worry me. We had coupons for various things, including clothes, so that was easy enough because we couldn't have all that many. The college used to take in our ration books and give us back loose soap coupons. I remember thinking, 'I'll buy myself a really expensive, really wonderful block of soap.' There wasn't much of a choice, but there was one very elaborate one called Autumn Leaves, and it smelt of them. I can remember having baths for almost a year with that block of soap. I think perhaps these shortages brought about a levelling process. Also I think adolescents were fairly used not to compete in clothes – you had your school uniform and another dress and that was it. There wasn't competition there.

I got my degree in 1942, and then suddenly I had to get a job. As a woman you could either go into the services or teaching or the civil service. For teaching you needed another year's training, and I didn't want to do that. I'd heard hair-raising stories about the services, so I thought they weren't for me. The only other possibility was the civil service, for which you needed to go for an interview before a board in London. While I was waiting for this interview, I went to stay with a college friend in Bognor. She was a very keen, patriotic girl – we *were* patriotic, even if the war hadn't yet touched us very much. She met me at the station on her bicycle, and she said, 'Come on, we're going to do land work, digging up potatoes.' So we dug up potatoes in the mornings, for something like tuppence an hour. Then we used to go to one of the British Restaurants, to be waitresses. We didn't serve out the meals, because that was considered the Lady Bountiful's job – she always served the meals with her hat on; I can still see her behind the canteen with this hat. We just took the trays to the people who ordered it – it was one and sixpence – and we had our dinner free. And then we went off again to the potato field. All this made me very healthy.

Then I got a telegram asking me to go for the interview. My mother had made me a costume, a kind of suit made out of bombed-out-shop material – it was all right, but it wasn't exactly *haute couture*. She'd also made a pink blouse out of an old dress, and I had a pair of old Clark's sandals, which cost five shillings. I had no clothes coupons to buy anything new, and what was worse none to buy stockings. So we scuffed about and found a pair of stockings with holes in – there was a thing that you didn't mend ladders, because if you put stockings on with holes in, it looked as though it had just happened. Of course I couldn't afford to have my hair done or anything like that.

So, looking horribly peasant-like, I breezed into Burlington Gardens. And in this room there were all these smartly dressed young ladies with hats and handbags and smart shoes with heels. They were being interviewed for assistant principal jobs, which was the lowest administrative level, but still quite a good level. Before the war it used to be on examination, and men only. And I thought, 'Oh God, it's no good.' Anyway, I was brought in, and there was this long table and a lot of people. There were two women on the board, and *they* had hats on. I sat down and the chairman said, 'I see you've got a very good reference from Mrs Stocks, and she says you've been looking after a blind girl.' I had shared rooms with her at college for three years, having been brought up with the idea of doing good works. Lady Stocks – she was then Mary Stocks – was our principal, and every term she used to try to persuade me to let this girl share with someone else. But I would refuse, saying I knew her ways. So I said, 'That's right.' And he said, 'What did they pay you for that?' And I said, 'Nothing.' 'Nothing? Oh. And what have you been doing since you came down?' 'Well, I've been working on the land, I've been doing waitressing in a British Restaurant . . .' And so it went on. I couldn't put a foot wrong. As a result I got a peach of a job in the Colonial Office.

Nowadays you get women in all grades of the civil service, but previously they had only been typists or clerical officers. This was the first time women had been allowed into the administrative level. Well, I didn't know anything about the colonies, so I hastily read up a bit. I treated myself to a plain little dress, with a detachable collar of the kind that you had in those days – you could wash it and put another one on, and it looked like a different dress. So I turned up at the Colonial Office, which was on the left-hand side of Downing Street. You had to have a special pass and you were sworn in on the Official Secrets Act. I thought, 'Good heavens, I'm going to learn an awful lot.' I never did, of course.

So there I was at a huge desk opposite my principal, Mr Big – yes, that was actually his name. He was a small man and he looked at me with loathing, and said, 'You're my assistant principal?' 'Yes.' 'Can you write a letter?' Me, with a degree in English, write a letter? 'Oh yes,' I said. 'Yes, yes, but can you write a *letter*?' Then he gave me a file – of course I'd never seen a file before – and I had to work out what I was supposed to do. I drafted a letter to some governor – we still had all the colonies, and things went backwards and forwards between us and them. There was the governor of the Bahamas, the Duke of Windsor, and he kept doing things and we kept sending him rude letters, couched politely. Anyway, Mr Big looked at my draft and tore it into little pieces and put it into the waste-paper basket. 'Right, now you start in the registry.' I was a bit shattered by this, but apparently he was well known as a difficult man, and he had run through dozens of assistant principals. He had worked his way up from office boy practically, and here was this little pipsqueak of a *woman* coming in, who he thought couldn't possibly cope. But by the end of the year I was still there, and still working for him. There were very few women in the civil service, though, there was resistance to us getting the jobs. I was particularly unlucky because I was young. The older ones were accepted more and managed better. But even they found it difficult, and none of the ones I knew stayed after the war.

In those days you could buy property for a small amount; places were ridiculously cheap because everyone thought London was unsafe because of the bombs. I remember once I was looking after this flat in Chelsea for someone who had gone abroad. There was a new girl in the office, Daphne, and I brought her back for a meal. It was all pretty basic, we sat there in the kitchen frying dried egg and sloshing it on to a plate. She then invited me back for a meal with her mother in St John's Wood. The first thing that staggered me was that a maid opened the door – this must have been about 1944. I gulped a bit and went into the drawing-room, where her mother was writing out invitations for a Red Cross Ball at the Dorchester. I thought, 'Gosh, what have I got into here?' So then we went up into Daphne's flat. They *all* had their own flats in this house. I was staggered by this. Then we went downstairs to have dinner, which was haggis, which was not on the ration. There was a very, very long *beautiful* table, and Daphne sat at one end and I sat at the other. Even people like that, who had plenty of money, were punctilious about not doing anything on the black market. They had a dinner party every Thursday, and the haggis was sent from Fortnum & Mason.

My sort of level wouldn't have done any black marketing in clothing coupons or anything like that, which people did do. We would have considered that not really the done thing. You could go out and have meals in restaurants without food coupons. So if you could get somebody to take you out to a meal, that was really quite a good idea. You had to be careful though. Sometimes, after you had finished a nice steak, you might see a notice saying, 'Horse is Provided Here'. I think if they served horse they had to put a notice up; whether you saw it was another matter. I remember having a violent argument with one man, saying, 'Fancy bringing me to a place where you eat horse', and he said, 'Well, you said it was very nice, so what's the difference between eating that and a cow?' Well there isn't any really, so I went on eating horse.

It was quite a nightmare going into the Underground in London. I found it very claustrophobic. I didn't shelter there, I just travelled on the trains. But people came down quite early in the evening and stretched themselves out on the platforms. Bunk beds were put up for them after a while. I remember feeling that I'd rather be in a house, however dangerous. There were accidents, though of course they didn't tell you about them at the time. But some people enjoyed it down there – they would have dancing on the platforms.

We loved the lunch-time concerts at the National Gallery with Myra Hess. They cost a shilling, and in the basement there was a snack bar where you could have beetroot sandwiches for about threepence. We went there often, my friends and I. We always knew what the Picture of the Month was. They used to put all the pictures underground, except for one small one, some tiny masterpiece. They would put this in the entrance, and all around would be pictures by the same artist, with interesting comments about him. And when there was an air-raid alarm, one of the wardens would put the picture under his arm and take it down into the cellars. I thought that was wonderful, because they had a different one every month and you could just concentrate on the one picture.

My only direct experience of a bomb was when I was living in Morden in south London, and we had one of those table shelters which you got underneath. My landlady had just put my fish and chips on the table when she said, 'Oh, it's stopped!' – meaning the engine of the flying bomb had cut out. So we all rushed underneath the table, and the whole house came down on top of my supper. I was more interested in the fate of my supper than anything else. But this solid and very unattractive table saved our lives. The French windows facing it were blown out, so we just scuttled out and went to the shelter. The police then came along and said we couldn't go into the house for the time being. So I just had to go to work wearing the same clothes. There didn't seem anything special about that, possibly because I was young.

Various men who came back from the colonies would take me out. They would take me to their parents' houses. That was more done in those days, but it didn't mean anything especially, it was just simpler to produce the food there. But again, because the men were in the war, you thought, 'Oh, I can't get too involved with him, he may not come back.' You didn't have time to get to know them particularly well. I wasn't brought up to think that this is a gay life and a short one, so the men you got involved with were much older, and usually had some kind of sad story behind them as to why they weren't in the war, or some disease to explain it.

At the end of the war, when Churchill was defeated, this was absolutely staggering to everybody in Whitehall. Grown men were going around absolutely stunned and amazed. They had no contact with the man in the street. But I could have told them what was going to happen. People wanted a change. Of course the civil service was going to have to work with the new government, and they weren't in the least in favour of that. They said, 'What about all these wonderful plans for after the war?' They weren't really in touch with reality.

England was very much a closed society before the war. People like teachers and doctors and solicitors had a certain cachet. And even if you weren't a churchgoer, the Church was there, the Church would tell you every now and then what to do, and even if *you* didn't agree with it you thought *good* people agreed with it – 'I may not be good myself, but there is a general feeling of an accepted morality, acceptable beliefs.' So it was easier to fit into the pattern. We were of a generation that believed what it was told.

Everything seemed more or less straightforward as far as the war was concerned. There was a war to be fought, we were on the right side, and therefore we would win. I don't think anybody ever considered we *wouldn't* win, even in the bad days during Dunkirk, which was very, very traumatic. But again it was an adventure – all the ships, not the hundreds and hundreds that died. Either the propaganda was very good or we were very gullible – after all, we hadn't been through too much before. Politics didn't impinge at all, but I think I must have been particularly stupid. I and other women of my age and upbringing were full of ideals but we didn't think deeply about politics. We were full of interest in music and art, and somehow that was enough. You read about the war, but you thought, 'Well, I'm doing my war work, what can poor little me do to influence it?'

The Shop Steward

The women seemed to enjoy the camaraderie of factory life, and were quite enthusiastic about the unions campaigning for equal pay.

Kay Ekevall

We'd only been married four months when war broke out. We lived in Edinburgh. I was twenty-eight and working part-time as a typist at the Scottish Peace Council. My husband was an engine-driver, and neither of us agreed with Britain going to war over Poland. We couldn't believe that the defence of such a feudal fascist state was anything else than a move to protect Britain's interests in Poland. So it wasn't until Germany attacked Russia that we felt we should join in the war effort, to defend what we saw as the vanguard state of socialism. We had always been strong trade unionists and socialists; we had supported anti-fascist refugees and the Spanish republican government.

I'd been a shorthand typist all my life, and never worked in a factory. But I applied to Redpath Browns' shipbuilding firm to train as a welder. At the time the government had made a deal with the trade unions so that they would be recognized and be able to recruit in factories. It became much more difficult for them to harass trade unionists, which they had done before. I remember the chief shop steward at Redpath's had been blacklisted for nine years, but as a skilled engineer he was now protected in his job. I soon became shop steward for the women, as few of them seemed to know much about trade unionism. We were in the constructional engineering union, and we had some amusing confrontations with the management. We would demand, say, protective clothing, and be immediately refused, and so we would say, 'Well, we'll see what the unions have to say about that.' And they'd cave in immediately. They had no experience of unions and seemed to be terrified of them.

My husband used to say the government couldn't organize a tea party, never mind a war. This was obvious from various incidents that happened at the factory. I remember, for instance, that the welders needed copper plate to build up gaps or holes in the steel. There was one small piece of copper available between all the welders, so we just had to wait for each other to use it. Then I heard from a friend working in a factory in England that they had so much copper that in their spare time they were making ashtrays from it.

As the employers could make a profit on overtime – it was cost plus 10 per cent – they had us on night shift, just standing about waiting for work. This often happened on the day shifts as well. Piece-rate workers were particularly niggled at this. Once there was a rush job, and it was all hands on deck for about a week. But the steel plates then just stood out in the yard, rusting away for about three months. As you can imagine, we treated the next urgent job with some cynicism.

Music While You Work was the rage then, but it would hardly have been possible to have it in the factory, what with the noise of the cranes and the hammers and the clogs on the steel plates, not to mention the wide-open spaces. So we had it in the canteen, deafeningly, so that you couldn't hear what anyone said. The only time there was anything like a hush was when everyone was swooning over Bing Crosby.

I remember on one holiday we had gone down to visit my folk in London, and we went to the pictures with my mother. They showed a newsreel in which a tank-landing craft rolled on to the Normandy beaches, and I found myself calling out in excitement, 'Oh look, I made those!' A friend who had worked in a factory in the west of Scotland said the same thing happened to her when she saw the ship she had worked on in a newsreel. Another friend had a husband working in the Glasgow shipyards. He'd been a printer all his life and was quite new to the job. I remember her saying, 'No wonder all the ships are going down.'

My husband worked all kinds of peculiar and lengthy shifts, while I was alternately on night and day shifts. Often we only met on the stairs going to and from work, and I just had time to say, 'There's a pie in the oven, and the bed's ready to heat up. See you tomorrow.' Or he would say, 'My shift changes tomorrow, so I shan't see you until six o'clock.'

Redpath's had never employed women before the war, as it was considered heavy industry. Women took part in most of the jobs, such as crane-driving, burning, buffing, painting, welding and such-like. I became a welder when there were both men and women trainees, but the men were paid more than the women. We had several battles over equal pay after we were used on the same jobs as the men, many of whom were as new to the skills as we were. By the end of my time we had managed to get close to the men's wage, but we only got equality in the case of the crane-drivers. On the whole the men didn't seem to resent the women, and the skilled men were friendly and helpful to the trainees. As it was an essential work industry, like the railways, I suppose they weren't afraid for their jobs. I believe there was some resentment in other factories at the dilution by cheap labour, and the unions campaigned for equal pay. But in heavy industry like Redpath's, no one thought women would be kept on after the war, so we were in a less vulnerable position. Spot welding in the electrical factories was the only kind of welding work that had been done by women up to then.

There were about thirty of us at Redpath's, and most had been housewives or done nothing more than domestic work in canteens, or office cleaning or light factory work. Only three of us had done clerical work, and the other two had given it up when they got married. The women seemed to enjoy the camaraderie of factory life, and were quite enthusiastic about the unions campaigning for equal pay, although they had no experience of belonging to a union before then. I think they found they could cope with quite a few new skills. I think the work gave them more confidence. Many of them, especially those with families of working age, would, I think, have been willing to carry on after the war. The younger women were glad to get back to their homes and start families. But even they would have been ready to take jobs, especially as the war had promoted the nursery system, which lingered on for a few years after 1945.

Before the war we had met a number of refugees from Czechoslovakia, Hungary and Germany, some of whom stayed with us in Edinburgh. They were popular in our circles as anti-fascist, but there was still quite a strong anti-foreign element about. When Italy came into the war, there was an upsurge of hooliganism against Italian shops and cafés. Many of their owners were third-generation British, but that didn't save them. We also met members of the Canadian and Free French forces, who seemed to be accepted amicably by the local people. And Norwegian and Russian sailors were also usually made a fuss of when they came ashore. The only two nationalities who seemed to arouse general hostility, both among the forces and civilians, were the Western Poles and the Americans.

It was clear that the Western Poles despised the Eastern Poles, even though there were doctors and nurses from both areas working side by side in the same hospital. The Western Polish doctors wouldn't mix with the Eastern ones. They were also very arrogant, especially when they were in uniform, and would push local people off the pavement as they strutted along. They had the best accommodation and rations of any of the armed forces, and their own hospitals and medical supplies. Later in the war I myself worked for a medical supply company and I found out that the Polish doctors had an allowance of £40 a month to spend on equipment – *twice* the average industrial wage – and openly said they were storing it up to take back to Poland after the war. So our boss refused to let them buy lease-lend equipment, saying it was sent for immediate use in hospitals in Britain.

The Americans were also resented, though not so widely as the Poles. They were especially resented by our forces because of their most luxurious conditions, accommodation and rations – and in some cases their attitudes to their own black troops. They were also resented because they had more money to spend on taking girls out and buying them scarce luxuries like nylon stockings.

During most of the war it was patently obvious that a great deal of luxury was being enjoyed by the wealthy and powerful. Children of the wealthy were evacuated to America, while the *hoi polloi* were in some cases carelessly and haphazardly evacuated to any old where. Sometimes they were evacuated no more than 3 miles from their own homes, so some of the older ones just walked back – that happened in Dundee. I remember in other cases they were sent to seaside places that had already been evacuated inland, or to places like Cambridge, which was surrounded by several airfields. Discrimination of this kind didn't endear the classes to each other. I think that people became more cynical, at least temporarily, about the government's capabilities.

The war took its toll on us. Late one night in February 1945, around midnight, my husband came off his shift in a dazed condition, with his speech all jumbled and not understanding anything I said to him. I rushed him to our doctor, who diagnosed it as vertigo. But it turned out to be the beginning of a long illness, with fits that became more and

more frequent until he died twenty-three years later. I was pregnant at
the time, and six weeks later our daughter was born. I had had two
miscarriages before, in 1940 and 1941, so we were very thankful that
she turned out healthy and lively.

Extract from a letter to F.W. Pethwick Lawrence MP

It has transpired since the appeals that the girls were directed to wash bottles in
breweries or to wash dishes in luxury restaurants, and that at the most appalling
wages. Surely, if luxury restaurants are allowed to employ girls they should be
expected to pay for the luxury, and not continue with the sweated labour they
were used to before the war. In any case, the girls resent being sent to such jobs
when they could undertake engineering jobs, and their general feeling is that
they should be directed to wash dishes in hospitals rather than in luxury
restaurants, if that is the only kind of work available for them.

I should be glad if you would present the case to the Ministry from this point of
view, and we, in our turn, will take it up again with the local trades council, who
have also received similar complaints from the Amalgamated Engineering Union
and other unions.

Yours fraternally
Kay Ekevall

The Student Volunteer

Most of the women on the factory bench had had only one job between school and marriage, and they seemed to find the work a stimulating change from all that making do and mending.

Joan Collins

As students we were expected to involve ourselves in volunteer work for the war effort. We were expected to do a minimum of forty-eight hours a month during term-time. I remember you had to produce a signed statement to confirm that you'd done this. In vacations we could take paid work if it was of national importance, as long as it didn't interfere with our set assignments. Since students were fair game for any organization which wanted a spare pair of hands, a lot of my time in the first part of the war was spent on voluntary work.

I was about to start at Bristol University when war broke out. I thought I would take an honours degree in history and then do teacher training. Teaching wasn't my first choice of career, but it was the only one that was subsidized. You see, if you agreed to teach for four years after you qualified, you could get a grant to cover your tuition and exam fees, as well as half the cost of residence in hall or approved lodgings. The other half you could borrow interest free from the local education authority, together with a very small grant for books and travel. But you had to pay all this back during the four years you were contracted to stay in teaching.

I don't know how far this was peculiar to Bristol, but as students were in the age group most likely to be called up, they made special wartime arrangements. I remember that art students were allowed to enter for an honours degree, but you were assessed every half-year, and if you failed any of these tests you could be called up. Also, if you didn't meet the university's rules of conduct you were liable to be tipped out, although you could appeal to be reinstated, and many students were. I remember in my first term a group of us walked out of the service of dedication in Bristol Cathedral because we objected to the militant phraseology of the sermon. At the school I had been to some of the teachers were members of the Society of Friends, so I grew up with the belief that war wasn't the right way to solve political conflict. Anyway, we were sent down for two weeks. We were reinstated, but I felt after that we were being kept under surveillance in case we became subversives.

So I compromised by trying to avoid voluntary work which involved making or handling weapons, or raw material for weapons. I managed this most of the time. We all had to take our share of fire-watching, which played havoc with our seminar and lecture timetables, so you needed quite a lot of ingenuity to get to the essential lectures and study periods. I remember that if you were on fire duty this didn't count as cutting a lecture, so some of the less popular staff found students were suddenly very civic minded.

If there was a red alert or an actual raid, we then came under the command of the local branch of the National Fire Service and we could be drafted off the university premises. One night a grocery warehouse got a direct hit and thousands of tons of sugar and jam went up in flames. The smell of hot jam or coffee still brings back that night. In the same way, Dvorak's *New World Symphony* brings back the night the Colston Hall and most of Park Street in Bristol were destroyed. I remember the hall was cleared after the orchestra had finished the symphony, and a gang of students, including me, who had volunteered to fight the fire, all yelled in defiance, 'Pom, pom pom pom/Pom de deedle pom/Pom de deedle pom pom/Pom de deedle deedle pom', and so on.

I felt we were often given jobs that were particularly dreary, so that we shouldn't develop an exaggerated idea of our importance or give the idea that being a student was a soft option for the privileged. The fact that we might be a little brighter than most didn't seem to register.

I worked for a time in a small munitions factory in a converted warehouse with fourteen other women. Most of them were married volunteers, but we were working under a male foreman, and he was paid. I think we were making a small piece of a bomb-aiming device – this was the one time I wasn't able to keep to my intention of not working on weapons. I remember we worked a half-day shift, mornings one week, afternoons the next. Most of these factories had only a very short-term life. We were told the work was experimental. But I wonder now if it wasn't just a means of absorbing a supply of women who wanted to do something useful.

I then worked in a hospital kitchen, and this was more rewarding. It began as an emergency measure, when an air-raid disrupted the traffic and the regular staff couldn't get to work on time. I remember we got meals on duty and a free bed and a bath, and a chance to do our washing with unrationed soap. It certainly gave me a chance to learn about cooking for invalids and about special diets. I shall never forget washing the mince under the hot tap before cooking it for the 'gastrics'.

The kitchens were part of Matron's territory, so the only man on the staff was the pig-bin man. I don't think any of us were exactly Amazons, but we were expected to handle great sacks of flour and vegetables, pans full of soup and hods of fuel for the stove. I think that alone would have given a modern trade union a thousand fits.

I remember we rather despised the female relations of university staff for choosing rather ladylike kinds of war work, like joining the uniformed volunteer organizations. But once we became involved we realized the jobs they had were very risky ones. They often had to drive ambulances with minimal lighting, going through lanes which were completely without lights and signposts. They would have to meet, say, a train-load of wounded men at a remote railway siding and take them back to base hospital. It was the same with the crews of the mobile canteens and laundry vans which went out to the badly blitzed areas; they were under great stress, emotional and physical.

I also worked in the university canteen. I think the war provided a welcome break for the women I met there and in the factory. Most of the women on the factory bench had had only one job between school and marriage, and they seemed to find the work a stimulating change from all that making do and mending. As for the university wives, without their canteens they would have been very cut off from the community. They were not usually practising academics and the social occasions at the university had disappeared.

Early in my degree year I had been one of a group of students who had been quite badly hurt when an unexploded bomb blew up in one of the university buildings. We shouldn't have been there, but we had taken a short cut to get to a lecture. If I had been injured on duty I would have had free hospital treatment, but in this case you had to pay according to your means. As these were non-existent, one of the consultants fixed it so that, when I was fit enough, I would work as a volunteer clerk in the lady almoner's office.

One job that was almost exclusively done by students was making visits to sites for barrage balloons, or isolated searchlight and ack-ack posts, in pairs. We had no particular instructions. If we met a group of servicemen we liked, and they liked us, we would temporarily become part of their outfit. We'd do odd jobs like mending socks and shirts, helping with letters home, scouting round for birthday presents for their families, organizing magazine exchanges, or just playing cards or draughts or dominoes with them. The idea was to try and humanize their existence, which was a very isolated one.

I needed most of my vacation to study, but I put enough time in during the holidays on the family farm to qualify as an auxiliary member of the Women's Land Army. So I got my free pair of dungarees and wellington boots. I also had brief contact with the Ministry of Information. One of our history teachers used to work for them, preparing news-sheets about the war effort and people's experiences in England, which would then be sent to the Empire and America. As he was blind, we would read aloud from newspapers so that he could make Braille notes. We would describe the appearance of a Blitzed street, or report formal interviews with victims and their helpers. Sometimes we would be his escort for a journey. The perks were to be about when distinguished guests came. This was how I had a number of brief encounters with Eleanor Roosevelt and General de Gaulle. I also met Churchill on several occasions. I remember once he took a good strong swig from the bottle of rhubarb wine which had come from our farm. It had put most people under the table, but he remained quite unperturbed.

Once I did a bit of unpaid broadcasting. Parts of the BBC had been evacuated to Bristol, and the schools broadcasting unit was in the same building as the university's department of education. I remember being involved with an episode of *Toytown* made from a hospital ward where Uncle Mac – Derek McCulloch – was a patient. I should have been in the hospital kitchen, but at the last minute I became Laetitia, Larry the Lamb's little sister. I was really thrilled to read the lines.

I think almost everything I did was new for a young woman from my background. On a farm, wives and daughters had their set task, so they didn't usually go off and work in offices and factories. Very few made a clean break and went to university; the more usual way was to go into teacher training or nursing. I don't think university students had ever worked in term-time before; of course most of them didn't have to consider it. My father had made it clear that he wasn't willing or able to subsidize me as a student. I was one of a new breed of really poor students who were able to get some creature comforts because of the voluntary work that the war threw up.

In most of the work we accepted that the men were the bosses, but after that we were on pretty level terms. For example, when we were fire-fighting or on fire picket we weren't protected from danger. Even when a job was beyond our strength they usually sent another woman to help, we weren't replaced. The only place I met real resentment was from the men working on the farm, who I think saw me as a threat to their overtime payments. I remember one of them said as I was pitching hay into a wagon, 'If thair's be so clever why's can't find thyself summat usin' the brains and leave the proper work for the likes of we?' Also some of the women in the factory and hospital kitchen were a bit suspicious of our motives. They needed convincing that we weren't afraid of work, that we could do the practical tasks as well as most of them.

Teachers who qualified during wartime were likely to be directed to their first appointment, and go to schools where men had been called up. Once you qualified you were dropped in at the deep end, with no probationary year or consultations with a tutor. My first appointment was to a small mixed grammar school on the outskirts of Ely. I was to replace a man who had joined the Air Force. His subject had been modern languages, mine was history, so there was a general shuffle round and I ended up by taking general subjects with a form of thirteen-year-olds, and teaching maths and geography to other classes. And when the craft teacher retired I taught survival sewing and cookery to the boys until a new teacher could be found. But the job came to an abrupt end when the original teacher came back.

For many women, moving away from the home area to work was a new experience. Perfect ladies were no longer to be exempt from soiling their hands. So after the war going away to work became acceptable, instead of being a confession that you were unable to find a job near home. I think people who would otherwise have had very severe but dull lives found themselves in demand, and rose to the occasion. Of course at the end of the war the attitude to women working changed again – witness the way day nurseries were shut down. But I think people soon realized that many women didn't want to scuttle back to the kitchen and the social round. There was some feeling that women who went willingly to jobs which had previously been reserved for men were 'no better than they ought to be'. Even in work where mixed company was already tolerated, for example in teaching, we felt that the male teachers didn't quite know whether to treat us as potential girlfriends or as colleagues, so they used to switch from one approach to the other.

I think the war made a lot of people revise their priorities and learn to do without material rewards and privileges. There were plenty who made big personal sacrifices for others, but I think most people had an eye open for a chance to exchange favours or get a bit of something on the side. Organized efforts like the evacuation of children or the conscription of women were approved of in principle until they touched people personally. Then you would find, for instance, that large houses with previously unoccupied space became overnight the headquarters of some fine-sounding organization, and there was no room for evacuees. In the same way, mothers and daughters and servants became essential to the war effort at home as the time for call-up to their age group approached.

I don't think class barriers were undermined, although we were aware that they could be surmounted. I think we tend to remember all wartime relationships as being better, just as we remember the lovely summers we had when we were children. Most of us were determined we would not be beaten, and we took every opportunity we could to show that we could carry on whatever happened. I think because communal living was thrust upon us we made the most of the experience, and found ourselves on friendly terms with many kinds of people who would not have crossed our paths under ordinary circumstances.

We still had our prejudices, of course. Pacifists were regarded as cranks, all Germans were bad, whereas the 'Eyeties' were seen as poor blighters who had been cheated by 'Old Musso'. I remember there was an Italian prisoner-of-war camp near our village, and we had two of them working on the farm when my father was ill. They would sing at the slightest provocation. I remember one cow wouldn't give down her milk until she had a few bars of 'Santa Lucia' sung to her.

On another occasion a German plane came down in our cornfield, but the pilot was dead. As the body was taken away I remember thinking that he was only a boy, about the age of my brother, and what a horrible waste of a life it was. Those of us who were young felt that our parents' generation had made the mess that resulted in the war. When it ended we felt they should get out of the way and let us have a go. It was our chance now.

The Timber Yard Worker

Some of the women were very rough types, and the language was foul. *I had a great friend who started with me, and she was in tears at the end of the first week, and left, she couldn't stand it.*

Betty Jones

If you were married and above a certain age you had to do war work, unless you had a child under fourteen. Eventually the service wives were called up as well, but I was only part-time because my husband came home for meals, as he was living out of camp in the RAF.

I worked in a timber yard in Berkshire in the afternoons, for which I got one shilling an hour – I had one pound at the end of the week. I suppose there were above a hundred of us; it was in the open air, although we did have a corrugated roof over our heads. We all worked at a bench. The foreman showed you for about five minutes what you had to do, while you stood there in fear and trembling. We were making army huts for American soldiers, and we had these sections of wood which were slotted into the bench to make the framework for the huts. We knocked up six or seven in an afternoon, but I never saw a finished one. We were all women except the foreman, and a funny old boy who used to come round hobbling on a stick and say, 'Blow-up', which meant you could make tea. He was a terrific bully; if he saw somebody slacking off, he would call you everything under the sun.

The yard was separated off into sections. There was music playing all the time, and we sang, with our scarves around our heads and dressed in our dungarees, the usual sort of dress. We all went on bikes to work with our tool-bags on our handlebars, with hammers and so on. You had masses of nails which you often pinched. You were allowed to take back home any firewood you could carry, as they reckoned you couldn't take very much on a bike. I'm afraid I was the ringleader on this. It was 1941 and we had just got married, and I thought, 'Ah, stools, we must make some furniture.' So I measured all my bits of wood very carefully, so there wouldn't be any sawing needed, and took all these bits the same size home, four large ones for the legs and then six slatted ones cut to the right length, and two crossbars, and enough nails to knock it all in, and that evening we had a stool, which my husband painted the next day, and that would be that. I don't know how many stools I made in this way.

But the awful thing in the yard was loading these heavy things on to a lorry. That was when I had a miscarriage, so I had to leave and go on sick leave for six months or so.

A lot of the women were RAF wives. Very few of them stuck it out: husbands went overseas and they went home to look after perhaps an elderly mother or something like that – there were ways of swinging these things. We were all living in digs and none of us wanted to stay there. Some of the women were very rough types, and the language was *foul* – oh, I certainly learnt a lot. I had a great friend who started with me, and she was in tears at the end of the first week, and left, she couldn't stand it. It was terribly heavy work, I was absolutely whacked by four o'clock. We were standing in the mud all the time, in a freezing wind, it was a pretty cold job actually. We were awfully sick of this bang, bang, bang all the time, everybody hammering like mad. Of course you had an awful lot of black nails in the beginning, with hammers descending on your fingers. But it was the only war work going in that part, and it was only a couple of fields across from where I was living with Mum at Wendover. At the start I was put with four very rough types, and they'd all been there for ages, and they were very good at it. I didn't like it here, but who *did* like their war work? You just had to do it and hope to get the war over as quickly as possible. Looking back now it all seems very funny, but at the time it was just a job.

My mother was a bit amazed at my doing this sort of work. But she herself was a terrific war worker. She ran the food office in Bridgwater in Somerset, she used to issue the ration books. The first three months of the war Mum and Auntie Mabel got up early and departed every morning for the town, Auntie Mabel to the Red Cross and Mum to the food office. Goodness knows what would have happened to the rations without Mum! She was terribly strict about it all, much to the amusement of the family. I'd say, 'Can I have an emergency card?' and she'd say, 'Only if you give me your ration book, dear.'

The black marketeering was terrible, it was very widespread. Up in Anglesey, where I went later in the war, they didn't seem to know there was a war on. The only thing they were short of was tea. They had masses of farm butter, eggs, home-cured bacon and lard. Everybody's son was in the Merchant Navy, and they all came home with cases full of tinned fruit and what have you. No, there was no problem in Anglesey. That's why we went there for holidays, you always got marvellous food and you could build up your strength. It wasn't black market, it was just the farmers had so much.

I always used to use the phrase 'make and mend do' – I didn't know it was wrong. We all had to do that, and that was when the second-hand clothing shops started, so you could get things without coupons. I remember going up to London many a time, on the scrounge. There was a place that my sister knew about in Baker Street where you could buy model clothes without coupons. Fantastic. If you had the money you were in the black market, and clothing coupons were passed around like mad.

If you had a pregnant mum staying with you it was jolly good. If you were having a baby you could get special emergency rations, you could get a huge lot of butter and eggs, and milk, which was usually rationed. I think the authorities had learnt a lot by that time, because everybody was having babies during the war. Husbands were going overseas, so people were madly trying for a child, and lots of people got married in the early part of the war, particularly in 1939 – so there was a great spurt of babies in 1940.

Food was a problem though, you never went away even for a night without taking your emergency cards, so that your hostess could cut off your meat coupons; or else you took your rations for the night. We were a bit strict about food, we wouldn't have black market food for anything.

I don't think we suffered very much with clothing. I was terribly lucky, because we got married the week before clothing rationing came in, and so I had six of everything new. What we got up to was nobody's business. I remember going down to stay with a friend in Exmouth, and she said, 'I've just found out there's a shop in the town and they sell floor-cloth material by the yard.' I said, 'What, without coupons?' 'Yes', she said. So we went. And she made a skirt and I made a sun frock out of it. And we were cycling one afternoon in a terrific heat wave and a convoy of soldiers came past. As I was leaning over all they could see was my bare back. One of them yelled, 'What's the matter with you, run out of margarine coupons?' For the first six months you used your margarine coupons for clothes, they hadn't got the clothing books ready.

Everybody helped everybody else, especially when there was bombing. I was working for a while in a restaurant near Reading, and the owner also had a shop in Southampton. And the first night that Southampton had a Blitz, which was a terrible one, his shop went and a lot of his staff were killed. He laid on a special train-load from Southampton to Reading. And he had them all in the restaurant that day, and we fed the lot. You'd never seen such food: they had as many eggs as they liked, as many rashers of bacon. They came in their dozens, we all stayed on to help. That was the sort of thing you did.

I remember servicemen had priority for everything, until the Blitz. In the restaurant you had to offer men in uniform two eggs. Nobody else was allowed more than one. But as soon as the bombing started and the civilians were put through it, that all stopped, and they were treated the same as civilians.

We used to live from one news bulletin to the other. Everyone used to go straight into the house and switch on the radio. You listened to the radio because the papers were so thin; because of the paper shortage, there was practically nothing in them. The day we were married we ordered the taxi to fetch us from the reception at six o'clock. We were coming down the stairs, and the best man came rushing up the stairs and said, 'For God's sake don't come down yet, they're all glued to the radio, listening to the six o'clock news.' And we had to stand and wait at the top of the stairs for quarter of an hour, waiting for this blasted news to finish before we were allowed to go away.

A Kind of Schooling

We were enormously interested in the technical side of the war. We all became experts on aeroplanes, tanks, and so on. We knew far more about these things than about the things we were supposed to be studying – as I was frequently told.

LONDON BOY

Exams were going on, but people didn't swot and things like that, we were all doing other things. I'd joined the ARP, I was in the Guides, I was helping to run a Cub pack, and we helped at the hospital one night a week. Revising for exams was the least of our problems.

LONDON GIRL

We were all issued with tiny pieces of blotting paper, and one teacher went slightly off her head about its misuse. She gave one boy a tremendous lecture about the merchant seamen risking their lives to bring all these supplies to England.

SHROPSHIRE BOY

We spent many hours in those dark and damp shelters. We passed the time by chanting the tables, reciting poetry, and just sitting.

ESSEX GIRL

On the day the *Bismarck* was sunk we were having singing lessons. The music master told one of us to open the door. We sang 'Rule Britannia'. Then he ordered the door to be closed again.

MANCHESTER BOY

During fire-watching the physics and chemistry masters, who had been in the First World War, would regale us with stories of their war-time lives. So the humanity of the staff came over more than it had done.

CHESHIRE BOY

Formal schooling was a major casualty of the war. Evacuation, the break-up of families, the bombing of the civilian population, the call-up of teachers, the requisitioning of buildings, the shortage of materials – all contributed to the turmoil and dislocation of the normal timetable. Yet though children experienced suffering and tragedy like everyone else, the resulting experiences were not all negative ones. If most of them spent less time on traditional subjects, with implications for later qualifications, they often found themselves on a crash course in citizenship that had other equally important benefits.

The physical and organizational problems were most acute in the early part of the war, especially during the two periods of evacuation. In towns and cities many schools suffered direct hits or extensive damage. Of those unscathed, a number were taken over by the Army, or used for other purposes, such as rest centres by the Civil Defence services. Meanwhile, in the country and the 'safe' areas, schools became horrendously over-crowded, classes enormous. Home children mixed uneasily with evacuees and, in some cases, refugees. Staff changes were a regular feature. Gone for most of the war were the younger male teachers. Into their jobs came older, married women – previously barred from teaching – and an assortment of clergymen, retired teachers, conscientious objectors, and many others without any formal teaching qualifications. To the delight of many pupils, male teachers appeared in girls' schools for the first time, and female teachers in boys' schools.

Some children initially had no schooling at all, for weeks or even months on end. Many found paid work, and never returned. Others frequently played truant, spending time in the cinema, collecting shrapnel in the street or playing for hours on bomb sites. In the early months, significant numbers went to school in the morning or the afternoon only, since premises often had to be shared between two or even three separate schools. Others received part-time schooling in the form of home tuition. Not surprisingly, there was a significant increase in delinquency, malicious damage and petty theft by young people during this period.

Life within school was often dramatically different from what it had been in peacetime. Playgrounds and playing fields were dug up for shelters, or converted into allotments. Cadet corps, air training corps and girls' training corps sprang up. Individual schools adopted a minesweeper or destroyer, or saved money to help 'buy' a Spitfire or Hurricane plane. Assembly became the occasion for reporting the progress of the war, for instilling pupils with patriotic fervour, even chauvinism; or, more sombrely, for a roll-call of present and former pupils who had become casualties of the bombing, or been killed on active service.

Lessons were constantly interrupted by air-raid alerts, or the real thing. Children, armed with the necessary iron rations, spent many hours, sometimes the whole day, in the nearest shelter. There, teachers attempted to keep up both their spirits and their education, not always successfully. Some older children had to sit their exams in the shelters. Examiners took such circumstances into account: it was rumoured in some areas that a solid air-raid in mid-exam was worth an extra grade. Some children sitting for 'The Scholarship' during the Blitz period were assessed simply on their previous work, and only borderline cases actually had to sit the examination.

In many schools the curriculum was directly affected by the war. Maps showing the battle for Europe were used in geography. Art lessons offered an opportunity for creating posters for War Weapons Week or National Savings Week. Older children sometimes even helped the war effort directly by making small munitions in school workshops. History became current affairs, with outside speakers much in demand. In the country, evacuated city children who had difficulty in identifying a cow were suddenly exposed to nature studies. Yet other schools tried as far as possible to retain the traditional content of lessons. A widespread problem, though, was the acute shortage of materials as basic as paper, pencils and exercise books – at least in state schools. Ingenuity and improvisation were the order of the day as teachers tried desperately to harvest scarce resources.

Many traditional school rules went by the board. Uniform became an increasing problem, especially when rationing was introduced, and many schools turned a blind eye to infringements. Nevertheless, some teachers still tried to enforce the accepted notions of proper dress, even at the height of the Blitz. Corporal punishment was still the norm in most schools, primary as well as secondary, but some of the sadistic practices that took place in certain isolated villages still came as a surprise to many educationalists and parents, as well as a shock to evacuated city children. On the other hand, there were plenty of examples of friendlier, more relaxed relationships between teachers and pupils, brought on by the need to face danger together.

Inevitably, children in country schools were less dramatically affected than their counterparts in the town and city schools, except perhaps during the three evacuation periods. But most children's education was in some way disturbed by the war, even if some of them gained by the experience. Yet the shock given to the school system did increase the momentum for the kind of radical reform that was marked by the 1944 Education Act.

The State Schoolgirl

All the teachers were very old, grey-haired people, and none of them seemed human.

Kate Eggleston

I was at primary school when war broke out, in Nottingham. As a small child I can remember the evacuees coming. We were horrible to them. It's one of my most shameful memories, how nasty we were. We didn't want them to come, and we all ganged up on them in the playground. We were all in a big circle and the poor evacuees were herded together in the middle, and we were glaring at them and saying, 'You made us squash up in our classrooms, you've done this, you've done that.' I can remember them now, looking frightened to death. They were poor little East Enders, they weren't tough at all, they were poor little thin, puny things. They used to be very quiet, and they only used to talk to each other. We weren't friendly with them at all, we were very much apart, we just ignored them.

It was prejudice from the teachers from the word go. When the evacuees arrived, they were pushed round from classroom to classroom in a big bunch according to their ages, in no welcoming way. All the existing children had to sit three to a bench instead of two, so we all moved up, and the evacuees sat down by the windows, which must have been the coldest and the draughtiest place in the classroom. I remember that we were put into sets, and that the 'duffers' were the ones that sat by the window, so all the evacuees were in the duffers' set. The top sets always sat nearest the corridor by the radiators, so they had the best places. Every Monday there used to be a few less evacuees in the classroom, and the poor kids were obviously *completely* unhappy, and their parents just took them home again. When Monday morning came the classrooms were rearranged. Gradually there were fewer and fewer evacuees, until there were none left at all.

All the teachers were very old, grey-haired people. The headmaster had TB, so he wasn't in the war anyway. The only young teachers we had were very young women, who I gathered later were still going through college. The headmaster was a horrible man, and none of the teachers seemed human. When I went on to the grammar school there were no young men at all, they'd all gone – except one with an artificial leg, he'd been invalided out.

Once again there was prejudice, this time against the Jewish children. We had a handful of refugee children. They used to opt out when it came to reading the New Testament, and just sit quietly. The teachers didn't like this. I can always remember them getting into *terrible* trouble with one teacher. She said: 'You didn't ask to be excused from this lesson', and the poor little child sat there and said, 'But I thought you knew I was a Jew, and we don't read the New Testament.' Of course she knew perfectly well. But I remember they were always talked about in an unpleasant way, not only by the children but the adults as well. They'd say, 'They've come from nothing, they've got no money, and look at them now, they've made money, Jews are like that.' One of these Jewish kids got an entrance pass to the boys' high school in Nottingham, which picked off the cream of the children from the whole county. These entrances and scholarships were highly prized in our school. And there was immediately talk: 'How did *he* get it? He must have had some influence somewhere.' But the lad was clever, and that was that. But the Jews were disliked. We had no idea what had happened to them before, and we didn't care.

We lived in West Bridgford, a suburb of Nottingham. It was divided into two halves by a canal, which were known as the tanner and bob sides. We lived on the bob side. It wasn't the slums of Nottingham, it was a better area. Most of them were three-bedroomed houses. I remember when people came round to see who was going to have refugees, the controversy there was as to who was going to have to move bedrooms. The prejudice against the evacuees was terrible.

Most of us at the primary school lived within a mile's radius of the school. I remember you had to practise running home when there was going to be a raid, because there were no shelters in the school, and you had to see how long it took you. On the whole the war didn't come into school work. But there were never any materials that I can remember. We never had any new books, and the ones we did have always had their pages coming out. The only colour books that we had were history books, and they were purple ones with colour pictures in. You know how at that age you don't know the meaning of some words – 'history', 'geography'. I always knew history as 'that coloured subject'.

At secondary school I had three different versions of *Macbeth* to read the text, because there were so many pages out. Where there were pages missing in one version you went and got another, and hoped the page was in that one. History there never went beyond 1914. We never had any visitors to talk, there were no current affairs people. What there was, was rampant imperialism; I don't think I knew where the Middle East was. I can remember doing 'Where are you going to all you big steamers?/ If anyone hinders your coming we'll starve' – that type of poem.

On the whole I think you got more of the war at home actually. My father worked at Boots the Chemist, and he would come home every night by six o'clock to listen to the news, to hear where the bombs had dropped. He was in the Home Guard, and I remember him dressing up for duty every night. He was a very, very scientific man, and he worked out that his unit, which was on duty every night, always had more air raids than anyone else. He was one of those who kept a graph of everything. He worked awfully hard, he didn't get an awful lot of sleep. A lot of it was a waste of time, though, as we didn't get a lot of bombs, they tended to go to Coventry. When we did have the odd bomb that became a real talking-point. Once when there was devastation in a part of West Bridgford, everyone was out looking at the great crater on the bowling green. It seemed huge to my young eyes.

My father was too old to go in the forces, he'd been in the First World War. Most of the children of my age had their fathers at home. A lot of people were working in munitions; we had a big ordnance factory not far from us. I remember the man next door worked there, and one day there was an explosion and he damaged his hand very badly. I also remember one child at the grammar school who was always late. When he was finally asked why he'd been late so many times he said that he'd been bombed out. All the children on his council estate groaned, because he'd been bombed two years before and was still living on it as an excuse.

I can remember people coming to the school and talking to the children about 'make do and mend'. You didn't waste a thing in the war, not a thing. You learnt how to alter your clothes, make them bigger, put panels in your skirt, and goodness only knows what. Every weekend the paper used to have things on 'make do and mend'. You didn't throw anything away at all. My mother wasn't very good at sewing, but she did her best. We had a big rag-bag which everything went into, to be turned into dusters when they were too torn to be of use. And second-hand clothes – you lived on second-hand clothes. I can remember my cousin sending down a trunk of clothes which probably weren't even new when she'd had them. I lived on that trunkful for absolutely years. You had new underwear, but not new top clothes. I can remember wearing the same dress for years for the Sunday School anniversary. When my brother went into long trousers he got all the coupons that year. My mother never got anything, nor my father. He got his Home Guard uniform and shoes free, so he used to garden in those shoes to help with the coupons.

My mother was at the age when she was excused work so she could look after us. For her one of the chief worries was food; she was always worried sick about that. If you had an egg at tea-time that was the exception. Usually you had bread and butter and jam – bread and scrape as it was always known, because you scraped the butter on and then you scraped it off again. We didn't have a knife and fork at tea-time, except on special occasions. I remember also you had to save up for weeks to buy special things for Christmas. I can remember one year our buying suet to go in the Christmas pudding, and it was rancid. You could get chicken sometimes, it was supplied by the milk lady.

I always remember going to the butcher's. I was a very frail child, and I hated the smell of blood and the sight of animal dripping. The times I used to queue and then come home with a face as white as a sheet, and I'd say to my parents, 'I haven't got the meat, I felt ill in the butcher's', and they'd say, 'Oh, never mind, we'll have something else today.' Fortunately we had a garden and an allotment, so there were always vegetables in our house. The food queues seemed to stretch for miles. I remember one of my friends always had money in her purse, because her mother used to say, 'Now if you see a queue on the avenue, you've got to get in it, just buy whatever it is. Here's half a crown. You're not to spend it on anything else, but whatever you see a queue for, go and get it.'

One Christmas a fox got into our hen roost, so instead of chicken we had rabbit. But you couldn't get things cleaned, you couldn't buy them ready done because they were short of labour. I remember my father going down the shed to clean out his blessed fowl and coming back with a face as white as a sheet, saying, 'Well, if I've got to clean a fowl next year, we're not having one.'

There was a lot of black market going on. We were registered with the Co-op, and you never got anything extra from the Co-op. But my mother used to go down to the butcher's and give him a bit of tea, and he'd give us a bit more meat. Milk was a great shortage too. My mother had colitis and had a medical certificate to say she could have extra milk, but as I would never have tea I drank it all. I was a very malnourished child. I always remember the school doctor coming and saying to my mother, 'This child is malnourished', and I pricked up my ears, wondering what 'malnourished' meant. My mother went scarlet.

You hardly ever went out, and you didn't have holidays; nobody in our area went away at all. You could go into the country, but you didn't go running off to the seaside, because there was no petrol, and anyway the seaside was blockaded. For amusement you played in the garden. There was civic entertainment in the park every summer. One event I remember was the circus; I remember being thrilled to bits with the lion. It was all to give the populace something to do because they couldn't go on holiday.

You tended not to go out after dark – especially in the winter – because of the blackout. You stayed in and played board games like Ludo, and knitted and talked and listened to the radio. A lot of children were very keen on *ITMA*, but I used to just sit there and say, 'What's funny about that?' and my family would say, 'We're all listening to it now, we'll explain later.' The sense of humour seemed to be above my head, but perhaps I was just a little bit too young.

We were brought up with a hatred of Hitler. He was a figurehead, and we hated him. We had a dartboard I remember, and we used to throw darts at Hitler's face. I can see that dartboard now as clearly as anything. All Germans were horrible, the only good German was a dead German. I didn't *know* anybody German, but that was what we were brought up to think, both at home and at school. The headmaster used to go on about the war. Wings for Victory I can remember – we used to do 'weeks' when everybody had to give money to help build Spitfires. There was a terrific amount of savings, you were always saving stamps to help the home economy – except there was nothing to buy in the shops anyway.

There used to be quite a lot of soldiers about. You know how parents are always saying, 'Don't go anywhere with strange men.' Our mother said, 'A lot of these soldiers have had nasty experiences in the war, and they don't always quite know what they are doing. So you mustn't go off with any of them.' And so to my mind, all the badness that was available from men was caused by the war and their experience in it.

For my mother the epitome of the war was the blackout, which she hated. As soon as victory was declared on VE Day, I remember she took off all those wretched nets that had to be glued to the window in case of bomb blast. I remember too the great rejoicing and the parties all the children had everywhere. We all got a shiny silver sixpence and a mug.

The Country Teacher

The first day I was there the police came up, because three of the seven-year-olds had been soliciting Americans for their older sisters.

Mary-Rose Murphy

Teacher training college was out in the wilds of Berkshire. The college had been evacuated from London to Cold Ash, a small farming community. The village itself didn't have much to offer, and we didn't have any come and go with the local people. We were ringed with American camps, and there were dances at Newbury at the Corn Exchange – Cold Ash didn't even have a village hall, so there weren't any there. There was one bus from the village, and the first time you got on the driver gave you a ticket. Thereafter he just looked at you and nodded and didn't bother. It was a shilling return into Newbury, which was 5 miles away, and he used to stop at all the cottages, picking things up and taking orders. And then halfway to Newbury he'd stop and ask who was going to the pictures, who was going to the Corn Exchange, who was going to be late. He then announced his times of coming back. That bus was a public service. No one was refused: you sat on each other's knee, you stood, you sat on a crate of chickens. People put themselves out, especially in the villages, which had always been close-knit communities, and became even more so.

The college was housed in a big orphanage, but it was very, very cramped and narrow. It had to be because lecturers were doubling in subjects, there wasn't room to have a classroom each, only very specialist subjects like needlework or biology had one. The rooms were *terribly* small, and the refectory was used for lectures as well as meals, and for music too. And the great attic was bunged up to the top with inflammable material, and we used that for lectures too. We had very small rooms ourselves, little cells, and we were very much thrown on each other. There were only three single rooms, one for the students' president, two for the infirmary. So if there were more than two people ill, they had to be nursed in their own room. And if there was an epidemic of German measles, you just shared your room with the spots and the lumps. Blackouts were a fearful bugbear, and on hot nights it was awful. One of the nuns went round each night, at intervals, to make sure the blackout was in force.

Education materials were lacking. There was a *terrific* paper shortage, and when we did have paper it was full of little wood-chips. It was wartime standard paper, which had imperfections that would never be passed nowadays. Biros hadn't been invented, it was fountain pens and ink. I remember our Indian ink running out, so when you were doing maps you had to do it in fountain pen. You couldn't get fountain pens very easily, so many people used ordinary nibs, and dipped. It was very primitive. Coloured pencils were very hard to get. Very few new books were being printed, so we used the textbooks that we had already.

The college lecturers used the war in various ways. The art lecturer used to show us the beauties of the countryside. The biology lecturer used the wild flowers. We used to cycle everywhere; the student nuns used to cycle in their habits. As there was very little petrol, it was very difficult to get visiting speakers to come. Travelling was so difficult: you had to have your identity card, you could never find your way anywhere, there were no signposts, you couldn't come by car, and trains were erratic. One or two people came in uniform and told us about cadet corps, so that those who were going to be senior school teachers would know about that. We did have C.S. Lewis, who came to give a lecture on medieval literature. And we had a man come to talk about aspects of air-raid precautions, most of which we knew already, because most of us had done fire-watching and things like that.

There was a village school at Cold Ash, and we used to go there and do teaching practice. There was one boy who was twelve, and still in the infants. He was perfectly bright, perfectly normal, but in his first year in the juniors he'd been rude, and the head had told him to apologize, and he wouldn't. So she said, 'You're a baby, go and stay with the babies until you apologize.' He was still there five years later. He was perfectly happy, he used to come out with the little ones, join in their PE, and love it. Otherwise he just sat and got on with work himself, and nothing was done about it. They didn't have inspectors or anything around.

In a lot of the village schools you had supplementary teachers. The only qualifications were that you had to be over eighteen and vaccinated. I was horrified: I knew unqualified teachers, but this was a third category. They were all right. They came in as more and more of the men teachers were being called up, so it became nearly all women staffing the schools. Then there were the unqualified teachers. Several of them had been pupil-teachers and never gone to college, but carried on in the school. In those days one could still find people who had gone to a school at five, become a pupil-teacher, either stayed on or gone back to college, come back to the same school, and reached retirement there, spending their entire lives in the one school. People who changed a lot were considered gadabouts and unstable. You got to a school and you stayed put.

Teaching practice was a bit of a problem. The lecturers came together to see you because of petrol rationing. They were only allowed so much, so they came in a bunch. It was like a complete inspection, you got the whole mob. You felt very nervous when they came.

I was given top infants in E.P. Collier Infants School in Reading. The first day the police came up, because three seven-year-olds had been soliciting Americans for their older sisters. Of course they were below juvenile court age, so they could only be told off. They just laughed. We were terribly shocked, but the kids weren't. I remember that first day the headmistress welcomed us by saying that she herself would serve our lunch. The first course was just vegetables and gravy. The second was suet roll with custard, and when we ate the roll we found it was a meat roll.

The rural schools varied. They were mainly church schools, built with high walls and higher windows, so that children didn't get distracted but light came in. They had great tortoise stoves that were usually polished to a high shine. In the winter they went out, though the senior boys were very good at lighting them. The girls quite often did the washing up for the meals that came in from Newbury. In some of the schools the boys and girls were segregated for break, but not in all of them. Some children were still sewn up for the winter: you could tell those ones a mile off! You couldn't afford to have PE kit or shoes – shoes were five coupons, and you couldn't give up five coupons for a lesson. So the senior boys would just strip off their shirts.

The schools were all-age and very often only divided by a curtain. If they weren't divided like this, the children at the back of both sets got the best of both worlds, so to speak. You followed one teacher and then you followed another, your ears flapping and your head turning. Tables were generally all recited together, and hymns. So even the five-year-olds would be sitting chanting, 'Twelve twelves are a hundred and forty-four, twenty-two yards one chain, ten chains one furlong, eight furlongs one mile.' All these things the whole school would do together. Rote learning was typical in these schools.

The regime was very strict. You got caned for talking, for turning round, pretty well for sneezing. As a student you didn't cane the children yourself, but you were there when it happened. Most of the schools didn't have staffrooms, and the head did the secretarial work by coming in early. Of course if there was only a curtain, you could hear everything that was going on. As a student it made you feel very nervous, but it did lead to good discipline, because the head could hear everything.

In one school I was in, in Greenham, they had just three history books in the senior part, and I think it was the same for geography, so they knew them fairly thoroughly. It was there that we had a confounded Flying Fortress plane over the way, which revved up every hour, on the hour, so that you had to stop work until it took off.

We taught reading with big reading sheets that came over the blackboard, with sentences and three-letter words, because it was phonic. So you got 'A Pig in a Wig Did the Jig'. Rural children were familiar with pigs, but were a bit baffled by wigs and jigs. Another one was 'Nell Fell She Hurt Her Knee'.

For my inspection at one school we had just done reading round the class, which was forbidden – our lecturers said it shouldn't be used, because the children wasted their time while others were reading. Nevertheless most schools did it. Some didn't, because the bright children could work out where their bit would be, and then dream until it came. So sometimes you changed the order.

After I got my certificate I started teaching at Cove County Infant and Junior School. The head said, 'This is your class, dear,' and off she went. I looked at this mass of wriggling worms and I said, 'Sit down.' They all sat, and I thought, 'There's nothing to this lark!' Then I took the register. We weren't shown how to do the register at college, because we were told each county had its own system and that someone on the staff would show us. Did they, Hector! Anyway, I looked at it, and the system seemed easy:

you put a red mark one way in the morning, a red mark the other way in the afternoon,\ a black ring if they were away, an H if they were away for hospital treatment, an X for infectious disease, a T for treatment, and a V if they were away for holiday – during the war holidays were staggered, as many parents couldn't take them during the holiday time. There were two faults for which you could be dismissed from teaching: one was moral turpitude, the other an error in your register.

Suddenly one of the children came up to me and said, 'I feel sick' – and he was, all over the register. I didn't know what to do. Next to my room was the one where the women did the washing up. I dashed in, and there was a tall, gaunt woman, with a green overall and a whistle on a lanyard round her neck. I said, 'One of the children's been sick over the register.' She gave me a look of withering scorn, came back into the room, picked up a small chair, put the boy outside on the chair, then took a floor cloth and went over the register, and then went out again.

A couple of minutes later I looked up and saw all my class going out. I said, 'Hoy!' One of them turned round and said, 'Siren's gone, miss.' The tall woman came in again and said, 'The hurricane lamp's behind the piano in the hall; your shelter's the fourth' – and off *she* went. So I went into the hall, found a hurricane lamp and went outside. There were eight shelters, and I finally located mine by the racket. I hadn't matches to light the lamp, so I couldn't see what was going on, though I soon gathered what was. There hadn't been any sirens for a while and the shelters were full of water and frogs, and the boys were catching the frogs and putting them down the girls' necks. Of course I couldn't catch them. We had four more sirens that day, and each time my class were first out and last back. Not unnaturally I came with matches the next day. They also had to take their gas masks to the shelter and back again – oh yes, you were caned if you forgot your gas mask.

You couldn't get books, chalk, things like that. We used slates instead of books and old supplies of chalk. The children all wrote on slates except the top infants who had books. I discouraged them from spitting to wipe the slate clean, but they always used to manage to knock their little mugs of water over. We counted on little cowrie shells, I found a big supply of those. But we had no apparatus, none of the fitting-together Fisher Price dinky toys. There was none of that, you just couldn't get toys. We couldn't get balls either, and courses began on how to make balls with papier mâché and string. They didn't bounce, of course, but we could teach rolling and throwing and catching.

The food was mince, because the authorities felt mince was suitable for infants. So you had children up to twelve getting mince day after day. There was no thought about diet, although there was a lot in other ways: the free orange juice, the milk, everything that could be given to the young went to them. We were deprived, the children got it, which I think was fair.

They used to pay for their milk then. Every Monday I used to collect dinner money, milk money and national savings – the milk wasn't free until the Labour government came in. The savings weren't compulsory, but even some of the poorest managed, though a few didn't. It was a sixpenny stamp every week: some children brought in their sixpence, some brought in half a crown. There were also children on free school meals. I used to call them up to hand in their money. When I realized I hadn't called some children I said to the head, 'This one's . . .' and she said in a whisper, 'Oh no dear, very poor family. Free.' But I'd seen the kids' eyes when they just sat there, looking glum. So I thought, 'Right, we must get round this.' So I used to call them up as well, so that they didn't feel left out. As I called each child out, I used to chat to them for a couple of moments. I had a couple of books piled up, so no one could see what each child was giving.

There was not a lot of poverty, not compared with that in the cities and in the slums – I had a cousin who taught in Glasgow, so I'd heard about that. At least all our children had clothes. Some of the girls came to school in very pretty nylon dresses made out of parachute panels, which you could get on the black market. Big families used to swap their clothing coupons for cash – very illegal, but all the more fun for that.

This was a big school with eight classes, and the head just sat in her office; I didn't see any more of her after the first day. I just had to use such common sense as I had, and get on with it. I found a kindred spirit across the way from me, and she gave me a lot of help. We just did the best we could.

In general you just turned your hand to what was available, and got on with it. You went and commiserated with parents when the worst happened. You gave the children extra hugs and love. I remember they used to have their diphtheria injections at school. I used to keep some sweets by and pop one in after the injection. The school doctor would come, and the terrified child would stand up on the table, clinging to me like grim death.

The war didn't upset the very young children, because they didn't know any different. The older ones were upset, those who could remember their fathers, and the fathers who didn't come back. Also those who found themselves with new brothers and sisters, and 'uncles'. Nearly everybody sprouted a Canadian uncle, and there was inevitably a rise in the population. The resentment was always against the woman, however, and not the Canadian. 'No better than she should be, husband off at the war, and she'd done this' was the attitude. I was very friendly with some people who kept a brothel down in Cove that was much used by the Canadians. I had one of their children in my class, and the first day the parents came up in a body, not wanting their children to sit next to this child. But I managed to sort that one out, because I had one mother who had been up twice complaining about whoever her child was sitting next to. So I put this particular boy next to the little girl, and the girl next to the wall. Not even that mother could come up a third time and complain.

There were a lot of dads missing, and an awful lot for some of them to get used to when they came back. There was a lot of shaking down, which was difficult to do, difficult to understand. And of course reconciliations where those could be made, with some fathers accepting 'foster children'; or walk-outs when that wasn't accepted, with the wives saying, 'Well, I don't know what *you* got up to.'

Although the war ended in 1945, other things didn't. Rationing went on, shortages went on. Everyone said, 'We must work for peace, I don't want my kids to go through what I've gone through.' Yet, although one wouldn't wish war on anyone, in some ways we're depriving our children of hardship, which perhaps can sometimes be a good thing. Perhaps things are a little too easy. Ideals I think sometimes need a little hardening.

How did we get through it? I remember while I was still at school, we were machine-gunned by a Jerry who had nothing better to do. And Miss White, a member of staff, was going up the drive from the Anglican church. She simply put up her umbrella and continued on her way. It was the British spirit. We were an island, we had never been overrun since the days of the Goths, and if the Goths were coming back, bad luck: we just felt they couldn't.

Ethel Robinson and her husband on their wedding day, 1940.

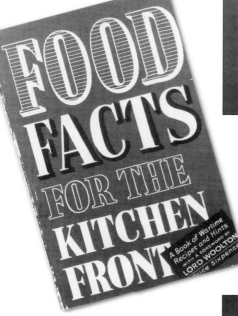

Jane Barham as a seven-year-old in Cambridge during the war.

Gwendolen Potter during the last year of the war.

"DIET for the Expectant Mother"

John Howell (back row, second from right) and fellow Welsh cricketers, 1945.

Cynthia Gillett, wartime girl guide: 'You saluted the flag as you walked round the field.'

WILL'S CIGARETTES

PROTECTING YOUR WINDOWS — A SANDBAG DEFENCE

Jean Stafford and her father, 1942.

Dennis Briggs and fellow evacuee, safe in Oxfordshire.

Thank you, Foster-Parents... we want more like you!

The Secretary of State, who has been entrusted by the Government with the conduct of evacuation, asks you urgently to join the Roll of those who are willing to receive children. Please apply to your local Council.

WILLS'S CIGARETTES

EQUIPPING YOUR REFUGE ROOM —B

Mary Wolfard in her clerical days at Cirencester.

Lettice Curtis: 'There was some opposition to women pilots to start with.'

WOMEN

please lend your support a little longer ...

let's work together for

PROSPERITY

Mary Davies (left) as a young civil servant in London, 1943.

Kay Ekevall on the river at Cambridge, 1940.

AN APPEAL TO WOMEN

Will You drive to the Rescue?

LONDON VOLUNTEER Ambulance Service

WILLS'S CIGARETTES

REMOVAL OF INCENDIARY BOMB WITH SCOOP AND HOE

Joan Collins on graduation day in Bristol, 1944.

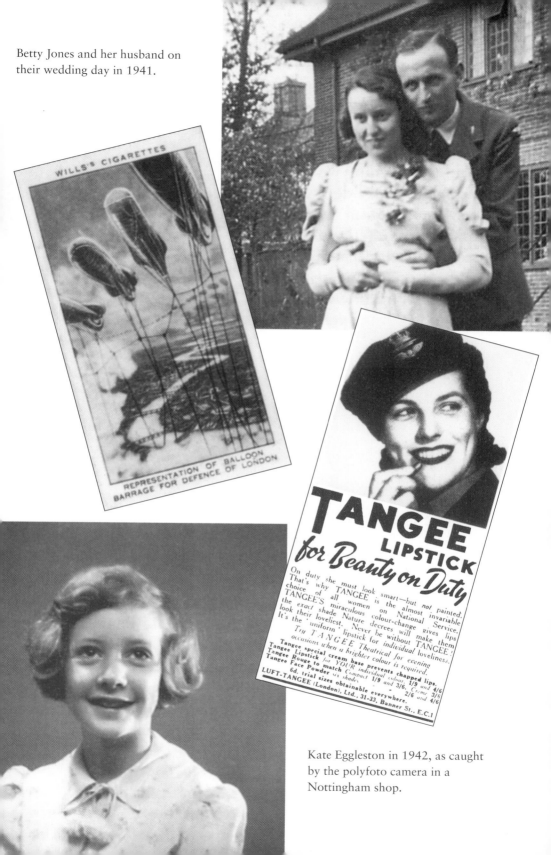

Betty Jones and her husband on their wedding day in 1941.

WILLS'S CIGARETTES

REPRESENTATION OF BALLOON
BARRAGE FOR DEFENCE OF LONDON

TANGEE LIPSTICK
for Beauty on Duty

On duty she must look smart—but not painted.
That's why TANGEE is the almost invariable
choice of all women on National Service.
TANGEE'S miraculous colour-change gives the
the exact shade Nature decrees will make them
look their loveliest. Never be without TANGEE:
It's the 'uniform' lipstick for individual loveliness.
Try TANGEE Theatrical for evening
occasions when a brighter colour is required.
Tangee special cream base prevents chapped lips.
Tangee Lipstick for YOUR individual colour. 1/9 and 4/6
Tangee Rouge to match Compact. 1/9 and 3/6. Creme 3/6.
Tangee Face Powder in shades - 2/6 and 4/6
6d. trial sizes obtainable everywhere.
LUFT-TANGEE (London), Ltd., 31-33, Banner St., E.C.1

Kate Eggleston in 1942, as caught
by the polyfoto camera in a
Nottingham shop.

Mary-Rose Murphy as a young teacher, 1944.

Constance Holt while editor of the wartime *Woman's Own*.

Extracts from the diary of a Suffolk teacher, 1939–40

17 October. Today we had our first air-raid warning. We had just gone over to have dinner and had got as far as our soup. Everybody was busy talking about an air raid on Hull that morning when our hooter began bellowing forth its horrible note. I ran to get H, who was in bed with a temperature, and I knew she would be frightened. I picked up her eiderdown and we went into the trench. The other children were there complete with gas masks, E looking as white as a sheet, and saying, 'I feel frightened', over and over again.

On the road outside the school air-raid wardens had sprung into activity – they looked so completely ineffectual and frightened despite the tin hats they were wearing that it made one want to laugh, and at the same time it made one want to cry. We lit the lamps in the dugout and the children were reading books about Peter Rabbit and *The Adventures of Henny Penny*. By and by they got tired of this, and began using the dugout as a gymnasium, turning somersaults on the crossbar.

The effect of this our first warning was to make us feel very sleepy, but instead we must begin digging on the ramp of our dugout, which refused to drain properly and is deep in mud. Every night now I see that the children have their clothes ready in case we have to get up in the night – they are very good about this and do a lot of straightening out for themselves – particularly when I am ready to turn out their lights! They also secrete private supplies of sweets in their gas mask cases, and then try to forget about them so that they get a surprise one day. The forgetting part of this doesn't seem to work too well, and quite often before breakfast there is a scuffling in the hall where the gas masks are kept – someone is liquidating his private store.

11 November. Everybody seems to be in a state of expectation today, and there are rumours all around of an attempted invasion of the Suffolk coast. What truth there is in this it is difficult to say, but we do seem to have a terrific number of soldiers in this part of the country.

While we were playing golf this afternoon we heard a sudden roar of planes, and looked up to see nine approaching from the sea. One wondered what they were about, and certainly hoped they were ours. Aldeburgh seems to be in a particularly nervous state ever since they heard from the wireless propaganda station that they had been heavily bombed.

Always on the coast the war seems so much nearer, it's like being on the boundary line: here we are playing golf, and just over there, on a strip of the sea where warships are convoying boats, you feel the war has being. Soon I suppose we shall have planes crossing this boundary line, and making us participators in this senseless war which nobody wants.

25 November. F came into my room today and began saying: 'I've never seen a Siegfried, what does it look like? I've often been down to the sea, but I've never found one.' It seemed a pity to enlighten her.

7 February. We heard rumours of some toy balloons floating in our direction. We heard that they might contain poisonous gas, and N came over and told the children that if they saw any balloons lying in the grounds they were not to touch them. We heard afterwards they were balloons which were being used for meteorological purposes, and quite harmless. Funny the things we have to tell children nowadays.

11 February. When S came back from a shopping expedition this afternoon she said, 'We seem to be short of everything except soldiers, and I'm glad we're not short of them or else Hitler might win the war. In fact perhaps he will win the war – ooh! I can't think what it will be like if he does, but somehow I don't think he will. Do you?' To which I replied, 'I don't know.'

11 May. We heard this morning that Hitler had invaded Belgium and Holland, giving us a very worried feeling that our time is coming near. We the grown-ups feel very tense, but fortunately the children, who have heard so often that Hitler has invaded somewhere, seem to be not at all disturbed. S said, 'Last night I saw a plane going to Holland, then it came back, and then it went again,' just as if it were a terrific game.

15 May. This morning we were awakened at 4.30 by planes passing, and later there was a series of explosions which rocked the house terrifically. On the news we heard that most of Holland had capitulated. A meeting was called at school, as it had been decided that it was time to paste paper on the windows to prevent the glass from flying; so there were no fixed lessons. However, I took my children into the hut, because they were rather frightened about things. After the terrific explosions of the early morning, I moved their tables into the middle of the room away from the windows. I said, 'That's in case the windows break, so you won't get cut with the glass,' and they took it quite calmly and made no comment. All the windows have now been pasted with strips of paper, and look very ugly.

23 May. E and P have a new game. They have found an old tin which they sound every evening as an air-raid warning. Then they go inside and fetch their gas masks and go into the shelter where they stay for a while.

7 June. Today was spent in packing up the children's clothes. They are going home tomorrow while we look for a school in a safer area. We hope there is not a disturbed night because they leave so early in the morning.

8 June. Unfortunately the siren went again last night about 11.15. The children were harder to wake than ever, and kept getting back into bed again as soon as we had stood them on their feet. But eventually we got into the shelter and made beds there immediately, and so they went to sleep at once. This time we only had to stay there for an hour, and when the all-clear went the children were sound asleep, and so we left them and they slept until 6.30. E said, 'I was never so surprised in all my life when I woke up, I couldn't think where I was or what had happened.' We managed to get up in time and they have all gone on the train. It was sad to see them go, but also a relief, because I am sure we will have a lot of warnings like this now.

The Public Schoolboy

We were under firm instructions that if the air-raid warning went we were to go down into the basement, and put on our honour not to discuss the exam questions, or take any books down with us.

David Howell

When war started I was in my second year at Chigwell, a small, independent boys' school in Essex, a boarding and day school. I had started out as a day boy on a county place, and travelled from my home in Ilford, 4 miles away. I had a younger brother who was evacuated to Ipswich. The compromise for me was being sent as a boarder to Chigwell.

During the Phoney War period the main difference was that the school was organized on a war footing. Air-raid shelters were dug, a land girl was hired, and part of the extensive playing fields were given over to the production of vegetables. The school was doing its bit. Concrete shelters were dug in odd spots around the grounds, and the blackout system was brought into operation. We had air-raid drill, and when the invasion scare started in the summer of 1940, and a ban was placed on the ringing of bells, instead of lesson change being signalled by bells, we had somebody from the corps blowing a bugle.

Some of the younger masters went off to the forces immediately. The main difference was that membership of the junior training corps became compulsory instead of being voluntary, as it was before the war, when it was the officer training corps. The OTC had contacted perhaps the majority of the boys. One became eligible to join at fourteen. As far as I could tell, there was no great feeling that membership was some outrageous imposition, it was taken as normal.

During the Battle of Britain my parents decided that my brother and myself ought to be evacuated, after a number of near misses on our house. We went to a village 4 miles outside Northampton called Kislingbury. After a year we went back to London, things being fairly quiet. So back I went to Chigwell for the rest of the war, where I followed the traditional academic curriculum. Chigwell prided itself on its classical tradition, which meant that everything else was neglected. The head himself did a lot of the sixth-form classical teaching, but he had other commitments during the war: he was on various selection boards for officers, which involved attendance in London, so he was away. The senior classical master was in the RAF, so we were left in the hands of the junior one. And most of the masters had duties allied with the war, either in the Home Guard or as air-raid wardens.

By now the corps had expanded. There were two officers, there was a captain in charge of the school force, another master who was a lieutenant, and we also had a branch of the air training corps. There was some logic in making corps membership compulsory, since at eighteen you were called up unless you had asthma or very flat feet. It was not a great bone of contention. There was not all that much militarism or jingoistic flag-waving. There were admittedly one or two boys to whose heads office went. There was one company sergeant-major who was known behind his back as Die Führer, and one or two others who flung their weight about. One of them suggested that on corps days the boys should salute officers every time they passed them. But the masters who were the officers said they wouldn't have it, they would be spending all their time at the salute. In addition there were occasional exercises, the corps had a field day, there was an annual inspection, and we had pep talks from visiting speakers from the War Office.

Having lectures and outside speakers was popular because it meant the cancellation of classes. I still remember vividly some visiting speakers. One was a daring young man from the Fleet Air Arm, who helped to sink the Italian fleet in Ankara and was involved in other hazardous activities. There were also two old boys, who had found themselves prisoners of war in Italy when the Italians surrendered. When the prison gates were opened they walked out and down half the length of Italy to rejoin their colleagues. Somehow they were able to assemble some photos, which they exhibited on slides, prefacing them with remarks such as, 'Interesting building this, I'm afraid I don't know what it is.' After several castles and cathedrals had appeared unidentified in this way, it became a standing joke. They did cause one master to walk out when they said one of them had been taken short in Rome station, and went into the wrong lavatory, thinking *Uomini* meant Women. He realized his mistake just in time. But I don't think our headmaster was one to get visiting speakers to enliven our social consciences or quicken our interest in the world around us. I remember one very boring old colonel, whom even the head addressed as sir, who talked about dog-breeding.

There was an escape for the more pacifically inclined into the air training corps, which recruited at sixteen. This did a lot of pre-flying training, the emphasis being on groundwork and calculations – we learnt the mysteries of Morse and wireless. It was run by the science master, an agreeable if lazy character; he saw this as quite a pleasant way of doing his bit, but he didn't take the military side of it seriously.

We followed the war news avidly. There was little else in the papers. The only paper taken in the library was the *Daily Telegraph*, but of course one had access to other papers at home. We had a school debating society, and a mock election at the end of the war. Chigwell was in Churchill's constituency. The Conservative candidate modelled himself to a comical extent on our great leader: he got about ninety-six votes, the next candidate getting about twenty-five.

I was able to engage in a bit of subversive activity, because my mother was working for Victor Gollancz the publisher, as all his male staff had been called up. So my introduction to politics was Michael Foot's *Guilty Men*, which was passed around the sixth form, and proved wildly popular. But I was told to stop wasting my time on this political nonsense and concentrate on Higher Cert.

The head was a strong Conservative. I remember he once asked three of us in the classical sixth how we would vote after the war, and what our general political views were. One boy said Labour, and one said, 'Conservative – and I hope the Germans and Russians fight each other to extinction', which struck me as being the most appalling heresy; by this time there was an enormous amount of goodwill towards Russia. In general we took an intelligent interest in the war, and of course elder brothers and fathers were involved in it.

It seems astonishing that we took it so stoically, with air-raid warnings at any time of day or night. When my brother and I went home at the end of the day, we didn't know if our mother would come back from London, we didn't know if we'd find any house. One flying bomb crashed not far from the school while we were all in the dining hall. As I remember, no boy was killed or injured as a result of enemy action, and neither were any masters.

I vividly remember school food, which went from the mediocre to the unspeakable. We had mincemeat, potato or cabbage, some kind of milk pudding, a lot of stodge, with sauces that became more and more watery. Somebody had made a killing in salted cod in Iceland, which stank to high heaven. I suppose it had a lot of protein, but that was its only virtue. At one stage lunch consisted of rather watery soup, based on onions, followed by hunks of bread and cheese – that was our economy measure. Good red meat, which was rationed rather strictly, we had twice a week. After the American invasion we had such delights as spam – spiced ham – and prem – pressed meat. One wag said that in that case dried eggs, which were in plentiful supply, should be called dregs. Then there was a baker in the local shop who produced fresh hot rolls, which were our mainstay during break. Sweets were rationed, the making of ice-cream was banned after 1942, on the grounds that, though it was popular with children and invalids, it had no food value, and was a diversion of scarce resources. All meat became scarce. Some extra account was taken of the needs of growing children, so there was an institutional ration as well as a family ration. So our diet became increasingly monotonous. There were pies which were based on potato and carrot and – we thought it was sawdust – soya beans.

The other difference was school uniform. Chigwell's uniform had always been fairly simple: a dark jacket, dark grey or black trousers, a white or grey shirt – if it had a stiff collar it had to have a tie-pin through the lapels – a plain black tie, and the school cap, from which only prefects were exempt. Now all clothing was rationed, and the number of coupons was grossly insufficient for almost everyone. There was a thriving black market. Even those who wouldn't normally dream of using it felt it necessary to clothe their children with the aid of the black market coupons. So our clothing became shabbier and shabbier, and blind eyes were turned. Jackets became anything in tweed. The blazer, which previously had only been worn to and from games, was countenanced at other times. Shirts became grey instead of white, which was a great advantage. As the tie-pins ruined the collars, they were quietly dropped. We blossomed out into other trousers: you couldn't always get grey flannel, so we had to have what the Army didn't want, which meant dark green or dark brown corduroys. Much though the head cast a disapproving eye over some of the more exotic wear, he couldn't do much about it. Games kit became more varied: shirts used for football had to do for cricket as well, and fewer and fewer boys wore white trousers or even white boots. One had to make do.

I don't recall that we were ever told to be careful in our use of paper or ink or anything like that. And we didn't have the same set books year after year, because the one thing you *could* get during the war were books. So if the masters decided it was time for a change, then thirty brand-new copies of *Thucydides* Book Seven or *The Selected Poems of Robert Browning* would appear.

I remember there were Ministry of Food inspectors who went round checking on alleged hoarding. This was very unpopular, and quite vicious, particularly in the early stages of the war. There was a great deal of bargaining and bartering, and those who didn't take sugar in drinks had a ready-made currency. There was some spectacular evidence of black market operation at Chigwell. The licensee of the local pub had two boys at the school. He was found guilty of black marketing on an advanced scale and sentenced to, I think, three years in prison and a large fine. His two boys left the next day and transferred to a school in Colchester where their dad was in prison. This was the Awful Warning. Examples were made, sometimes of fairly harmless people, of people who were thought to have gone over the tacitly permitted limits.

The most dramatic incidents for us were the School Cert. and Higher Cert. exams in 1944. We were under firm instructions from the examining boards that if an air-raid warning went, we were to go down into the basement, and put on our honour not to discuss the exam questions and not to take any books down with us. There were of course masters down there to see that we didn't actually cheat, but it was a golden opportunity to do a bit of revision inside one's head. I remember our exams being interrupted at least twice. On our return we were to put on our paper, feeling rather heroic about it, 'Paper interrupted by air-raid warning for one hour twenty minutes', or whatever the time was. I'm convinced that this was how we all passed.

The City Teacher

*In school the children responded magnificently. There was
no panic, no confusion, they followed the routine to the
letter, without prompting.*

Eileen Jameson

When war broke out, I'd just started teaching at a junior school in
Middlesex; I'd moved there from one in Hertfordshire. I can't
remember for how long now, but for several days education in Southall
came to a standstill. We were just outside the London area, where
evacuation plans were being put into effect. Children whose parents wanted
them to leave before the expected bombing started were being sent away.
Our school was closed until a decision could be made about the children's
schooling. I remember we all felt very strange, no one knew what to expect,
we lived in a vacuum. The weather was idyllic, and I spent the time
mooning about with a colleague.

Eventually someone suggested the parents ought to be consulted, and so
the staff were sent off all round the catchment area. We had to ask the
parents if they would like the children to be taught in groups in people's
homes in the area, where they would be safer. The reasoning was that if a
bomb fell on the school there could be heavy casualties. It wasn't a very
satisfactory plan, as each teacher would have had to cope with a group
with children of different ages. I have a vague memory of it being tried out,
and being found to be unworkable. In the end the school did reopen.

When the siren sounded the alert, we all had to follow simple instructions. The teacher had to pick up her register and be sure she was the last one from the room. When she arrived in the shelter – which actually was the school corridor and cloakrooms – she had to check all her class were present. You had to keep a pile of books on your desk: I remember mine were an arithmetic book, a poetry book, a large story-book and a song-book. The children also had to have a pile of essential books ready in a corner of their desks, as they wouldn't have time to look for them. They had to pick up a jotter, an arithmetic book, a reader and a pencil. No orders were given, the children just stood in absolute silence, and then moved in single file to the shelter, smartly and without running. They knew speed and order were of the essence.

My class were given a large and fairly airy cloakroom near an outside door, so they had rather more air and space than the unfortunate children squashed on the corridor floor. Even so, during the longer raids the air would become decidedly fuggy, which wasn't surprising when you think there were more than forty children crammed together like this. I remember once they were there from just after assembly until after eight in the evening. Another time we had a whole day of alerts. We were like yo-yos, up and down, up and down. Luckily there were no incidents during those raids, though we were prepared for them; we had a first-aid box and iron rations in biscuit tins for every class. We also had a chemical toilet in the corner of the classroom, as we couldn't risk the children going over to the lavatory block when there was a raid on; the falling shrapnel could be very dangerous. Incidentally, when the night raids replaced the daylight ones, the children would collect shrapnel in the morning, and display it on the front of their desks. You could really score over your classmates if you could produce a gleaming brass shell-cap.

During the hours in the shelter I tried to keep to the timetable. But I also used to give the children a break from sitting on the gym mats by having mini exercise sessions. We stood up for short singing sessions, with plenty of fun songs, action songs, rounds. We also used to do miming, and tell stories and recite poems. We tried to stop them being bored and frightened.

I remember during the Battle of Britain we could hear dog-fights going on above us. We could see the tiny wisps in the sky, and we used to wonder if they were vapour trails or puffs from the Spitfire guns or simply smoke from damaged planes. My eight-year-olds were too young to grasp much about the true import of the war, but they knew from the older children, and the fact that their dads were conscripted, their mums doing war work, the rationing and so on, that these weren't normal times. But in school they responded magnificently. There was no panic, no confusion, they followed the routine to the letter, without prompting.

Of course when the night raids started it was the parents' turn to cope. The children spent night after night in their own shelters in their gardens, in very chilly and cramped conditions, often from sunset to sunrise, so they were very tired and dark-eyed in the mornings. But I think we were probably even more tired than they were. As well as the broken nights we had to keep watch for incendiaries falling. We were split into teams of four. As there were only twelve of us on the staff, our turn came round rather quickly. We did a full day's teaching, dashed home – in my case to digs – had a wash and a meal, if rations allowed, and then returned almost at once for fire-watching.

I remember we had iron bedsteads and hard mattresses and a blanket each in a downstairs classroom, which had protected and blacked-out windows. We couldn't switch on the lights, and so we had to patrol with torches, but they didn't give out much light because they were dimmed with black tissue paper. We used to make sure the outer doors were locked, but sometimes they rattled, and we found it all rather spooky and scary – I think we would have found bombing less frightening. There was one woman in our team who had the most terrifying nightmares, she let out demoniacal screams and moans and she talked in her sleep. Another woman was close to a nervous breakdown, or so we thought. She would come back from her patrol round the building shaking, swearing that someone was there in the darkness. She'd heard soft footsteps behind her, or someone had brushed past her in one of the cloakrooms, or she'd heard someone breathing in a corner of a classroom. We'd make her return to the spot so that we could show her that there was no one there, but we could never convince her. So we were always relieved when morning came. Then we would dash home – provided there wasn't an alert on – have a quick wash and breakfast, and then come straight back to school. I don't know how we did it.

I remember one small incident. We were constantly reminded on the radio and on hoardings to watch our tongues and give absolutely nothing away. One day one of the teachers set a composition on the topic 'My Father'. She discussed the kind of ideas they might use with the children: what Dad looks like, what his hobbies are, his habits, what work he does, where he works, and so on. And she was reported to the police by a parent, as a possible fifth columnist. When she was interviewed she said, 'What me? A bloody fifth columnist? Come off it! With a husband serving in a

Royal Navy frigate?' Of course she was exonerated. She was very angry at first, but she ended up having a good laugh. You had to laugh, if only as an antidote to all the pressures.

In the autumn of 1943 I became pregnant with my first baby. But this wasn't considered a good enough reason to be excused fire-watching. I remember telling the head that I wasn't looking for a way out, but that I was genuinely worried for the baby. But apparently I couldn't be spared. Anyway, my daughter was born in June 1944, during a night when our area had what was probably its worst raid of the war. When she started school five years later the teacher in charge of the reception class, who had taught before the war, told me she had never had such a highly strung class. She said that almost without exception the children were a very unsettled bunch. They were quick to laugh and equally quick to cry, and most of them tended to be apprehensive, especially about noise. These were the children whose mothers were living under great tension during their pre-natal and toddler months, and of course many also had fathers away from home or in the forces.

Letter from a teacher during the first Blitz on London's East End

Monday 9 September 1940

Dear Peter,

I would like to have written a nice cheerful letter but things are pretty grim here. After spending all Saturday night and all Sunday night in a public shelter miles from home and feeling worn from lack of sleep, I've just been bundled down another at 5 p.m., and I'm wondering if it's going to last till 5 tomorrow morning. It's no use trying to tell what some parts of London look like. Sufficient to say it took me two hours to get to work this morning, and then after so many detours that I lost track of where I was.

People are tight-lipped and strained. AFS and ARP personnel are tired, dirty and unshaven, but still fighting. You can judge for yourself when I tell you that Winsor School is just a burnt-out shell; Lathom has one corner completely gone; Woolworths opposite the station is literally just a rubbish heap, and huge girders lie about like twisted hairpins; and a dozen other places in and around the station are just the same. And East Ham is lucky compared with scores of other areas in the whole of the eastern area of London.

For many people the worst disaster is the shambles which used to be Beckton Gas Works. It's surprising how disappointing it is not to have a hot drink of some sort, and to be told at Toni's and the Co-op that you can't have a hot meal of any sort. Nothing is more ironical than the supposedly encouraging story in the press of East Enders worrying about the Sunday joint after the raid. Considering it took an hour to boil a cup of water, and later the gas failed completely, it must have been pretty heroic to get the Sunday joint ready and hot meals for Monday.

Tuesday

I tried to get this finished yesterday but it was impossible. By the time I'd had something to eat last evening the horror had started again. Nothing I could say could faintly describe the terror that fills everyone. Every crumbling crash seems to mean the next one is going to be overhead. The din is nerve-wracking and unending – no respite – no sleep – only the company of your own deadly imagination, and as you look around you see each one is thinking and dreading what you are. You try to do something but it dies in your hands. Some lucky ones manage to find room to stretch out and they sleep fitfully, only to wake pale and nervous as a particularly close one makes everything rock and heave.

How bad it really is can be judged by the fact that today several families that evacuated from Hornchurch have just moved back there. But what can I say that will give you a real picture? It's just hopeless to try. Today still no gas, no electricity in the morning because the East Ham and West Ham power houses were hit, no transport, no milk, only a skeleton post. Some places are a little better, some a little worse.

No school today, all teachers detailed off to help with the soul-destroying job of emergency relief. I was sent to the Methodist Hall in Sixth Avenue. There I have to take the names of the homeless people, provide food (without gas), and try to beg, borrow or steal transport to get them to some place where they can find a roof – Thundersley, Chingford, Epping – anywhere. I won't tell you of the harrowing sights and stories, as you can easily imagine it yourself. At six o'clock I was relieved and tried to get home, but too late. A wave of bombers with fighter escorts passed right across as I pedalled like mad.

It's just gone 9 p.m. and we're waiting for the usual nightmare to begin. I'm forcing myself to write on to keep me from listening to the waves of bombers passing one's head. Three have gone by already, whether ones or hundreds I can't tell, but the old cool indifference is all gone. The number of people who still stay in houses during raids grows even less. The idle watchers of dog-fights are nearly all gone. People are no longer ashamed of their fear, and the shelters are full to suffocation. (The death roll of those killed in public shelters must be terrific.) Here goes another wave of bombers and the staccato of machine-gun fire; it alternates with the shattering crashes of what I hope is gunfire and not bombs. I must try to get some sleep now, altho' the noise doesn't sound like a restful lullaby. I hope I can finish this off and send it off in the morning. If it goes on like this I'll have to cut my losses and get a flat in the West End.

Wednesday
This morning on duty at Herbert Read clearing house. On the way past St Gabriel's Mr Sands called out to stop me – aerial torpedo on Belgrave Road or Street – still getting the dead out. In East Ham Alec Ford stopped me – public shelter gone in High Street – haven't got to the bodies yet – and so it goes on. At this clearing station the refugees panicked during the night and refused to stay, and threatened to sit on the debris of their homes if they weren't evacuated at once. The officer in charge is almost hysterical with fatigue and nerve-strain.

I'm sorry to have written so depressing a letter, but I've written cheerfully to most people who have families in London, and the words have stuck in my throat, and it does me good to loosen up a bit. How long we shall be able to keep a stiff upper lip I don't know, but this sort of work doesn't help. Trying to write in an atmosphere of sobbing women and men too is a little difficult, and when you think it may be your turn next it becomes a little futile to think at all.

Meanwhile, if the receiving officer can find a householder to receive the woman and two children referred to in the enclosed form; if you can do that then the woman can evacuate and receive a billeting allowance. Otherwise there is no school scheme for the evacuation of children with mothers.

Write soon, I've not received a word for days from anywhere, and it makes me feel more hemmed in than ever.

Pete

Taking It

I remember my mother saying, 'If there's another war, I'll put my head in the gas oven.' But she did nothing of the sort, she just got on with it.

MIDDLESEX GIRL

If the Germans had come, it certainly would have been guerrilla warfare. As Churchill said, we would have fought street by street.

CHESHIRE WOMAN

I heard a bomb in the distance, so I said, 'Come on, can't we sing louder than that?' So the children shouted the songs. The head said to me afterwards, 'You're much more useful than your predecessor: he got under the table and cried, and called on the Virgin Mary.'

BRISTOL WOMAN

During the air-raids I never saw anybody in the hospital show the slightest sign that anything was happening. I was sometimes in the operating theatre, and nobody batted an eyelid.

LONDON WOMAN

My grandmother kept an old sword in the corner that someone had given her. She was going to slash any German that came in.

LONDON GIRL

As the war developed people's attitude changed. They were either getting a bit desperate or apathetic about things, losing faith in how it was going to finish.

LONDON MAN

As Prime Minister, Churchill at one stage was asked by an American journalist, 'How are you going to win the war?' 'First we shall see we do not lose it,' he replied. This characteristic remark neatly summed up the essence of the battle on the Home Front. For the civilian population it was above all a war of survival, of individual and collective endurance, of keeping in place, in face of the utmost provocation, as much as possible of the fabric of normal daily life. In the end the British people showed that they could, in the phrase of the time, 'take it'. But only just.

The achievement was certainly a remarkable one. Over the country as a whole, 2 out of 7 houses were destroyed or damaged during the war. In the centre of London, 9 out of 10 were damaged in some way; and many provincial cities suffered similar devastation. At least 60,000 people – half of them in London – were killed by enemy action, while 87,000 were seriously injured and 150,000 slightly hurt.

Yet though the casualties were heavy, the German bombers ultimately failed to achieve their main objective, which was to bring British war production to a halt. Even the heaviest and most effective air raids failed to cause more than a temporary disruption to the essential parts of the wartime economy. While factories and buildings were demolished, machines and equipment often remained intact, or at least usable; and as long as there were men and women to continue production, the country's economic life could continue, and the planes, tanks and other armaments could roll off the assembly lines. Attendance at work remained surprisingly good, despite the grievous dislocation. People did, on the whole, carry on working, even among smouldering ruins and with the minimum of equipment.

Yet this was not just a question of grim defiance or patriotic fervour, though such sentiments were often present. As in peace-time, there was a need to earn a living. Work, whatever its deficiencies and drawbacks, also gave a shape to life, and provided human contact. Though there was absence, much of it tragic, there was never absenteeism on a significant scale. Neither was there any total breakdown in law and order, even after the worst of the raids, when sometimes as many as 1,000 people were killed in one city in a single night. There were certainly some reported incidents of looting, though defining it in wartime is not a simple matter. There was also anger and frustration in many communities at the failure of local officials to keep people informed, at their tendency to get bogged down in red tape or petty territorial intrigues, or simply at their manifest incompetence. But such feelings do not appear to have turned bitter enough to push people on to the rampage, or provoke insurrectionary action.

There was, quite justifiably, widespread fear during the Blitz period, and in some cases nothing less than panic. This frequently led to wholesale flights of entire communities into the countryside – or 'trekking', as it was somewhat euphemistically called at the time. So Londoners escaped in droves to Epping Forest during the grim days of the onslaught on the East End. In Belfast 100,000 people left the city for the country after major raids. Only a fraction of the population spent their nights in Southampton in the immediate aftermath of the Blitz on the city. In Clydebank, near Glasgow, the working population took to the moors; in Liverpool, Coventry and Portsmouth shattered civilians trekked to the surrounding suburbs and villages; in devastated Plymouth they found shelter in farms, barns, hedges and ditches in the Devon countryside.

Yet many of those who trekked were the same people who continued to turn up for work. People generally adapted remarkably well to their new circumstances. The widespread despair and panic that had been predicted by the authorities before the war never materialized. On the contrary, people's mental health seemed to improve. The suicide rate went down, among both men and women, as did the number of admissions to hospital for 'nervous' disorders. Drunkenness figures declined by more than 50 per cent between 1939 and 1942. Of course there were bomb-related diseases and illnesses, but not to a degree that might have mattered.

What, then, caused the civilian population to endure the raids? Various answers have been put forward, many touching on the supposed qualities that make up the British character. Doggedness, a sense of humour, quiet resilience, a misplaced feeling of superiority, the capacity to improvise, a lack of imagination, a love of one's country, coolness, stubbornness – somewhere in the list is the mixture that ensured survival, though different individuals have their own formula. Where there is near unanimity is in the crucial role played by Churchill, who, in Ed Murrow's succinct phrase, 'mobilized the language and made it fight'. He was, perhaps, the country's most formidable war weapon. In his famous speeches, with their deliberate and skilful blend of realism, humour and inspiration, Churchill somehow instilled in most British people a determination that their land would remain their own, come who or what may. His presence in the Blitzed areas, complete with cigar and siren suit, seemed to produce the same effect. On such visits the morning after a raid he would often throw out the question, 'Are you downhearted?', to which the standard reply of the people around him, many of them just made homeless, was 'No!' And, when it really counted, they weren't.

The Magazine Editor

*We were aware that dreadful things were happening
around us, but you'd get quite exhausted if you got too
involved with other people's distress, so we just went on
with our ordinary lives.*

Constance Holt

I was much more frightened of the war before it happened than when it
began. We'd heard that another war would be the end of civilization.
I remember just before the war going to the H.G. Wells film *Things to
Come*. The film was full of cars distributing gas masks, and hooters and
alerts, and everyone rushing about trying to get away from things. I was
very unnerved by this, but when the war actually came I felt perfectly calm.

When war broke out I had been editor of *Woman's Own* for a year. I'd
come up from the bottom really. After I came down from university there
were simply no jobs. I borrowed some money to do a secretarial course.
Then I applied for jobs all over the place; I took three in one day because I
was so worried. Finally I got a job in the fashion pattern department of
Newnes and Pearsons the publishers, answering letters about cut-out
garments and things. Then when *Woman's Own* was launched I got the
job of answering appreciation letters. Then I moved on to being a sub, and
then editor.

At first it seemed to me the magazine didn't reflect the war much,
certainly not during the Phoney War. Then the readers started to write in

with problems about meeting another boy and being worried about 'the boy over there', and of course chaps worried about their girls. We didn't depress people by worrying too much about that, but we answered the letters. I used to keep a general eye on the letters myself. I remember after the raid on Coventry, which was a mighty affair, we had a letter from there posted the day after.

The letter was from a nurse, and she wanted to know how to improve her skin and her hair-do – she was expecting her chap home on leave. Not a word about the bombing, though she must have been involved, being a nurse. She had obviously sat down in the corner of an air-raid shelter or a hospital ward and written to *Woman's Own* about her face. And I said to my assistant, 'We shall never forget this.' And she said, 'But we're the same.'

She was right. Ordinary work for the magazine went on as usual. We never lost an issue. We always had reserve copy in hand, a whole issue ready for printing, in case everything got bombed. This was a lovely store, because when we didn't like a thing we'd got, we were always borrowing from the reserve issue. Then of course you were on your honour to put something back, with the editor's approval.

We had a problem page, and we always came down on the side of the angels. Leonora Eyles did our problem page, she was quite a character. My assistant and I had to sort through the letters that came via Leonora, and we were responsible for the replies that went out, because Leonora didn't know a thing about love and things like that. She was always telling people about her book *Common Sense about Sex*; every reader got a notification of the book. But we let her do a certain amount. She used to tell people off for being silly and selfish, and say that they should forget themselves and put others first. We used to warn people about being unfaithful, we were rather strict about that. But if it had already happened we suggested the best thing to do was forgive and forget.

We used to have cookery and garden features, a baby service, a household tips section, fashion and knitting, three stories, as well as news and features and an editorial. Knitting and all that practical kind of thing went very well. People always knit, don't they, and they certainly did in the war. We talked about every aspect of life for women – clothing when clothing coupons came in, and so on. But men used to read it too. Packs of magazines were sent abroad to various fronts, and we used to get letters from the men. They used to write in to the beauty column, they wanted to look good when they came home on leave to see their girlfriends.

Our print order didn't reflect our total circulation, because people used to lend their copies to five or six other readers. Our circulation when the war began was half a million, although the readership was much more than that. Of course the print order was kept down because of the shortage of paper. We couldn't print any more because pulp wasn't coming from Canada, and everything was being saved and saved and saved. So we had to go down to small print, make the pictures smaller, and tell the dear reader how we were placed. We felt they all supported us with great loyalty.

I felt that we were doing a job of morale boosting, and after a year or so even the government ministers realized that women's magazines had an influence. In a practical way the Ministry of Food would see that we had plenty of material about the coming shortages well in advance, so that we could arrange cookery recipes that were suitable. They gave us press conferences earlier than the daily newspapers because we had full colour for certain pages, and we went to press three weeks ahead. They used to send a minister or one of his representatives to see us in the Publishers' Association headquarters. Also, as time went on, they prepared us for the health service, which was then being planned. But they never put pressure on us, we were completely free to publish what we wanted.

The services run by women like the WVS used to have meetings to which they would invite the editors of the women's magazines. So we who were normally in competition with each other were all round a table together. Of course we didn't plan together. We had our own views about what would be helpful, and we were careful not to disclose how we were going to use the information. But we did get to know each other and become very friendly.

During the Phoney War our offices were evacuated to Great Missenden in Buckinghamshire, but the staff protested, and we went back to our offices in Covent Garden. I remember when war was declared everyone rushed out to buy Tampax and deodorants, because we didn't think we'd be able to buy them again. But it soon became business as usual. I don't think any of us were callous, we were aware that dreadful things were happening all around us, but you'd be quite exhausted if you got too involved with other people's distress. So we just went on with our ordinary lives, but with a changed routine.

We were at Tower House in the Strand, which was the fire-watching post for the area. We all had to do our share, and it was rather fun really. They made dormitories for us out of empty offices, and we used to go down there while the alert was on, taking all our stuff with us, talking to the art editor on the stairs about whether blue would be better than green, and things like that. We knew the work had to go on, so this was better for all of us. It seemed quite normal to be fiddling with roughs or reading proofs or manuscripts. I remember one group used to stay down there all day, working on the new *Chamber's Encyclopedia*. They were always very busy with these huge tomes and piles of notebooks. I suppose they couldn't really keep heaving them all the way up and down three flights of stairs. I used to call them 'the ants'. I also remember that our managing director was very unpopular; he used to snore, so people avoided him. There was a girl from the Southampton Street Post Office there too; she was rather jolly and popular with the editorial people. We all thought she was most conscientious because she used to sit up in bed trying to get her stamps right. The men, bless their hearts, were very protective of the women, and when the alert went to go out on the roof, they would be inclined to say, 'Don't bother, girls, we'll see to it.'

When France fell I was up in Penrith for the weekend, and heard the appeal by Eden on the radio, and before he had finished people had gone to join the Home Guard. I came back to London and that night, because all the Channel ports had been taken, so the enemy was bang opposite us, the wardens came round to re-check our gas masks. But we didn't seem to feel any different. I remember going in to the office next morning, and there was an artist's agent who had come in to show me a drawing, and she said, 'Oh, Miss Holt, isn't it terrible!' And I felt rather priggish in a way, because I said, 'What's terrible?' and she said, 'Well, they might come now.' And I said, awfully sententiously, 'But they might always have come, they wanted to come, they planned to come, and now we know where we are.' I think at the bottom of our hearts there was a feeling that the French were out of the way, the decks were clear now, and it was them and us.

In the block of flats in Holborn where I lived they turned the basement into a shelter, with nice little bunks at sixpence a week each. I put curtains on mine because I liked a little privacy, especially when I was in my curlers. I remember some enterprising hairdresser from nearby set up shop in the flats. You had none of the bother of appointments, it was first come, first served. My job in the morning was to kick the gentleman next to me, who was married to a lady on the other side. 'Would you mind giving him a good kick?' she said. He liked to be lower down, and I was to kick him to wake him up.

People did talk to each other, but I've always found that London people do when they're gathered together for any purpose. It seems to me that bus queues burst forth into conversation, and I don't think I always start it. Most of the tube stations were taken over as shelters, as there weren't enough big public shelters that people could get to. Russell Square station was one of these. I remember on stray occasions coming back from the theatre by tube, and when I got out at Russell Square they had put bunks all along the platform, and you'd see women putting on their face cream, doing up their curlers and getting right for the night. Of course you'd politely not stare at them because they were in their bedrooms. I remember there was a little bit of snobbery about stations. I heard one woman say, 'Oh, us and our family go to Regent's Park now, it's nicer people.' And the children used to go for rides on the tube. At least their mothers knew where they were, and it was much safer than the street.

As the war went on we used to get the all-clear by midnight – before that it wasn't usually until the morning. But if we'd already gone to bed by midnight, we'd stay there. But one night I remember the all-clear didn't go, and it was time to get up, and nobody liked it. Then somebody who went up to Fleet Street came in and said, 'Oh, it's pilotless planes'; she'd heard the rumour. And do you know it was hateful. I don't know why it should be any worse than the earlier raids, but we felt they were things that were not in human control. We had a whole summer of that, the buzz bombs.

Even so I used to go down during that period to Weston-super-Mare to my parents' home, to get some good sleep. There were these notices all over the place saying 'Is Your Journey Really Necessary?' But I used to go down every Friday on the train leaving platform 1 at Paddington at half-past six. The alert was *always* on, and it was always on when I got back. You didn't know where the thing was, you just carried on. I remember once hearing a buzz bomb approaching just after I had come out of Waterloo station. When the thing stopped we all fell flat on our faces, hundreds of us who were steaming across Waterloo Bridge. That was quite a scene. Sadly it landed just near the station and killed or injured a lot of people. I had caught an earlier train than usual, otherwise I might have been one of the unlucky ones.

Radio was very important. We didn't have handy portable ones or covered-in ones, they had these great big batteries, a wet one and a dry one, which were terribly heavy. We listened like mad to J.B. Priestley on Sunday – it was our Sunday School duty. He was marvellous. He just gave a general talk, about life as it was, as it might be, as it had been in his youth, the qualities of the English, and so on. He gave us a boost, you know, with his examples of dangers in the past. He didn't go into the worst side of the war, but it was always something a little relevant. The talks were called *Postscripts*, and nobody would have missed them.

I also remember people in the Houses of Parliament would go home early for Gracie Fields if she was singing on the radio. And we wouldn't miss the shows like *ITMA* with Tommy Handley, though sometimes we would miss bits because it would fade off when there was an alert. I remember when he died, suddenly, they had a memorial show the following week. I listened with a journalist friend of mine, and there were tears falling down his cheeks. That's what people thought of Tommy Handley. We were grateful to him – you're always grateful to people who make you laugh, you never forget them.

There was also the radio doctor and Lord Woolton, on the *Kitchen Front* programme. Lord Woolton was extremely clever, the way he pulled out the stops and made you feel you'd got something. The rations went up and down, so he'd say, 'There'll be less bacon next week, but there'll be carrots, an awful lot of carrots.' So then you had the radio doctor telling everyone how good carrots were for you, and in the magazine we published recipes using carrots, and using parsnips where before you might have used bananas. And of course there was the Dig for Victory campaign; everybody with a strip of earth was doing it, taking a little allotment if they could find one. Allotments had been around at the beginning of the First World War, but they became popular again. Of course it was not very popular to make fancy gardens when food was needed.

I don't think the war was all doom and gloom, people still managed to have fun. Often people saw it as the happiest time of their life. You didn't feel dreadful to feel it, though you didn't say it at the time. I know it sounds corny, but this business-as-usual idea really was in operation. The war didn't seem to alter people's behaviour, although the community spirit deepened. When you got anywhere near where a bomb had fallen, you knew there were people being dug out, you knew that they were gone, and of course offices had gone and fires were burning. But your mind was so focused on the fact that we were going to win the war that you carried on as normal.

The Stockbroker's Daughter

I was convinced that I was going to be buried alive. I would just say, 'Dear God, please let me live to grow up, I don't want to die, I want to be alive so much.'

Pat Kettle

When war broke out I was at Burgess Hill School in Hampstead with my two brothers, a typical product of the Hampstead Garden Suburb. My father was a socialist stockbroker who preached revolution, and who was hopeless moneywise. He was a Jew, while my mother was anti-Semitic, and always married Jews, so the whole thing was absolutely batty. My parents fought like cat and dog, literally – blood, teeth, everything – so I developed scholarly tendencies and fantasies as a protective measure.

When war actually started we were on holiday at my uncle's house in Burnham-on-Sea. My brother and I were left with an old lady and her two companions, while the adults went back to London. We were noisy and impossible, and eventually we ran away; we went to the station with one and sixpence. So we came back to London. My younger brother then went with Burgess Hill to Cranmore, and I went to the Friends' School in Saffron Walden. My elder brother went to another Quaker school, Sibford.

I arrived before the beginning of term in this very strange atmosphere, there were only some three or four children there. Gradually within a month or so the school filled up. There was an enormous cross-section of people there, a lot of Spanish and German refugees, it was a haven for them.

You also had the old Quaker families, and others on reduced fees. The teachers of course were pacifists, so we discussed the rights and wrongs of war with them. There was no celebration of nationalism or warlike feeling, we were in no way led to feel hatred of the German people. The Quakers are not a dogmatic people, and nothing was pushed upon us. But I was quite determined that if the war was still going on when I had to be called up, I wouldn't fight, I would go on the land.

Although my father had talked a lot about the First World War, you don't have a clue really. Although I knew war was a bad thing, there was an element of excitement that something was going to happen. The first bombs started in the summer of 1940, when the invasion was expected. Looking back on it now, it was quite ludicrous. All us children had a little attaché case at the end of our beds, in which we put all our belongings. And we were instructed that when the Germans landed, we would pick up our cases and follow our teacher. God knows where we would have gone to! I don't think that I was really frightened then, I don't think the penny had dropped. It wasn't until the bombing that I became shit scared – and remained so for the rest of my life.

During the first bombing we had I was ill and down in the 'san'. I remember what I thought was a thunderstorm, and being caught out of bed. I didn't know what was dream and what was real. We had to get out and sit with the nurse. At other times we used to bring our mattresses down and put them on the floor in the practice room, where there were no windows. Looking back I think how appalling it must have been for the teachers. I remember the first night we slept downstairs, I dreamt that I was in the sea, and I peed and wet my mattress, and I was *absolutely* horrified, and everyone was so nice about it.

Saffron Walden was a very cold place – most of my memories of it are of being cold and hungry and getting terrible chilblains. I wrote letters back home complaining about the education. I was absolutely passionate about painting and painted all the time, and thought the art education was appalling. Otherwise, life there was a mixture of pleasure and horror. I remember in the summer lying in the fields with a friend, reading *Gone with the Wind*, which we weren't allowed to, and being fascinated by the sexy bits, and at the same time watching dog-fights up in the sky. I remember one plane particularly, circling on fire, and then crashing just over in the field. This I have had recurrent nightmares about ever since; I must have been more frightened than I realized, I have been absolutely phobic about planes ever since.

After two years I came back to London, and went to Henrietta Barnet, which was considered a 'good school', though I thought it absolutely *frightful*, and loathed it. We had a headmistress who used to go to church in the lunch hour to pray for the heathen Jews to become reconciled to Christianity! I refused to wear a school hat, and I can remember being publicly dressed down by the history teacher, who said I was just the sort to become a communist and land up in jail. I was absolutely dumbfounded, I couldn't understand why a communist should end up in jail. But these were the attitudes. I didn't admit to being half-Jewish, and felt very guilty about that, it used to quite haunt me. There was a lot of anti-Semitism among the staff – I think the Jewish girls were thought to be inclined to be too clever. There was an attitude that their numbers should be limited, the fear was that they were too bossy and would take over.

To me education was a retreat from reality. The war impinged instead on what happened *outside* school. School was the time where you got away from what was actually happening. You could study something that had nothing to do with the war. I was lucky, as I was believed to be a talented painter, and I had a very good art teacher, Kay Allen. She was probably why I went on to art school and became a painter, she was the only one who supported me, and I had the run of the art room. My mother was mad about men, and she had American lovers. She took me round to meet her lovers – until they started looking at *me*. But I got into trouble at school because I did paintings of Yanks picking up women in bars and pubs. Kay Allen accepted them, but the other teachers thought them absolutely *disgusting*.

Because my mother was out on the gad, all the domestic chores fell on me at a very early age. I loathed it, I resented coming back from school in the dark to a house that was empty, and then doing all the cleaning. It made me terrified. My father was a warden and was often out, and my teeth chattered all the time. At first we didn't have a shelter, and we used to sit in the sitting-room downstairs. My mother used to give me chewing gum because she couldn't stand the sound of my teeth chattering. I used to have these dreams: all my dreams were landscapes, peaceful landscapes and beautiful colours, and I used to like to go to sleep during the day. Then we got a Morrison shelter, and I used to go under that with my mother; my younger brother slept through everything upstairs, and didn't seem to mind. My friends also didn't seem to be as cowardly as I knew myself to be. I was convinced that I was going to be buried alive. My mother used to do her best to divert my mind: we used to look at the rust patterns, or talk about Leonardo da Vinci, and I would just say, 'Dear

God, dear God, please let me live to grow up, I don't want to die, I want to be alive *so* much.'

I had many, many anxieties. My mother did once take me to a GP when I told her that I had a lump in my throat, but he just said I ought to get out more and meet people. I remember once a shell took the chimney off our house, and an incendiary bomb set the cat on fire, and we all had to get out in the middle of the night. There I was as usual, teeth chattering, clutching my sketch book, filled up with brandy or whisky to keep me quiet. I never saw any dead bodies, but every time my parents fought I used to run out of the house, and wait until the noise had stopped, and expect to go back and find a dead body. When my parents were fighting at night, I used to lie in bed and hear their voices. Looking back, I can see they were under incredible pressure. But I had all sorts of psychosomatic symptoms. When the blackout was drawn I wanted a light outside the window, so that I could see that I hadn't gone blind. I didn't dare tell my parents that, and they wouldn't let me have a light on, and the curtains were drawn tight, and I *knew* I was going blind. You see, nobody was bothered with kids then, there wasn't the concern with adolescents then. I started to read Freud when I was about thirteen to see what was the matter with my parents.

I was terribly aware of my mother being frightfully sexy. She liked a good time and pretty clothes. She used to work at Rainbow Corner in Piccadilly, and she used to bring back chocolate and chewing gum for us, and all sorts of delightful things to eat. Women friends who are older than me had a riotous time going out with blokes from a very early age. People talk about permissiveness as though it started quite recently! I was the one who 'didn't', I was in love with poets who were dead, but my friends and contemporaries were 'at it' from *very* early on. There were lots of men around in London, and if your tastes were for going out and dances, you were OK. But I was in reaction against all this. I wasn't a joiner-in, I couldn't stomach all the knees-ups.

The physical aspects of the war have run very deep. I hate wasting anything, I eat anything that's left on anybody's plate still. If I'm out I have to rigidly control myself, I can't bear seeing food being wasted. I'm sure this is because one's dreams as a child were of *food*. My husband says it was the same when he was a prisoner-of-war: they used to sit and write down the menus of what they would eat when they got out. I used to steal cheese from the larder because I was hungry, and my mother used to do her nut. It affected one's attitude to life, but in a good way, because you appreciate, you never take for granted *anything*. In a way I relished that having nothing aspect, of making the most out of what you've got. I still do it. People laugh at me, I make all our food, grow all our own vegetables in the country. I mind everything, I don't throw my clothes away, I can't bear to. I think it becomes a bit obsessional, but it's a pleasure, actually. I've never felt that domesticity was a bore, it's a challenge.

During the war the whole way that we worked, when you only had a small amount of money, was to say, 'Right, we're going to live really well with whatever we have. We haven't got much, but we've got a little, what can we get that you don't have to pay for, how will we use this and that?' My mother learnt to sew and made our clothes out of curtains or anything to hand, things from jumble sales. But the kids today at school or college, they think it's bizarre that one should want to use old things. But this is because they come from true poverty, which I didn't. So I think the war was a marvellous upbringing, if you survived it you could survive anything. Certainly my life has been chequered since, but I reckon the war gave me survival skills.

When the war ended I refused to celebrate anything at all, I just couldn't join in. I'm doubtful about the community spirit, or rather I think it's dangerous. They club together because they're hating somebody else, and this is irrational and bad to my mind. I believe in a community spirit, but not because you're attacking somebody else. And that's what it was, wasn't it, a common enemy that brings people together: if you're attacked, you respond. But I don't like the building up of the feeling that everybody on the other side is bad, and that we're the goodies.

Extract from the diary of a London man, 1944

Before Bill and I left the train we saw a flying bomb crash to earth, followed by the all-too-familiar plume of smoke and dust. At Waterloo amazing scenes met my eyes. Some 10,000 people were waiting to get away from it all for the weekend, with bombs flying overhead. I felt bewildered, but on to Dulwich. At the Elephant there was evidence of a recent incident, with crowds, ambulances and the like. The next shock greeted me at Alban Road, where another fresh incident met my eyes, where a pub and a petrol station had received a direct hit and, along with adjacent buildings, were reduced to rubble. Rescue squads were busy at their unpleasant task, and everywhere there were scenes of great suffering. Most significant I thought was the human wreckage drifting out of the doss house opposite: cut, bleeding, dazed, they presented a pitiful sight. War seems to strike only those people who have always suffered, the innocent, the dispossessed. The last straw came at the King's Arms, which had been hit again. The remains of what had once been a bus were lying near the pond, an un-recognizable mess of jagged metal. Cushions from the bus were everywhere, and I needed no telling about the tragedy that had occurred. Bodies were being brought up from the wreckage, and altogether it was a very depressing scene.

The Jewish Refugee

*Old Charlie said, 'You don't understand us. Now we're rid
of these bloody Frogs we're really going to go.' We went
home that evening thinking, 'These people are totally
insane.'*

Martin Goldenberg

I came to Britain because of the situation in Vienna. It was a year after the
takeover by the Germans, who were enthusiastically received by
the Austrians. If anything, the Austrians were fiercer in their persecution of
the Jews than the Germans ever were.

I had been living with my stepfather and mother and stepsister in Vienna,
in the first district. I was studying medicine, while my stepfather and
stepsister were solicitors. My mother had been a teacher before the First
World War, while my real father had been a regular officer in the Imperial
Hapsburg Army. He died in 1920 when I was just two and a half.

When the Germans arrived I was immediately thrown out of university,
and my stepsister and stepfather were deprived of their ability to carry on
with the law, since all Jews were removed from professional work. My
brother-in-law, who lived in Kashmir, sent us money, and it was thanks to
him that we were able to exist for a while. He tried to get us entry visas to
India, but by the time they arrived I was already in England, and when war
broke out my parents and stepsister were trapped in Germany. She died in
Auschwitz with my mother.

The Nazis threw all Jewish children out of state schools. In Austria and Germany there was no private school system, so that meant there were thousands of Jewish children with nowhere to go. So the Jewish community, in cooperation with Jewish youth movements, tried to organize some kind of schooling, to get these kids off the streets and out of their terrible homes where there was nothing but misery and despair and fear. I had been quite prominent in the Boy Scout movement, and we operated these kind of youth clubs. One day the Jewish community in Britain managed to get permission for 600 children to come to England, pending the granting of immigration certificates to Palestine, to receive appropriate training. I and a friend, Fred Dunstan, were asked to join a refugee transport to come to England. As there were no facilities for the children in England, the Jewish Refugee Committee decided to open up tented accommodation in Kitchener Camp, in Kent, an old First World War transit camp for shipping troops to the continent. It consisted of large barrack huts in a state of total disrepair. I was among the first to arrive there, in March 1939.

The camp was near Sandwich, and there were local people who made it their business to invite people to have tea with them. I was taken aback by the ignorance of some people as to what was going on in Europe. I remember Fred and I and two or three others were invited to take tea with the family of a naval officer, who was away. They were kindness themselves, but totally ignorant of what was going on – the Empire seemed more familiar to them. I remember the son, a naval lieutenant on leave, was very enthusiastic about a friendship visit his ship had made to Kiel, where he had found his opposite numbers in Hitler's navy 'absolutely splendid chaps', who we ought really to be friends with. We refugees looked at each other in amazement, as if to say, 'Doesn't he know who we are, and what this is all about?'

In the camp we watched the Territorial Army on Sunday exercises. This really frightened me. They were smartly turned out, with well-creased trousers, their puttees carefully arranged, highly polished boots, white gloves stuck under their epaulettes. Yet they were carrying ancient rifles, which they must have used in the Boer War, and some were carrying just cardboard cut-outs of tanks and anti-tank guns. We thought, 'What nonsense is this, don't they know what people are like over in Europe?' When you have seen them marching down the Winkstrasse in Vienna in columns of battalions, deliberately trampling down all the grass to show their power, their tanks, their artillery, and of course their unbelievable discipline. . . . We thought, these people don't know what's going to hit them when the war starts. But I soon learnt that it was because of this that these people were not going to lose.

In June we moved to Great Engham Farm in Ashford, Kent, which consisted of an ancient farmhouse, a large cowshed, stables for horses, pigsties and chicken runs. On a large field we erected marquees, which were expected to accommodate 600 refugee children. In the end we only received 300; the last transport crossed the border into Holland after war had been declared. The children were distraught. They had gone through some terrifying experiences, a lot of them had been put on the trains by parents who were mad with grief, and they didn't know where their next stop would be. When we heard Chamberlain's announcement on 3 September, we called everyone together and I made a speech. I tried to give the children some reassurance, telling them of the huge resources of the Allies, and that while there was going to be destruction, they would be preparing themselves for the task of rebuilding after victory was achieved. In the end all the children were dispersed to farm camps, to get agricultural training, or to schools.

I wrote to the War Office to offer my services, but received a polite letter declining from Colonel Margesson, the Minister of War. So I continued to look after groups of children. I worked for a short time in Hale Nurseries in Hampshire, where the boys and girls were housed in a number of greenhouses. They were soon moved from there, because I found that they were being exploited and had no educational facilities whatsoever. I remember the owner said in so many words that we shouldn't make unreasonable demands, as we ought to be grateful to have been kept alive.

So I moved to another farm in Braunton, near Barnstaple in Devon, where I worked with another group of youngsters. I found the English parochialism there quite amusing. I was having tea with some farming people, and the talk turned to the undesirable prominence of foreigners in Barnstaple. I was beginning to feel very uncomfortable, until I realized that they were talking about the manager of Boots and the cinema manager and others, and these 'foreigners' came from Yorkshire or Lancashire. To me this was just totally amazing. They didn't treat *me* as a foreigner, I was simply out of their ken.

I also found, even in the spring of 1940, that the English were totally unprepared for war. One day we were having lunch on the farm in Braunton, all these youngsters I was in charge of, the local farm workers, and old Charlie the foreman. We were listening to the radio, and the news

WILLS'S CIGARETTES

LIGHT TRAILER FIRE-PUMP IN ACTION

Pat Kettle in 1940.

Martin Goldenberg in 1944.

Nine-year-old Barbara Benjamin (right) with her family, 1940.

ARP LOOKS TO YOU

VOLUNTARY SERVICES

Sidney Greaves in 1945.

Olive Markham shortly before the war.

BEFORE
THE
TRIBUNAL
A SHORT DESCRIPTION OF THE REGULATIONS
TOGETHER WITH SOME ADVICE TO APPLICANTS

ONE PENNY

Issued by
THE NATIONAL JOINT ADVISORY BUREAU
6 ENDSLEIGH STREET
LONDON
W.C.1

Ernest Beavor (front left) and his family in 1945.

Pacifist Bernard Nicholls: 'There was an acceptance of my position, though it was seen as rather odd.'

Think of the wounded
GIVE TO THE LORD MAYOR'S
DUKE OF GLOUCESTER'S APPEAL FOR THE RED CROSS AND ST JOHN
FUND

Please send your gift to the Lord Mayor, The Mansion House, London, E.C.4. Envelopes should be marked 'Appeal' and cheques made payable to 'The Lord Mayor's Fund.' Alternatively you can subscribe to your local collection.

Alex Bryan in 1940.

Joyce Dennys during the war.

Nellie Town and her husband before the war.

John Dossett-Davies on 'report and control' for the civil defence in Witney.

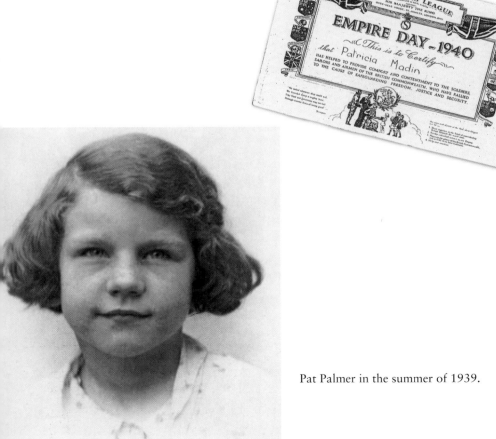

Pat Palmer in the summer of 1939.

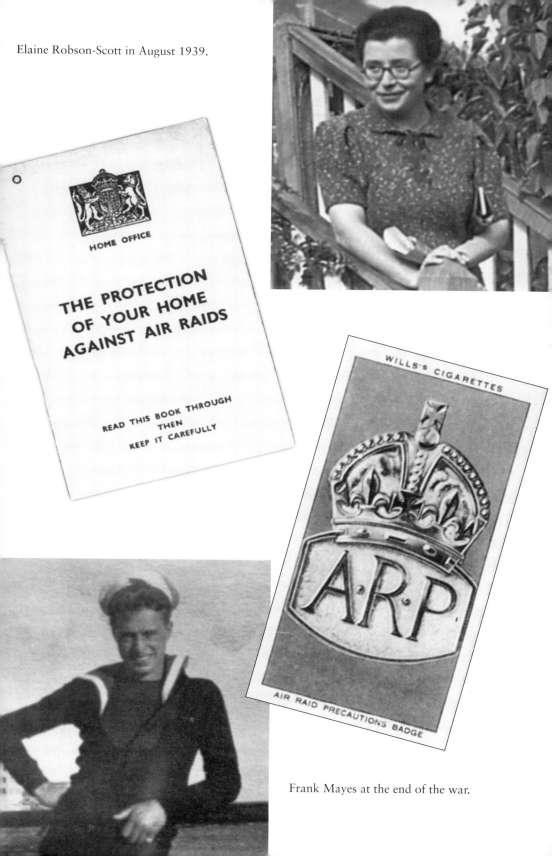

Elaine Robson-Scott in August 1939.

HOME OFFICE

THE PROTECTION
OF YOUR HOME
AGAINST AIR RAIDS

READ THIS BOOK THROUGH
THEN
KEEP IT CAREFULLY

WILLS'S CIGARETTES

ARP

AIR RAID PRECAUTIONS BADGE

Frank Mayes at the end of the war.

Doris Nicholls on her wedding day, 1942.

WILLS'S CIGARETTES

A VENTILATED GAS-PROOF SHELTER

FIRE GUARD HANDBOOK

FLEET AND CROOKHAM DISTRICT

Irene Gillon in 1942.

came through that Pétain had sued for an armistice. We refugees thought we might as well go and cut our throats right away. But old Charlie said – and he was applauded by his mates – 'You don't understand us. Now we're rid of these bloody Frogs we're really going to go.' We went home that evening thinking, 'These people are totally insane.' And in the evening the Local Defence Volunteers came out with shotguns and pikes, would you believe it? But when we were discussing this among ourselves, I said, 'I don't know how they are going to win the war, but they are not going to lose it. People who do this cannot lose, they never know when they've lost.' It was a courage born of ignorance of what they were up against.

I felt that if it hadn't been, not for what Churchill did, but the way he spoke, things might have turned out differently. One listened to him and one somehow felt reassured that, as he said, maybe the British people were the lion, but he gave the roar. Radio of course was very important, and we were very impressed by the calm and objective tone used by the BBC. I and many of my friends listened mainly to news broadcasts. To hear reverses and military defeats admitted, destruction by air raids admitted, that was impressive, because we knew that on the other side they were not going to say these things. It was confidence-inspiring. There were also the famous morale-building shows like *ITMA* and *Much Binding in the Marsh*, which showed us that the British had this tremendous self-confidence to laugh at sacred institutions, at their own foibles.

In June there was an enormous campaign to arrest and intern so-called enemy aliens. We were in a protected area, near Bristol. One day the local police sergeant came to the farm and requested Fred Dunstan and myself to accompany him to our quarters, all very friendly, where he said, 'I've got orders to pick you up, they want you in Barnstaple. Take a toothbrush with you and a piece of soap, you'll be back in a day or two anyway. Do you mind if I look through your belongings?' Well, we had no real belongings, we were not allowed to take anything with us from Germany except 20 Reichmarks and a small suitcase, in which we had a spare suit. When he went through our belongings he found in both Fred's and my papers the acknowledgement from Captain Margesson, thanking us for our offer to do military service, and saying that he would eventually come back and take advantage of it. 'Now I know where they got your names from,' the sergeant said.

We had not expected *anything* of the kind to happen, particularly since people like ourselves were the obvious first victims of the Germans, so why should we be a danger? That there might have been spies among us is of course possible, how can one tell? But we felt rather bad about the fact that we were swept up all together. The round-up seemed haphazard. Most of the people rounded up with me had been evacuated from London University, because some of the faculties had been evacuated to Bristol. Among them were lecturers and professors who had been academics in Germany and Austria and Czechoslovakia. We read in the papers that there had been opposition to them in areas of high unemployment such as South Wales, on the mistaken assumption that these refugees were going to take their jobs away. There certainly was some opposition, presumably from the right-wing fascist element, but in general people were not unfriendly, just uncomprehending.

We were taken to the police station, where there were a number of other people whose existence we hadn't known of. It was all very jolly, because we thought we'd be back home in a day. The policemen's wives made sandwiches and tea for us, and everything was on a very friendly basis. Then they took us in coaches to Barnstaple, where we spent the night in the cells. Again it was all very happy and friendly. Then it became a little more unpleasant, because they took us in coaches down to Paignton, where we were accommodated at Butlin's Holiday Camp, surrounded by a fence and barbed wire, and guards who were, well, Dad's Army – Local Defence Volunteers with fixed bayonets on their ancient blunderbusses, making little remarks like, 'Why not shoot the buggers right away?' So we were not really happy. But we stayed there only for about a week, and then a group of us were moved to Prees Heath Camp, near Shrewsbury.

We were taken, not in cattle trucks, but in a proper train, under guard. At Shrewsbury we were marched through the town under military escort. This was humiliating, to be treated like an enemy. As we left the city and walked along some country lane, the soldiers who were guarding us, who were a mixed bunch that had come back from Dunkirk just before this, to our amazement started to recruit us to carry their rifles, their tin hats, their packs. The whole thing turned into a walk through the country. This seemed strange to us, particularly those older than myself who had served in the First World War in the German and Austrian armies. They were absolutely appalled by such slack discipline, saying things like, 'You can say what you like about Hitler, but *he* would not allow his soldiers to do this sort of thing.' They were right. We felt we were in a different kind of place, the military had a different feel about them.

When we got into this tented camp we had a very nasty surprise. It was a huge compound, subdivided into separate compounds. One compound was inhabited by German sailors and merchant seamen who had been taken off ships. These people were Nazis to a man, or if they were not, many felt they could not afford to appear anything *but* Nazis. So we said we were not going to share a camp with these people. The camp commandant said he appreciated our point of view. He asked us to accept that he would do whatever he could to change it. And he did, these people were removed, probably to a prisoner-of-war camp.

We were confined in rough conditions, sleeping ten to a tent on straw, with very crude ablution and sanitary facilities. But among us were Germans and Italians who had lived in England almost all their lives, and were in the catering trade. They were chefs, and a large number of the Italians were ice-cream manufacturers or pastry cooks. With the rations we were given we had a *magnificent* cuisine. Every morning the guards patrolling the barbed wire used to stand there with their mess tins, waiting for their coffee and croissants. The guards even supplied some of their own rations to be processed by the cooks. So it was really a pleasant atmosphere. We had a camp orchestra, with many members of the Berlin and Vienna Philharmonic among them, who were allowed to have their instruments. There were several professional actors, and when we had amateur theatricals some of the officers went down to London to theatrical costumiers, to bring costumes up.

They began to recruit us for agricultural work. It was a little bit like a slave market. There was no compulsion at all, but every morning those who wished to do it would parade outside the camp gates, and the farmers would come in their carts and cars and horseboxes, to take us to work for the day, and bring us back in the evening. They were not allowed to pay us, they paid into the camp administration, and the camp issued us with camp currency, which were army dog-tags with numbers on – pence, shillings, pounds and so on. They were only allowed to feed us, and they often gave us cigarettes.

We worked like maniacs. For one thing, we were happy to be out there doing something. Secondly, we felt we were doing at least this minimal thing to defeat the Germans. We just loved being with these people, the way they treated us, the way the farmer's wife set out the table, we had magnificent meals. Whenever we arrived at the workplace the corporal and the two men of the guard would immediately detail somebody to look after their arms and ammunition and tin hats while they were having a kip, telling us to please whistle if we saw the orderly officer's van come round the back.

In the camp I had no complaints whatsoever. I felt that at a time when we all thought the very existence of the country was at stake, we were treated in a very gentlemanly fashion. To those of us who came from central Europe this was a surprise, because the authorities there, even if they had not been Nazis, would not have acted this way to presumed enemies. Of course there were others who were quite bitter at not being taken at face value as valuable members of the British community. Naturally, we were all very upset at being confined. We felt that if the Germans ever landed, well, there we were, all ready for them.

There were a large number of us who could have been put under pressure because of our families. I know when my doctor brother was picked up shortly after the Nazis came into Austria, he was taken to Dachau concentration camp. When he came out it was not easy to recognize him, because it was a nasty experience. He was summoned to the Hotel Metropole in Vienna, which was the headquarters of the Gestapo, and there he was interviewed by Adolf Eichmann, who then was just a minor-grade SS official. He said that Eichmann said to him, 'Well, how did you like the camp?' My brother stood there with his knees shaking, and said, 'It was very nice, very good, we were treated very well.' And Eichmann said to him, 'Look, don't give me this rubbish, don't tell me that, I know what goes on there. You can tell anybody you see, just tell them. Why do you think we keep these establishments? You tell anybody who wants to hear what goes on there. But when you get out of the country' – he had been released to go to Palestine – 'then remember that you have got your family here.'

So it is quite possible that they might have put pressure on people, saying, 'Either you cooperate, or there is Auschwitz or Treblinka', or not even that, just a rifle butt on your head – finished. So it was not totally unjustified to look at us with a certain amount of suspicion, and try and weed out people who might be unreliable, or in a particularly vulnerable position. I never heard of anyone like this, but that doesn't mean they didn't exist.

Then came the time when Herbert Morrison, the Home Secretary, decided to allow people to come out of internment under a number of headings: important war work, special qualifications, armed forces. I was let out and able to join the alien Pioneer Corps. I just had a medical and that was that. I was given the King's shilling and swore an oath of allegiance. We wore uniform, and were given some kind of superannuated weaponry. It was not exactly an élite unit, but at any rate we were out.

After a while I got a commission. I was doubtful about this. I thought, here I am, an enemy alien, standing here on the parade ground with a company of soldiers in front of me, and I speak with a thick German accent. What are they going to say? But if I gave an order they carried it out. Nobody ever said, 'Who the hell are you?' or anything like that. On the little brown officer's identity card that I carried it said 'Enemy Alien'. I later went through the Middle East with this thing, and people just saluted.

I think the British became less insular as a result of the war. It was not just us German Jewish refugees. Millions of people had served abroad. There was also a number of governments-in-exile who maintained their own armed forces – the Free French, the Polish Army, the Czech Brigade, the Norwegian Navy. They were spread out in camps and harbours all over the country, so people became aware there were other people around them who didn't have cloven hooves, who were just ordinary people.

But I don't think people in England could really appreciate what it is like to live under a regime such as that of the Nazis, where you feel you lived under a totally arbitrary system. The authorities decide to do something, they do it. There's no legal framework for it, it's not going to be debated in the House, no ombudsman is going to listen to you. Then a group of people, Jews, are put outside the legal framework. This is a concept that it is impossible for people who have grown up in England to appreciate, that you live in a lawless society. There *is* no law, no framework in which you can say, 'If I behave in this way I'll be all right, and in another way I'll be wrong.' You knew there was one way in which you behaved where you would certainly be in the wrong, but the right could change from minute to minute. This is impossible to understand for anyone growing up in England.

When people talk about the yoke of the British Empire and all the subordinate countries, and how they suffered under the yoke of imperialism, my cousin, who now teaches at the London School of Economics, sits there rubbing the camp number on his arm, and he says, 'If that was oppression, I'll buy it any day.'

Extract from a letter to a friend from a transport expert working in London

20 June 1940

The worst has happened now, I hope. At any rate you will not be going to France just yet. Unless you go to Iceland or the Faroes, it looks as if you will be helping St George to fight the Dragon on our own soil. We are no longer able to seek out the Dragon in his den or near it, we must wait till he comes to us and leave him all the advantage of surprise and initiative which he is so quick to take. For some reason or other people in England still think that ultimate victory will be ours, and for some reason or other I still share their conviction. When we lose that faith, it will be time to surrender, but not till then.

Don't you think Churchill's speeches are magnificent? The more I see and hear of his work, the more I realize what a superman he is. How lucky we are to have such a man at such a time! He is the man to lead us because really it is for the Empire we are fighting. On that rest all the physical amenities and human comforts on which we can afford to base the ideals of liberty.

The Barrister's Daughter

*This plane came from nowhere. Instinctively we flung
ourselves flat, or dived into the ditch. He circled round and
came back again, repeating the performance about three
times. I was so terrified, I just remember this blind panic.*

Barbara Benjamin

When war broke out my family evacuated itself down to Bramshott, a
village near Liphook in Surrey. There was literally a dame school, with
about ten children. It was like a relic of something that had gone before. My
brother and I were only there for three months while my parents were
looking for a house in the Guildford area, but even at the time it was odd, I
found it very strange. I was only eight at the time. Before that I had been to
school in north London. When we moved to Guildford my brother and I
went to a little primary school just around the corner, and I hated that –
well, I had very mixed feelings, but I do remember that dislike. By the age of
eight I was a thorough snob, finding myself among a very different group of
children from those I had been with in London, and I think that was the
main reason for feeling that way.

My memories really start with the Battle of Britain, because we were
under the flight path between London and the south coast, so we had daily
air-raid warnings and all-clears. School was very strange, because an awful
lot of it was conducted in shelters, at the bottom of the garden. It seemed as
if we were down there most of the time. It was incredibly difficult; how the

teachers managed I don't know, I don't suppose we learnt anything for a minute. The shelters were cramped, dark, poky, round-topped ones, and I was glad that I was too young to think about things like claustrophobia. One of my strongest shelter memories was being sustained by Horlicks and Ovaltine tablets. I'm not sure if this was part of the regular diet, or just my mother's contribution. I don't remember eating down there. I do remember having books, but I don't suppose we could have written very much.

I wasn't scared so much at school, but at home it was very, very frightening. We had no shelter, and we had raids at night – I think they were trying to get the railway line to Guildford. Hearing the sirens go in the evening, my parents either shoved us under the stairs in a poky little cupboard, or we had to go under the dining-room table. I was terrified by the sirens and then the planes going over. I can still remember the throbbing, listening to it getting more and more intense.

There was one particular incident that was highly dramatic, when I wasn't frightened at all, because I didn't realize its significance. We used to come home for lunch, because it was so near. One day my brother and I were wandering along with some other children – it was a beautiful summer day. Obviously there had been no warning, otherwise we would have realized what was happening. We looked up, and there were these planes around, and then suddenly little puffs of smoke. We were standing there gawping, absolutely fascinated by all this, and then my mother came rushing round the corner. We were obviously late coming home, and she could see what was happening. She was quite hysterical, and yelled at us all, 'Can't you see what's going on?' and she grabbed us and scuttled home with us.

There was another incident. My parents had been told that there was a lagoon on the south coast, a deep inlet near Pagham, which had not been mined or shut like the rest of the coast. Some friends of friends knew the owners, so we went down there with another family and their son. Eventually we three children were able to go to the lagoon, while all the parents went to the cinema in Bognor. We went down this long lane, and then a plane came from nowhere, it just appeared, and all of a sudden it came down low and started machine-gunning people in the lane. It was absolutely unbelievable, it must have been a madman – I don't think pilots on either side just went for civilians normally, they had no reason to. He must have been trigger-happy or completely berserk. Instinctively we flung ourselves flat or dived into the ditch. He circled round and went off, and came back again, repeating the performance about three times. I don't remember anybody being hurt, I was so terrified. I can just remember this blind panic. It seemed like hours getting back to the hotel, although it was probably only ten minutes' walk. But the drama wasn't over, because the parents weren't back when we arrived, so we had nobody to collapse on to. And when they did arrive, I don't remember telling them anything about the incident, because it was all overshadowed by the fact that the cinema they went to had had a direct hit the performance after they were there. So it was rather a dramatic holiday and we didn't repeat the experiment.

The war impinged a lot on our daily lives. Guildford was particularly over-populated. Not only were there evacuees like ourselves but there was also a large military hospital in Dorking. So you had a lot of soldiers in blue wandering around on crutches and things; and also there was the Aldershot barracks very near. And then the Americans arrived, and that was another element.

So food was very scarce, and I can remember queuing up for hours with my mother, and being sent off to another queue while she stayed in hers. You had to queue for absolutely everything. I was also gradually aware that people in other areas weren't so badly off, especially in country districts. We spent a couple of holidays on a farm, and were aware how better off they were for food, living off the land.

I also remember all the business of gas masks. Even before the war I remember going down to the local recreation ground where we lived, and hundreds and hundreds of us queuing up and being issued with these things in a very makeshift way, and of course carrying them around everywhere in those wretched boxes, at least for a while. At Bramshott we used to have gas mask drills. I remember one Sunday morning, we had to go out into the lane and under some trees and put on our masks. I remember it vividly because I had my night-dress on, and I just put my overcoat on top and went out into the street. All I can remember is being so ashamed, because the coat kept falling open, and I was trying desperately to hide it.

My stepfather was in the Home Guard, and he went off and came back with this pitchfork, or whatever it was they had to begin with. Eventually he was issued with a rifle, and he was very proud of that. But my mother weathered the war years very badly, it was a tremendous strain on her and she had several nervous breakdowns – not that I knew what they were then. So our family life was very disrupted. My mother wasn't working; in fact, she'd never worked since before her first marriage. She wasn't capable of it – though I suppose if pushed she might have been. But I can't imagine her working for one minute, and I don't think it ever occurred to her. Married women didn't work, full stop. It was never discussed, and I don't think it ever crossed her mind. Being a married woman with young children there was no call-up, and so no pressure for her to work. None of the women my parents knew were working.

When my brother went to a prep school in Guildford as a boarder at the age of seven, I was very, very envious of him, because I was very unhappy at home. Then I became aware of a private school at the other end of town. I wanted to go there desperately, and I managed to persuade my parents to send me there. I don't know how they managed it, as my father was only a struggling young barrister. I went there for a couple of years and was very happy, I loved it. It was much bigger than the other school, but I was a big fish in a small pond, and I did very well there. By this time the Battle of Britain was over, so there were no more real dramas until the V1s and V2s, whose randomness was a real terror.

I don't remember the war as a topic coming into school at all. Early on I can remember distinctly having a weekly comic, the *Dandy* and the *Beano*: my brother had one and I had the other. There was an awful lot of propaganda in those comics. I can see now one picture particularly, of Mussolini, and I can remember the caption, 'Musso Da Wop is a Biga Da Flop'. That sticks in my mind. I do remember clearly listening to the six o'clock news with Alvar Liddell reading it. But my family were very isolated indeed. Although I used to go to friends' houses I hated bringing them back, mainly because of the atmosphere. I just wanted to be at school all the time, I hated being at home. My relationship with my father was very poor. It was a very, very difficult marriage indeed – they had only got married just before the war, so there was an awful lot to adjust to. They obviously had a very bad time. My father was drinking heavily, he used to go off to London, and there were always traumas about him coming home at night; if he wasn't back on time my mother suspected he had been drinking. So he never talked about what was happening up in London, it was a closed book. The life was appalling. And my mother never referred to her previous marriage to my actual father, who died when I was four.

Our family life was so bad that even my half-brother was sent to boarding school at the age of five, because my mother couldn't cope. So I was left at home to bear the brunt. I remember the usual thing, being a girl, of being expected to do more than the boys, and resenting it. I was very aware of the different ways boys were brought up, and I remember hating being a girl. I owe whatever Women's Lib feelings I have to those early experiences.

I'm just so aware of the difference the war made to the whole social structure. Life before the war was totally different to that after. It was absolutely unbelievable. Looking from a middle-class perspective, help in the home had just gone. My mother had a daily in twice a week after the war, but before it my brother and I had a governess – she taught me to read before I went to school. In fact I didn't go to school until I was six-and-a-half. We certainly had a living-in maid and a nanny before the war, when my father was alive. All that faded out during the war, which was an added trauma for my mother.

When you're a child, of course, time is endless. The war lasted half my life at that stage, it just went on and on and on, and I thought it was never going to end, it seemed like an eternity. On VE Day I was aware that grown-ups were prancing around in the streets, and that there was an awful lot of jollification going on. But I don't remember what I was doing. Memory is a funny thing – I know it's all there, but some of it just won't come back, which is a bit frustrating. I'm aware of privation and hardship all mixed up, with a very traumatic family situation, and it's hard to disentangle the two.

Account of the Blitz by a Hull secondary schoolgirl, summer 1941

Since August 1940 Hull has been one of the most badly blitzed areas in England, the worst Blitzes being during May, June, July when the main shops of Hull, such as Hammonds, the Co-op and Thornton-Varley's, were burnt.

The raid that affected me most was the one on Saturday, February 22nd, 1941. That night I was in the house of my friend Mary, and at about 8.30 the sirens sounded.

At nine o'clock we began to think the all-clear would be heard soon when, suddenly, all the guns on earth seemed to fire at once, and the Luftwaffe machines droned overhead.

About ten minutes later we breathed a sigh of relief. The Jerries had passed over without dropping any bombs – or so we thought.

Mary's mother said we had better go down into the shelter while we had a chance.

Just as we were beginning to think the Germans had forgotten about us, the guns started booming, and, once again, we could hear the drone of enemy aircraft overhead.

Suddenly, there was a terrific crash and the shelter door blew in and hit Mary's mother on the leg, not causing any serious injury, however.

We found it impossible to remain in the shelter, because of smoke and dust, so we climbed out and ran into the street. The scene at the other end of Rowlston Grove was one of devastation and ruin.

There were women, children and wardens running to and fro carrying sandbags and telling everyone to keep calm.

The fire engine came clanging down the street to put out a fiercely burning fire which a burst gas-pipe and someone's kitchen fire had caused. When we asked a policeman what had happened he told us a land-mine had dropped.

A warden came to us and asked our names and addresses as they wanted to check on people who were missing.

We then went to see how Mary's house had suffered. Though it was still standing, it was impossible to live in it again.

At 10.30 p.m. the all-clear sounded, and Mary came with me to our house to see how it had fared. We found it in a worse condition, and my mother, who had been at my aunt's house, was just about to come for me.

As it was impossible for me to do anything then, I went to stay the night in my sister-in-law's house and Mary went to her grandmother's.

We spent the next morning excavating what was left of our furniture and clothing. I spent ten minutes trying to find my gym tunic, which had been hung in front of my wardrobe, and my brother asked me if a rather dirty-looking object on the top of a wireless pole was it. So I shook the pole and eventually down came my gym slip.

Needless to say, I did not wear it again until it had been cleaned.

During the latter part of February and the whole of March I stayed at my sister-in-law's house until we got a new home in Portobello Street.

A Matter of Conscience

I found people tolerant before the war, if not understanding. But when it got going, and particularly after the fall of France, attitudes hardened distinctly. I remember being publicly prayed for as a sinner because I would not fight.

LONDON MAN

I got the feeling that those tribunals were going to let one or two people through every day, and to keep a balance they had to strike a few people off, and I was one of the unlucky ones. I didn't feel the system was fair in any way.

HULL MAN

At the tribunal I was asked about how the war problem ought to be dealt with. I said I thought the first thing you had to do was pray, to get your mind clear, before you rush in and do anything. This brought a loud guffaw from the gallery.

MIDDLESEX MAN

My friend's letters to me from prison were censored, but he told me later that the wardens used to treat him worse than the criminals. They would throw the door of his cell open, and say, 'I can't understand these chaps being scared to go and fight.' He was strong enough to bang their heads together, but he had to stand there and take it.

CARDIFF MAN

It soon became known in the office that I was a CO, but there was no antagonism. My colleagues remained friendly without exception. My boss said I should decide what to do: in his words, it was my conscience, not his.

LONDON MAN

The only pacifist I knew had been a conscientious objector in 1914, and had suffered greatly. In 1940 he was accepted by everyone.

LONDON MAN

'At a time when we are claiming, as against some other countries, that freedom of conscience must everywhere be honoured, it obviously is our duty to show that we fully respect it.' The sentiments are those of the Archbishop of Canterbury, speaking in the House of Lords four months before the outbreak of the Second World War. As his words imply, conscientious objectors were treated much more tolerantly than they had been during the First World War.

Most people saw the fight against Hitler as a fight against fascism, a system which explicitly denied both freedom of speech and conscience. To force COs to join the armed forces and kill for their country defied both logic and morality. This was a widely held view, endorsed by the government even before war started. Introducing the exemption clause to the Military Training Act in May 1939, the Prime Minister, Neville Chamberlain, told cheering MPs in the House of Commons, 'We all recognize that there are people who have perfectly genuine and deeply seated scruples on the subject of military service. . . . Where their scruples are conscientiously held we desire that they should be respected, and that there should be no persecution.'

This was a far cry indeed from the official attitude during the First World War. When conscription was introduced in 1916, some 16,000 men, encouraged by the influential No Conscription Fellowship, had refused to obey the law. 'I will make their path as hard as I can', Lloyd George had said. And so he did. Some 3,000 who refused non-combatant service were put into labour camps. Many others were drafted into the Army, and then court-martialled and imprisoned for refusing to obey orders. A small number sent to the front in France were sentenced to death, and were only reprieved at the very last minute. At one stage there were 6,000 prisoners of conscience in British prisons or camps. For the sake of their beliefs, 73 conscientious objectors died in jail or shortly after their release, while a further 31 became mentally ill.

It was partly in reaction against this shameful treatment that a more humane arrangement was put in place in 1939. All COs had now to apply to go on a register, and then appear before a tribunal. They would then either be exempted unconditionally; or on condition that they did non-combatant service in the armed forces; or that they undertook it elsewhere – on the land, in hospitals, with the fire service, down the mines, or with such bodies as the Friends' Ambulance Unit or the Quaker Relief Service. The tribunal was supposed to decide, not if the CO's views were right, but whether they were held sincerely and conscientiously. If it found against, the CO would then be liable for call-up. They did have the right of appeal to an appellate tribunal, but that body's decision was final. For the 'absolutists' who exhausted this procedure, prison was the final stage of their journey.

So much for the law. In practice, the decision did not depend solely on the merits of the case. Regional variations were striking, and much resented. For example, after two months of war, during which very little fighting had taken place, unconditional exemptions had been given in 49 cases out of 80 in Bristol, but only 6 out of 70 in Manchester, and an astonishing 0 out of 90 in London. Much depended on the outlook and background of the tribunal's members. In a famous confrontation with Fenner Brockway at one appellate tribunal, an eminent lawyer declared that 'It doesn't in the least matter what the Prime Minister said.' The views of the chairman, who was always a judge, were also crucial. Certain men quickly gained reputations as 'hard-liners', others for being more amenable after than before lunch. The London judge who argued that 'Even God is not a pacifist, for he kills us all in the end' was not untypical of this group, however dubious his theology.

Another critical factor was the kind of support the COs received. They were entitled to be represented by counsel, a solicitor, a union representative, or a relative or personal friend. Generally it was the more politically aware or better educated or connected that exercised this right. The Central Board for Conscientious Objectors, chaired by Fenner Brockway, did what it could to help, providing support and information for COs on how best to present their case. In some areas the Independent Labour Party organized mock tribunals, bringing in older pacifists to show potential COs how to handle hostile questions from a tribunal.

Most applicants opposed the war on religious grounds, believing it to be incompatible with the principles of Christianity. Others took the moral view that it was wrong to take a human life, though they were prepared to die for their country themselves. Many socialist COs based their case on a political objection to the war. Of the nearly 6,000 people to go on the register, around 2,000 were women. About 500 women were prosecuted for a range of 'offences', and more than 200 of them were imprisoned.

Tribunals were understandably less inclined to be objective if their neighbourhood had recently had a visit from German bombers. During the tense days in the summer of 1940, when invasion seemed a certainty, hostility towards COs increased sharply. Neighbours became abusive, employers sacked or suspended COs, and even the notorious white feathers from the First World War period made the occasional appearance. Yet few people now categorized COs as shirkers, however much they disagreed with their stance. And many COs did their own cause no harm by undertaking dangerous relief work during the worst months of the Blitz.

Appeal by a conscientious objector against a tribunal decision to refuse him exemption from military service

I conscientiously object to all wars, because war is contrary to the Christian ethic in which I believe. To destroy not only human life but anything which makes for good or is of spiritual uplift is directly opposed to Christian teaching as I see it. In trying to work out a philosophy of life, I have arrived at the conclusion that all human life has a purpose, and that to put an end to human beings is to deprive the world of a power of good. All human life is precious, therefore to kill is sinful. In view of this, I feel justified in appealing against non-combatant duties, for to do any such work would signify my acquiescence with the war. This does not mean that I am not willing to work for the good of my fellow-men. Above all, I desire my life to be of service to humanity. But I do not wish to offer to do one piece of work merely to escape another. My present aim is not to bargain for my liberty from the Army, but to prove the sincerity of my objection to war, and also to show that, given the trust, I will employ my time and all my powers in the service of others, according to the light within.

The Pacifist Prisoner

People who were in for robbery with violence got much more respect from the warders than conscientious objectors. They made it very clear that we were regarded as the scum.

Sidney Greaves

There was no history of conscientious objection in my family, who were Church of England. What really started me was a picture in the *Daily Telegraph* during the Abyssinian war, when the Italians were dropping mustard gas on the Abyssinians. The *Telegraph* published a picture which I can see quite clearly to this day in my mind, of an Italian tank with the cloth laid over its front for Mass, with the chalice and the patten, and over the crucifix was the gun of the tank, sticking out. It was so blasphemous that it seemed to say all that was needed to be said about the incompatibility of war and Christianity.

After that I began to meet members of the Fellowship of Reconciliation and others who shared my views. I was a very keen Anglican in a large church in Sutton Coldfield. As far as I know, I was the only pacifist out of the four or five hundred people there. No one showed the slightest understanding or sympathy, including the vicar. When I registered as a CO he told me that if I continued to serve at communion I would stop people coming, which I thought was pretty appalling. So I stopped going to that church.

At the start of the war I decided to register as a CO. My parents were considerably disturbed by this. I'd got a younger brother who was in the Territorial Army, and they didn't understand my position. They tried to dissuade me, though not actually stop me. But quite early on in the war I stopped being an Anglican. I read something in a book that brought me up with a jolt, and made me re-think my position. I went along to Friends' House in London, and found people there talking and thinking in exactly the way I was doing, and that led me on to become a member of the Society of Friends.

I had my tribunal in Birmingham, and I was given exemption on condition that I stayed where I was, which was working in local government. But I'd asked for *complete* exemption, I wasn't prepared to accept conditional, so I resigned my job. For the next six months I helped a friend who was a clergyman run his church youth work in the suburbs of Birmingham. During this time the bombing of Coventry took place, and I was very anguished wondering what to do next, whether I should go to London or stay in Birmingham. I was in the church one morning after a short service, and it was just as though I heard suddenly over my left shoulder, 'You will go to London.' It was a remarkable experience, it was so clear and vivid, so distinct. What really surprised me was that I didn't find it in the least alarming; I felt a tremendous sense of peace. So this of course settled the issue, and I went off to London.

It was while I was working in London that I had to spend six months in Wormwood Scrubs, for refusing to accept a condition. I went up to Bow Street, which was the top joint. I had a rather benign but stern little magistrate called Sir Bernard Watson. I made my statement as to why I thought war was incompatible with Christianity, and why I refused to accept a condition, that I felt conscience should be respected. He listened to it, and then sent me down. At both my tribunal and appeal, I felt that the authorities were going through the motions, I don't think there was any attempt to discuss my point of view with me, or probe. They just listened and said, 'Nothing doing.'

My parents were shocked at the thought of my going to prison. I remember before I went to court, I had a letter from a close family friend, delivered by special messenger before the first post. It was pages and pages setting out all the arguments against the pacifist position – which any pacifist thinks of in the first ten minutes – and begging me to stop, because I was going to kill my parents. This wasn't exactly helpful at the time. But the interesting thing was that, after I had been in prison, although my parents still didn't understand my position, and although they would never have said so, I think they respected me, and were quite proud of what I'd done. Our relationship was very much stronger than it had been.

My sentence was hard labour, which was supposed to involve sleeping for the first fortnight on bare boards. But they forgot to take my mattress away, so it wasn't anything but in name. We were locked up in the early evening, about half past five, and let out again about seven in the morning. There were the usual appalling unsanitary conditions, with a bucket in the cell. Slopping out in the morning was a dreadful experience, faeces and urine everywhere. We would be given breakfast and then taken to the workshops for a couple of hours, and then back to the cells, and then in the afternoon another session in the workshops. And then we were locked up again at about five o'clock for the night. It was very difficult to have any decent conversation with the other prisoners. Although some conversation did take place on exercise, it was not allowed, it was a matter of chance who you were walking with as you shuffled two by two round the exercise yard. It wasn't really conducive to any deep conversation.

I was in the tailors' workshop, and I was put on sewing buttonholes for overalls, until I discovered that the overalls were for the Royal Navy. It was against the law to ask COs to do anything connected with the war effort. So, being a very tidy-minded person, I said I would finish the overalls I was working on, but I wouldn't do any more. I was switched on to a machine making socks for prisoners, and spent the rest of my time making yards and yards of prison socks.

The warders on the whole were hostile to COs. People who were in for robbery with violence got much more respect from them. They made it very clear that we were regarded as the scum. There was a subdued patriotic bias. One or two of the screws were better, but by and large that was the attitude. But I don't think the experience was anything like as scaring as that of COs in the First World War. We had a very easy time compared with them.

Conversation was restricted, but I did get talking to a couple of young soldiers, who asked me what I was in for. When I told them they said I had made a very bad choice. They said, 'This is much worse than the Army.' They thought that I had weighed up the possibilities and chosen prison. They hadn't the remotest understanding of what had led me to this. In so far as we talked, that was the general situation with the other prisoners, they didn't understand; they thought me and the other nine COs in there were nuts. I knew some of the other COs, but we didn't have much contact, though we did manage some clandestine conversations.

In the evenings, if you'd behaved yourself for six weeks, you had what was called 'association', when you could go and sit round tables on the ground floor and chat. This didn't appeal to me very much, so I decided to stay in my cell and read. I got copies of *The Oxford Book of English Verse* and *The Oxford Book of Modern Verse* and things like that. There was a prison library, but it was hit and miss what you got – I remember I got volume two of *War and Peace*, but not volumes one and three. So I've read the middle, but not the beginning and the end.

As a Quaker I was able to stay in my cell and read while they had services in the chapel. Quakers, Jews and Roman Catholics were exempt, but for everyone else it was compulsory. The Jews and Roman Catholics were told to fall out, and the Quakers did as well, and all the others were marched off to the chapel. I went at first. You sat below the level of the aisle, and the warders marched up and down to see what was going on, so it was not conducive to a spirit of worship. At the end of the morning service the chaplain would read the headlines – and just the headlines – from the *Mirror* or one of the other Sunday papers, and there would be a lot of shuffling and general inattention, until he got to the football results, and then you could hear a pin drop. It was quite clear the mass of prisoners were far more interested in the football results than the latest news of the war.

I stopped going to the services after a while, because I thought the level of preaching by the chaplain was deplorable. For instance, he took the marvellous text from St John's Gospel, 'I am the bread of life', and in his sermon he said that jam was all right sometimes, but we wouldn't like to have jam every day. Saying this to people who never saw jam seemed to me very insensitive.

I remember during air raids there was a panic in the prison, because we were all locked in. If the prison were hit there was no way you could get out. Prisoners would bang plates, jerries, mugs, anything; it was an enormous noise. There was nothing you could do. You could see the searchlights outside, you could hear the crump of bombs, and they had anti-aircraft guns on Wormwood Scrubs common, just nearby, so there was a lot of noise. But it was very disturbing to be in that situation.

I remember the day I came out very well. It was a very nice day, and we were let out at about seven in the morning. I was taken back to a flat in St Peter's Street in Westminster and we had breakfast. And for some time I used to sit in a room and say to myself, 'If I want to walk out, I can go through that door.' The idea of being in a room that you could walk out of took some getting used to. It was quite surprising. But I think prison was a valuable experience, it was a period of very deep self-examination. One got to know oneself much more there. Although all this unpleasantness and squalor was going on, and one was fitted out with appalling clothes, one seemed to be living above it, one always felt it was going on beneath one. It was a marvellous experience, and I suppose this was because we were in there without anything on our conscience, which was different from somebody who had been put in there with feelings of guilt and resentment. Roy Walker was a CO who was in at the same time as me, and he took a very absolutist stand. He refused to cooperate with the prison at all, and spent, I think, all his time in the punishment block. He was on hunger strike a lot of the time. He set himself against the system, and I admired his courage; he certainly had a very, very tough time. But by and large the COs' experiences were very like mine, there was no brutality, no roughing up or anything like that.

After the First World War the COs who had been in prison were very articulate. As a result of what they said when they came out, there were a lot of reforms. For instance, we didn't have to wear the broad-arrow clothing, although it was pretty shoddy. We didn't have our heads shaved. I think the authorities had learnt to that extent; they'd had to, because of the publicity given to the conditions. But prison is always unpleasant, because basically it's the denial of freedom that matters. It doesn't matter how well you're dressed or how well you're fed. But the sordidness of the business all adds to this, and it's a dehumanizing experience. Everything was done to humiliate and dehumanize you. How anyone can claim that such a system is redemptive or restorative I don't know. It can only damage people whose personalities are already impaired.

Later, when I wanted to start studying medicine, I went to the Labour Exchange in London, and told them what I wanted to do. They showed me my envelope which was like a health service patients' envelope, buff-coloured, and across the front were two red-inked lines, and diagonally in red-ink capitals it said, 'THIS MAN MUST NOT BE GIVEN PERMISSION TO STUDY MEDICINE'. I can remember coming out into the street and saying to myself, 'Right, if I can't do it with you, I'll do it without you.' And it was remarkable how every time I came to something that looked like a brick wall, a door opened, and I got through to the other side. It happened repeatedly. I had applied to Sutton Coldfield for help towards my medical studies, and they just turned me down flat, because I had been a CO. But the LCC were much more tolerant, and they helped me, partly because I'd worked in London during the war. But none of the London hospitals would consider taking me, because I had been a CO.

POEM BY A CONSCIENTIOUS OBJECTOR, FEBRUARY 1945

'Give peace, Lord, in our time,'
The preacher said,
With solemn voice and look sublime.
'God rest our glorious dead.'
A stir swept through the congregation,
And grief and aggravation
Broke rudely in upon their orisons,
As mothers thought of slaughtered sons,
Or husbands killed,
Mown down by tanks and guns.
The deep-toned organ filled
Their hearts with passionate feeling,
Which grew with each crescendo
To a mighty swell,
As loudly pealing
Without diminuendo,
Their voices rose and fell.
What peace is theirs,
Or what use prayers,
When human effort plays no part
To quench the conflagration
These people did not start,
These people, aroused to indignation,
By a preacher's thoughtless supplication?

The Actor's Wife

The judge, who was almost asleep, gave him six months at first, but then somebody behind prodded him and said, 'The maximum sentence is a year, my lord.' And he woke up and changed it, and said, 'A year's hard labour.'

Olive Markham

When war broke out we were in Sussex. My husband David and I had already been to peace meetings. I can remember a very big one in London just before the war. It was quite frightening, National Front people came into the gallery and threw leaflets down. The hall was absolutely packed. A lot of people who were pacifists with us then changed over when war broke out. But David never changed.

During the early part of the war he was working with the Old Vic company. But as he was a pacifist, they always knew that he might have to leave at any moment, and so it was difficult to get jobs because of that. But Tyrone Guthrie was very good to him. As the company was on the move all the time, it took some time for the authorities to catch up with him. He didn't particularly try to evade them, it was just that being in different places, the Labour Exchange followed you about, and then you weren't there. So it just took quite a time.

Some people in the theatre were horrible: people like Athene Seyler and Edith Evans didn't want to know at all. But others, like Sybil Thorndike and Lewis Casson, were very nice and understanding. Alec Clunes was also very sweet, he was one of the few who offered me a job back-stage to earn some money when I was desperate. But managements were certainly very unsympathetic, it was all doing things for the troops. Also David couldn't do those war films at all. He said they were made to show how wonderful war was and just romanticized it. He refused to act in Noel Coward's *In Which We Serve*, which annoyed Coward, who then circulated all the studios, saying that David was very difficult and shouldn't be employed.

When he was arrested he was about to play the main part in a play called *The Power and the Glory*. It was a great success, and Richard Attenborough did it instead, and made his name with it. Instead, David went before a tribunal in Reading. The tribunals could be very different. If you went to Birmingham there was a pacifist bishop there, so nearly everyone who wanted to go on doing their own work, especially actors, tried to get to Birmingham. You almost invariably got exemption.

The judges were nearly always against the COs. It always seemed rather silly to me, because there weren't all that many, and I always thought they wouldn't make good soldiers anyway, and it was better to just let them be, and carry on with their own job. Sometimes I went with boys who didn't have any friends, or where the family was against them and the mother wouldn't come in. I always remember one tribunal I went to with a very young boy whose father had been shell-shocked in the First World War, and had had epileptic fits from the shocks. The father was totally anti-war, and terribly dependent on his son, who looked after him. He had a doctor's letter to say that if he was called up the father probably wouldn't live and would give up hope altogether. And the judge turned him down, because they said that wasn't conscientious objection, but a collection of circumstances which had made him not want to fight. And the mother was there, and she almost collapsed, and the boy went as white as a sheet.

The Reading tribunal was very bad, they were very anti. But David's way made it difficult for the judges to decide that it was a conscientious objection. It wasn't religious, you see. His attitude was that everybody is capable of murder in certain circumstances, and if I've got to murder somebody I'll do it because I have to, in my way, I won't have a gun put into my hand by the state, because I won't know what I'll do with it, and I might kill somebody I don't know, or children. They didn't consider that to be conscientious objection. The judge, who was almost asleep, gave him six months at first, but then somebody behind prodded him and said, 'The maximum sentence is a year, my lord.' And he woke up and changed it, and said, 'A year's hard labour.'

David then went to Winson Green prison in Birmingham. I remember we had a horrible goodbye. It was the first time I saw the other side of the police, who had always been very yes and no up to then, kind and gentle. And I saw them kicking him down the steps, and the handcuffs . . . The awful thing was, after we said goodbye, I found that he had taken my suitcase and I had taken his, and I had to run all the way back and change them over.

The other prisoners were terribly kind to him. There was a gang of housebreakers who were very nice; the leader said he would teach David how to break into a house afterwards, he'd show him how to open windows, and then he could join the gang. They all thought it was an awful shame that they were there, they were shocked when it happened. David said the prison was full of people who shouldn't have been there, lots of people out of the Navy and the Air Force who'd pinched watches and done silly things like that; people who had exposed themselves, and so on. He thought there were only two, both black market men, who you could say were perhaps in the right place. All they did was to plan how they would carry on with the black market when they got out! That made him think a lot about prison, what it did to you, and how useless it was.

When I first went to see him there I was terribly, terribly shocked. I suppose I must have been very naïve, it was just the fact of everybody being behind bars, that human beings could do this to other human beings. I was very young and it seemed really terrible to me. There was just this long row of bars, and all of us wives and mothers on one side, and the men holding on to the bars, just like animals really, and the warders walking behind. I was so shocked I just burst into tears. One of the prison officers, meaning to be kind, I suppose, and knowing that David wasn't a criminal, took him out of his cell, and took us both to a little empty room where there was just a bare table. And he sat at the head of it, and David and I sat on either side, and he said, 'Now you can carry on.' But I found that it was very much more difficult to talk under those circumstances, because where there was so much noise with everybody talking and the warders walking up and down, you could say all sorts of things. But here I couldn't think of anything to say, except to tell David about a peewit that had made a nest in a farm near where we lived in Derbyshire. I remember how useless it felt, talking just about that, with the officer just sitting there at the end of the table.

The warders were quite nasty on the surface, but in fact I think they rather liked David. He was reading *War and Peace* – you were allowed one book a month – and one of the warders asked him if he would leave it behind because he wanted it for his girlfriend. David was rather pleased with that. But people did get on with him: he had a very funny sense of humour, and he was a very original thinker. He could always make people laugh and get on with anyone.

But he was terribly pulled down by his time in Winson Green. They had to sew mailbags, which he couldn't do, and he got terrible sores on his hands. The diet was terribly bad. He tried to be vegetarian, but they didn't cater for that sort of thing. The prison doctor was *absolutely* against COs and really punished him for any little thing. I remember him telling me that he was once given a month's punishment for a really silly incident. He was on exercise, and the remand prisoners were in another yard. Somebody was smoking and David waved his arm in appreciation of the smell, and the guard said, 'Right, communicating with another prisoner.' So then he wasn't allowed to write to me for a month.

He was in Winson Green for two months. Wormwood Scrubs, where he was transferred to, was better, there was more communication, and it was generally easier. I don't know why, but it just was a jollier prison. But he didn't complete his sentence; he appealed from prison, and was released. He had been in this play *Pick-Up Girl*, it was American, I think. It was to do with prostitution, and produced by Peter Cotes, and it got very good notices. Queen Mary was very interested in the whole question: she sent her lady-in-waiting to see it, to have a report about it. And so they wrote a letter to the appeal court saying they thought he should come out and go on with his own work. So he came out, but was ordered to go into forestry, which he was quite glad to do. When he came out he was completely grey, and he couldn't talk. He had had flu and jaundice, and he just spoke in a whisper, which was horrible.

There was a lot of stigma attached to being a CO. We lived for some of the war in Disley, just outside Manchester. A lot of the people in the village didn't talk to me, or to David when he came down. It was more the older people. There was an awfully nice man there who had been terribly injured in the First World War, and who was absolutely anti-war. His son was a CO, and I tended to go and see people like that, just to get with people who were a bit sympathetic. Otherwise there were only two people in the village who had pacifist leanings, the lady who kept the confectionery shop and the postmaster's wife. They were always nice about David, but other people took the attitude, 'My son may be killed getting food for your children, what are you doing?' My thing was, I felt very strongly that I shouldn't register, I thought it was wrong to have an identity card. The police got me in the Food Office, and they said that if I didn't register I couldn't get my rations, and I would go to prison. They were so determined to get everybody registered, and I couldn't face leaving my children. My mother wouldn't have been able to look after them, and I just knew I couldn't go to prison. I don't know why I felt so strongly about this. It doesn't seem so serious now, but then it did. In the end I had to give in, and that showed me that you should never criticize people for suddenly turning round at the last minute, because sometimes you have to make compromises.

I had two children by then. They were born in a teaching hospital in Manchester, free. That was quite an extraordinary time. Kika's was quite a bad birth, and a few days afterwards, when all the nurses were at supper, the ARP warden came and poked his head through the hospital window and said, 'Your lights are showing and the bombs are dropping.' The blackout had come down somehow. But none of us could get out of bed, because we'd all had bad births. But as I only had stitches, they all said, 'Go on, Mrs Markham, you can walk.' I was very frightened, because I thought if I got out all the stitches would break. But everyone else was much worse, so in the end I *had* to get out, and crawl round the room holding on to people's beds, and ring the bell to get the nurses in.

David's beliefs caused difficulty in our families. I think his stepfather really thought he was a coward. His brother was in the RAF and terribly physically brave. He was shot down by the Germans over France and lost the use of his arm. My youngest brother, who I was terribly close to, was at Dunkirk, and he had a terrible time coming over. They were all on the beach in darkness waiting to be rescued, and they had to keep absolutely quiet, but one of his own men lost his nerve and fired a gun, and the Germans wiped out the whole of his platoon. My stepfather-in-law had been in the Royal Flying Corps in the First World War, in one of those very early planes which came to bits in the air, and he had been quite badly injured. And he was bitterly against David.

I can see now that my father was frightened in a way, he was worried about my brothers, thinking David's attitude might have a bad effect on them. He was completely irreligious, while my mother had always been religious. She was really much kinder about David's position, because she believed he was standing by his principles. David was not at all evangelical about his beliefs. He had a way of agreeing with a person first, getting them into an agreeable frame of mind. He was terribly good with my father, so much better than I was about arguing on the subject. If you're the child it's more difficult, of course, but I never really made it up with my father. He couldn't say one nice word about David, and I found that terribly hard to understand. I know it was very hard for him: I was the only girl, in fact I was the first girl born into our family for generations, and obviously when I was little I was devoted to him. But then I began to see a different side when I left school and met David.

Once I started thinking for myself I sent up for all these anti-war magazines, so I could hear the other side. Of course, the editor of *Freedom* went to prison – it was called *War Commentary* then. But there were quite a few little magazines which started up and tried to put another point of view. The police raided the offices of one of them and found the list of subscribers, and I was one. So they sent a detective out to interview me, just before Kika was born. I can remember the interview well, because my father was quite upset about a detective coming. I was so near to having the baby that I had to lie on the sofa; I thought I might have to rush off to hospital any moment. I hardly let the detective get a word in edgeways. I lectured him about being in such a dreadful profession.

In Disley I started a nursery school for children up to five, while David was in prison. I tried to get so-called middle-class people from the village to get together with the poorer people for the benefit of the children. We were given a room and we did get inspected, but we couldn't get a government grant because no one in the village was on war work, so we had to do it all by subscription. I wrote to all the actors I knew, saying could they give me a pound or two for the school, and they were terribly kind, and I got enough money to pay the salary of a teacher, and we were able to get some toys. It ran for two years, but it was very difficult to get the two lots of people to mix, though they did in the end. At first the better-off people didn't want their children to pick up 'accents' and silly things like that. I learnt a lot about children there: we used to take turns helping the teacher, though a lot of the women didn't want to go, so I used to go pretty often. If people were poor and couldn't pay we used to take them free. There was a certain amount of back-biting: people would say, so-and-so's got a job, she could pay, we're paying. But they knew I didn't care about money.

I never thought we would survive the war. That's really what made me decide I wanted to have children. David had had such an unhappy childhood, and I thought if I have a baby, he might perhaps have a year or so of family life, and then we'd all be blown up. I think this was just a personal feeling, because I was so shocked by it all. I didn't think we would survive at all.

Letter from David Markham to Olive Markham, Winson Green Prison, Birmingham

23 May 1942

My darling,

Who said there ain't no justice. This morning what should I find in my study but a copy of *War and Peace*!! It's true there are many people who would far sooner do 12 Months' Hard than read *War and Peace* – but that's not the point. . . . It's the Constance Garnett translation – 1,536 pages of it. Meanwhile, my mind is not at rest, but much calmer.

Today I was at last given my cell task, which I think I shall manage alright, though it entails very intricate needlework. Tomorrow my first Quaker session. Should be a riot – I speak in the vernacular. Tonight I'm hungry for the first time, a good sign. You'll definitely be allowed to answer this, and I see by the regulations I am allowed four photos, so if you haven't sent them already, send two in your next letter and the other two when you've had them taken. Better send pretty small ones, by the way. I *may* be allowed to write to you again in two weeks, as a first offender, but I'm not quite sure of this.

I now feel I would like a visit, darling; that's to say only if you would too. If by any chance you have already replied to my last letter, saying you would also rather not, then we'll cut it out and I'll write instead; but if reading between the lines you really want to come – OK. Just be prepared for rather strange conditions. And write down on a piece of paper anything particular you want to discuss, in case you should forget. You won't of course be allowed to give me anything – except the photos, if they should be ready.

Light of my life, sometimes I hear a train in the distance, or a dog bark, or the faint shout of a child playing, or more loudly, the exhaust of a motorbike, and these sounds are the saddest things on earth. Yes, after the first blind anguish it is better to sit down and write – especially if one is lucky enough to have pen and ink. Oh my darling, my memory lacerates me – not only my memory but the certain knowledge that now you are saying good night to B and E, and *now* you are perhaps gazing out the bedroom window and thinking, What good is all this? No good, but in the evening the mind will wander.

This morning I was standing on my chair looking out of my 'window', from where I can see the whole inside portion of C block, which is two-hundred-odd similar spy-holes, when I suddenly noticed a human hand among all the dirty brickwork. It was sprinkling crumbs for the sparrows.

Darling, I shouldn't love you so much if I didn't miss you as I do. Yes, the first few days are immeasurably the worst. And at the last everything comes back to *boredom*, which is worse even than the food. How can people ever go to prison *twice*? In one way, of course, it is understandable – one knows what one is 'in for'.

Let me know how Mum is bearing up, and anything funny from HBH's letter. And of course about the school. In fact almost anything. Only write small like this – well, not quite so small or you'll give somebody a headache. I'll close with a spot of Hebrews II: 'Faith is the substance of things hoped for, the confidence of things not seen.' Good night my dearest darling.

Loveandloveandloveandlove xxxxxxx
D.

The Jehovah's Witness

*People would say, 'If everybody was like you, Hitler would
be here.' And we'd say, 'If everyone was like us, Hitler
wouldn't ever have an earthly chance.'*

Ernest Beavor

I'd already consecrated my life to be a witness to Jehovah God, so when
war broke out I wasn't going to stop. During the First World War I had
been patriotic. I remember standing in Whitehall at the Cenotaph in 1918,
and the clergyman said, 'This is the war to end wars, these men have not
died in vain.' And I believed it. But when the Second World War came
along, I thought, 'Hey, there's something wrong here.' What sickened me
furthermore was that the clergy were blessing both sides. In Germany it was
'Gott mit Uns', and here it was 'God is with Us'. Yet the Bible flatly and
distinctly forbids killing one another. The supreme command is to love your
neighbour, but how can you love him if you kill him?

Since 1923 I had been a press photographer, I had my own agency. But as
the war went on the newspapers wanted pictures to do with the war.
I decided I would be a hypocrite if I carried on. So I gave up my firm to my
two partners. I had been doing voluntary work for the Jehovah's Witnesses
up to then, but in June 1940 I became what we call a full-time minister.

We would go from home to home, urging people to get hold of their
Bible and see why the war was being waged. It's prophesied in the
scriptures: Jesus said nation would rise against nation – note that, not army

against army, but whole regimented nation against regimented nation. That was what commenced in 1914 and happened again in 1939 with conscription. Patriotism was running high, people had notices in their windows: ARP, national service, and so on. Many people would say, 'My son's fighting for the likes of you.' And we'd say, 'No indeed he's not.' They also used to say, 'If everybody was like you, Hitler would be here.' And we used to say, 'If everybody was like us, Hitler wouldn't ever have an earthly chance.' I was once accused of eating the food 'our brave boys brought over'. I said, 'Listen, if people are foolish enough to sink boats, that's entirely their own decision. The food that you eat is the food that I eat, which is provided by the God that I worship, the Lord God Jehovah.'

Nobody was ever violent in their opposition to us. Mind you, you often receive what you deserve, don't you? You must guard your tongue. Often a soft and mild answer turns away wrath. When people say things without thinking, well, you must be balanced to hold your tongue. Your tongue gets you into more trouble than anything else. The scripture says, 'No man has ever tamed the tongue.' But Jehovah God can contain it. If you talk about the things in the Bible, then you have tamed it.

My parents had been Bible students prior to the First World War. They brought me up to respect the Bible, but I didn't pay any attention at the time. But as I grew older I got to think more seriously about it, and decided that I would tell people the good news about Jehovah God's forthcoming kingdom. So when I refused call-up, it wasn't so much a conscientious objection to what was happening. That was something beyond my control; if nations go to war that's their responsibility. I refused on the grounds that I was not going to discontinue what I was already doing as a minister of Jehovah God.

Once I had refused to have a medical, I had to go in front of a tribunal. What you say there is left to the individual Witness, because it must be an individual decision. To be swept away by what everybody else did is not the point, is it? Each individual stands before God, and it must be our own determination.

The tribunal was at Tottenham Court. I remember the magistrate, a Mr Fork, was rather intolerant, and a bit impatient. We mustn't be, that's the point. You see, emotions mustn't control: it is either the truth or not the truth. If it's the truth you must do something about it; if it's just sentimentality, well, it's foolish. After all, it was a very serious proposition.

When I went for my appeal, the man whose case was being heard just before mine was a sergeant in the Army, who had been arrested for robbing a church. Before either of us went into the witness box, this soldier said to me, 'You'll get two years.' I said, 'What about you?' And he said, 'I'll get off.' And he was right. His commanding officer was there, and said he was a very gallant soldier. So the judge said, 'Case dismissed.' I think in my case the magistrate had made up his mind before he started, because Jehovah's Witnesses were very unpopular during the war; people generally didn't understand why we were so resolute, which is understandable. I remember in his final remarks the judge called me the worst of my kind, and said that he had the utmost pleasure in giving me the maximum sentence. He instructed the jury to confirm this. I had been told that if I lost my appeal, my one-year sentence would be doubled. And that's what happened: I got two years instead of the original twelve months.

My time in prison strengthened me tremendously. For one thing, it gave me a chance to do something I'd never done before, which was to read the Bible right through. The conditions were a bit rigid in Wormwood Scrubs: we were locked up for hours on our own, from four in the afternoon to seven the next morning. But I was able to talk to people, and three of the warders became Jehovah's Witnesses. People thought we were a bit peculiar, although the staff were respectful. But there again, being balanced, asking people why they thought the world was in this state of confusion – many people just don't stop to think, they just get caught up in the euphoria of the time. But we mustn't be afraid of the truth, and the only way to find the truth is to go to the Bible. It says in the Book of John, 'The whole world is lying in the power of the wicked one', and that wicked one is Satan, and he's the one who instigated the war.

My son went to prison; he was eighteen. It wasn't easy for my wife, with her husband and son in prison, although she had our two daughters at home. Of course some of the women Jehovah's Witnesses went to prison too, to Holloway. Mind you, the Bible teaches you to be content, you don't strive after riches, and Christ Jesus said, if you seek first the kingdom, all those other things will be added. With the Jehovah's Witnesses there's no clergy/laity distinction, we're all doing the same thing, womenfolk as well.

We were absolutely neutral regarding the politics of our work. We had no links with other pacifist groups. We consider religion as practised on earth today by established organizations to be hypocritical. The Bible says we must love God and love our neighbour, but how can you love him if you kill him? For another thing, there must be no difference between the nationalities. It's a horrible thing, nationalism.

People did listen to us, I think they were more spiritually minded than they are today. War brings suffering, and many people who had lost their dear ones wanted to know if they would ever see them again. And we were able to say yes, the time will come when all the millions that have died are going to come back, and this earth will be restored to the paradise that God intended.

We were allowed to go on giving public talks during the war. But the British government took a line against us, they banned some of our literature, on the grounds that it was subversive. It was the same in America. At the start of the war some Witnesses were granted exemption, but as the war heated up the government got a bit more intolerant. I think it was Herbert Morrison, the Home Secretary, who decided that we were objectionable. We visited MPs and explained our position, but their reaction was quite intolerant.

Many of today's Witnesses were in the war, and learnt the truth when they came out, they saw the folly of it all. There are 100,000 in Germany at the present moment. During the war they were put in the concentration camps, and suffered tremendously – many were killed. Before the war they had refused to give the *Heil Hitler*. Hitler called us a 'brood'; he said, 'I will exterminate this brood.' Well, the brood is still here, and Hitler no longer exists.

Letters between a conscientious objector and his MP

3 January 1940

Dear Sir,

Last May I wrote asking for your interest in the cause of conscientious objectors, and you very kindly replied sympathetically.

During the passage of the Military Training Bill through the House, the premier gave certain definite pledges which provided that no genuine objector should be in any way penalized, but unfortunately these pledges are being flouted by the local and appeal tribunals.

In my own case, which was heard at Leeds, the chairman said that he did not doubt the sincerity of my conscientious objection, but to everyone's surprise placed me in the category for non-combatant service with a strong recommendation for the Royal Auxiliary Medical Corps, regardless of the fact that I strongly objected to any form of service with the armed forces.

Feeling quite unable to accept this decision, I have applied for my case to be heard by the appeal tribunal and am now awaiting some communication in this respect.

In this connection may I call your attention to the enclosed cutting from *The Friend*, from which you will see that appellants are frequently treated unfairly and discourteously; that no attempt is made to rectify the inequalities which are evidenced by 4 per cent exemptions by one tribunal and 45 per cent by another. Further, you will observe that Sir Leonard Costello said, 'It doesn't in the least matter what the Prime Minister has said.'

If I must suffer injustice personally for conscience's sake, I shall try not to complain, but my view of my duty as a Christian impels me to continue in the course which I have followed for the last four years, and although you may not agree with my view, I am sure that will not prevent you doing all you can towards the implementation of the specific pledges which have been given to genuine conscientious objectors.

I thank you sir in advance and remain,

Yours truly
J.W. Emburton

5 January 1940

Dear Sir
I am obliged for yours this morning and the enclosure.

Not infrequently a judge queries the spoken word of prime minister and politicians when interpreting the law, but I doubt if any of them are justified in taking up that attitude in regard to conscientious objectors.

However we are watching these events very closely, and more will be heard of them when Parliament reassembles.

It has been and still is our wish that objectors should have a square deal, and for my part I shall insist upon no less than that.

Yours faithfully,
T. Williams, MP

The Shelter Warden

*I think I had convinced them about unconditional
exemption by showing that I had already committed
myself to a course which involved giving up all prospects
of life and career, and living on a pound a week.*

Bernard Nicholls

I think my pacifism arose out of my Christian understanding. I was
brought up in an ordinary, middle-class family in Hertfordshire. It wasn't
until the late 1930s that I got round to thinking seriously about the
Christian implications of war. It was characteristic of the conservative
evangelical Christianity of the time that the social implications of the
gospel, not to mention the political, were not to the fore. It was a personal,
pietistic faith one had. In adopting the Christian pacifist position, I did so
from a very narrow base of life and understanding.

During the Phoney War period, I was still without anyone I could turn to
for help. I was stimulated in a bit of wider thinking by a very remarkable
parish priest. He was an old Cornishman, a bachelor, who used to have me
sitting in his study while he talked. Though he was a conservative
evangelical, he was a true one, with a rounded understanding of the Gospel
which carried into all walks of life. When I said that I couldn't see Christian
faith as being compatible with war, he was absolutely shattered. He was
outraged that I should think of contracting out and standing on the
sidelines. And the next Sunday he preached a sermon virulently attacking

the pacifist position. He finished it with a ringing statement that anyone who adopted this position could be neither a Christian nor a gentleman. At which point I was so overcome, I walked out. All credit to the dear man, he was so upset by that, he came round to my home during the week, and we became friends again.

The very fact that he had overplayed his hand meant that in the aftermath there was an acceptance of my position, though it was seen as rather odd, and no doubt many thought that I'd grow out of it. I can't say that I went on being stigmatized, nobody rushed round as they did in the First World War with white feathers and that sort of thing. And I can't recollect that I lost a friend through it, or was snubbed, or anything like that.

I went through a great deal of youthful agony about taking up this position, because I wasn't so self-opinionated that I was happy being the odd man out. I was also worried by my family's distress. Yet, in spite of my oddity, and the shame and disgrace it was felt that it brought on them, my family closed round me. Both my mother and father said they simply couldn't understand my position, but nevertheless I happened to be their son, and that was that.

When the war started I was with a printing firm, as an apprentice who had then moved on to the business side. My employer was marvellous. Although he objected strongly to my position, he was willing to let the law take its course. He said, 'I'm not going to victimize you, my instinct is to chuck you out on your neck, but I'm not going to. The law has been set up to deal with such as you, and we'll see what happens.' So I registered as a conscientious objector, and got called before a local tribunal. And because I had taken up what some called the absolutist position – I had indicated that I was not willing to accept a condition of any kind provided under the Act for Conscientious Objection – the tribunal threw out my application. I was placed on the military register, and left to object to that if I chose to do so, which of course I promptly did, and appealed to the local tribunal.

Meanwhile, I had come into contact with the Quakers. The secretary of the committee for sufferings suggested I went to the headquarters of the Fellowship of Reconciliation, the international pacifist organization, where the Anglican Pacifist Fellowship had a little office. So I joined up with them, and soon received a circular from the APF to say they were developing a little service unit of some of the younger members, in the hope that they might be able to serve as Christian pacifists when London became subjected to bombing. I became so involved that I was asked to organize and lead the group.

When the bombing began we found the ARP services didn't seem to mind who we were. We had adopted boiler suits as a suitable garb, which was very sensible. At night-time we acted as shelter wardens in the crypt of Dickens's *Little Dorrit* church in Borough near London Bridge, which had been opened as a shelter. In the day-time we went round doing what we could, helping people who were bombed out, trying to rescue bits of furniture from buildings, and so on.

The camaraderie was very real and practical. I have never had a very strong proselytizing urge myself, but one or two of our group were keen to give their witness or testimony. By and large people were just bored with this, it didn't seem to make two pennyworth of difference to them. What you wanted was help to get through each day or night, that was what mattered. Some of the APF officials were a little disconcerted about this, because they were long-standing Christian pacifists, and one or two of them had suffered in the First World War as a result of this. They hoped that, while we would genuinely assist in practical and humanitarian ways, our work would turn out to be a good witness for Christian pacifism. I said that most people didn't understand what it meant anyway, and there was precious little opportunity to try and tell them.

Another little contingent of the APF had joined up with St Martin's-in-the-Fields in Trafalgar Square, which was being opened up as a 24-hours-a-day centre for all sorts. For instance, members of the Canadian Air Force who came over early on used to go there as an alternative to the less desirable seductions of the West End. We began to gravitate there increasingly, and got to know the official Westminster City Council's ARP and shelter services. Around late 1940 the council's town clerk was the remarkable Parker Morris, who came to fame after the war in connection with housing. He realized that there were many large buildings, public buildings, shops and so on with the kind of basements that were being designated as shelters, but that there wasn't really the capacity to cope with this. And he persuaded the council to appoint as chief shelter warden a man called Copeman, who was reputed to be a communist.

Copeman came to me and said, 'Look, we've got a problem on our hands. When the siren goes, the police and the wardens see that everybody goes into the shelters. But here in the West End we've got our permanent minority of down-and-outs, and they all get bundled into the shelters. Some of them have seen these shelters purely as somewhere to go out of the elements. Some of them are meths drinkers, an increasing number are being designated as infested with lice, and some are mentally backward people, and they're causing trouble. In some cases shelter wardens are taking the law into their own hands and separating the sheep from the goats, and either shoving these people back on to the streets, or making separate wings for the undesirables. This just won't do. I've come to the conclusion that the only way we can cope is to make a special shelter, to which people can be sent if wardens feel that they can't cope with them. But it won't be a dump; in fact we'll try and make it the best shelter in London. It isn't a place that my staff can run. I've seen what you people have been doing at St Martin's, and I think it's a job for you. We'll provide the setting and the facilities, and you can get on and run it.'

So they requisitioned one or two of the arches under Charing Cross station, which had been used for various purposes over the years – one or two were bank vaults and there was an old theatre in one. Arch number 176 was taken over and set up as a shelter with a capacity of about two hundred. It had three-tiered bunks, and they made a large open area complete with a lovely fireplace that would have graced a country residence. They fitted up a marvellous canteen facility, much better than any in other such places, a medical aid post, baths, and lavatory facilities.

And so we began the Hungerford Club. It was in fact one of the most exclusive clubs in London, because you couldn't get in without a special pass from the Westminster shelter service. It was indeed a club for the privileged, and we made use of this point, it was one of the things that helped to create camaraderie between people not always noted for it.

I think the club succeeded in its aim. It certainly brought relief to the shelter situation. Also it was important from the police point of view. At first we were a little apprehensive in regard to the police, because many of the people had a record of a petty kind. They were the kind of people who tended to be picked up and shoved behind bars for a few days for some minor misdemeanour, either because they were hopelessly drunk with meths, been involved with some pickpocketing, or because the police got complaints from hoteliers that layabouts were sleeping on their ventilation grilles round the back of their hotels. What I did was to go along to Bow Street police station and explain to the inspector what was on, and he welcomed the development enormously. Often if he picked up one of those he knew was ours, he would get in touch. And sometimes they were willing, after a word from us, to let somebody out that otherwise might have been up in court on a petty charge.

Quite a lot of the men were veterans of the First World War, and a great many were very interesting people. They were odd ones out, contractors out of society, which in a real sense we were too. In due course they would ask us who we were, what we were doing, why we were different from the usual kind of social service people they were used to, why we weren't fighting. Some of them, particularly if they were a bit drunk, would get abusive and violent about this, but I think it was because they had difficulty in understanding our position. But these antipathies did nothing to undermine the basic mutuality that existed between most of them and us. The fact that some of us spent a night or two in the shelter if things were getting difficult gave the sense that we were sharing their sort of life. We did insist on certain basic things, but that was slightly different. But many of them were nonconformists like ourselves. I'm sure this helped us to be more patient than we otherwise might have been.

There were times when patience and control broke, notably with a tall, gangling young man, who had fallen early for methylated spirits. This was the chief evil then, a horrid trap, and he was right into it. We did our darnedest to get him out of it, and we got so far as to get him reconciled and back with his family. But it didn't last. One day he appeared at the door with his bottle, swaying. I suddenly lost control and just lashed out and hit him, hard, straight and full in the face. I was amazed at myself, but in fact it was quite a good thing to have done, because *he* was so utterly amazed by this, that it did what all our other patient work had not been able to do. It was a really traumatic experience for him, and led him back to his family. I've often thought about the implications of that incident.

The general atmosphere was one of considerable tension. Some unpleasant things happened. One night a young merchant seaman who had jumped ship came in. Increasingly Merchant Navy chaps who got involved with the submarines had horrible experiences, and when they came to London docks a small proportion would jump ship. They were under discipline in a way that they were not in peacetime, and they had to be rounded up as deserters. This one was from Newfoundland, a tough young man. He was brought in by a policeman who had found him in Trafalgar Square, who said, 'Look, this chap's been drinking, I think he's all right, can you give him a bed for tonight, and we'll hope to pick him up and straighten him out in the morning?' They did try to get these chaps back to their ships rather than deal with them in a copybook sort of way; a great deal of very humane work was done by the police.

We were pretty full that night, but I looked at our bunk chart and, being rather busy at that moment, directed him to a bunk. A short while afterwards there was a hell of a row, and I dashed down to see it. Something had gone wrong with our record-keeping, and one of our old stagers, who was in the tertiary stage of syphilis and was in a horrible mess physically and mentally, had a semi-permanent bunk, *his* bunk, and I had directed this young man to it by mistake. They had got into a quarrel, and the young man had pulled out a big knife and was there in a threatening position. I found it necessary to grapple with him, though I had no training in this sort of thing, and it was an anxious moment. Fortunately, as sometimes happens in those circumstances, a person's aggression suddenly slackens, and I could feel him relax in my grasp. But it could have been a thoroughly nasty incident.

During my early days at the Hungerford I was called to the appellate tribunal in Victoria. We were very hard pressed, and during the daytime we used to insist that everyone went out while we cleared up. On this particular morning I was very busy, and suddenly woke up to the fact that I had this tribunal. So I dropped everything and dashed there, just as I was, with dirty hands and a boiler suit, arriving out of breath. The appellate tribunal had the papers of the first one, and you had the opportunity of making a further statement. I have no doubt that it was extremely naïve and simplistic, but I remember having a jolly good discussion with the three members of the tribunal, and at the end of it the chairman looked at me over his glasses, and said, 'You are a very obdurate young man.' One of the other members was a trade union man. Not being very good at all these theoretical discussions about what the Bible might or might not have said, he said, 'Why are you dressed like that, what's all this about?' And he got me on to my work at the club, rather helpfully from my point of view. I'd said in my paperwork that, irrespective of what tribunals might say, I was sure that I was called on the one hand to the almost devastating act of contracting out of society, but at the same time I had to find ways of contracting back in, and my way of doing this was offering myself for humanitarian service. I felt somehow that this impressed the trade union man far more than anything I had written down, or any more theoretical point.

So the tribunal reserved their judgement, and a fortnight later I heard that I had been placed unconditionally on the register of conscientious objectors, which I came to understand later was a comparatively rare verdict. I think I had convinced them about unconditional exemption by showing that I had already committed myself to a course which involved giving up all prospects of life and career and living on one pound a week.

The verdict was very important to me, because it enormously increased my regard for the British way of life and sense of justice; the love of my country, if you like. Here we were in the Blitz, with my country saying that I wasn't obliged to go and dig on the land or work in a hospital, but that I could go my way without being in any way tied in with what was then fast becoming a total commitment to war. I could walk along the street and, if I chose, say, 'You can all get on with this, it's nothing to do with me.' This wasn't my attitude at all, as it happens, but I accepted it as a verdict of trust, and it enormously increased my sense of social commitment and obligation.

The Dissident Student

The air-raid sirens went at night, so we were locked in, and all the lights turned off. I could hear the prison officer going round from cell to cell looking through the spy-hole to make sure we were all there. Then there was absolute silence until the all-clear went. We were left in our cells, entirely on our own.

Alex Bryan

I suppose my father was quite an influence on the way my thinking went. He was a cabinet-maker and he worked with the North-Eastern Railway. He had been in the trenches in France, so he knew what war was. He had had some horrible experiences. It was obvious that it had affected him greatly. He came to see that there was no good to be gained from fighting wars. Before the Second World War broke out he was involved with the peace plebiscite. I went with him when I was just a boy at school; we went from door to door handing in questionnaires. Almost unconsciously my thinking developed along the lines of pacifism.

I went up to university at the time of Munich, but I was not very optimistic about Chamberlain's promise of peace for our time. I suppose this stimulated me to think further about pacifist ideas. I'd heard father talk about Quakers in York. He belonged to an adult school and used to find speakers for the Sunday afternoon meetings. As there were two Quaker schools in York, he called on some of the staff there. I used to go with him on visits of that kind, and met these people. And so, on the

Sunday that war was declared, I went to my first Quaker meeting, in York.

When the university term began I made contact with the Friends in Sheffield. I knew that my turn to register would probably come very soon, and that I needed to be ready for this. I discussed it with some of my friends, and became quite certain that I should register as a conscientious objector, and that furthermore I would ask for complete exemption. I had decided that my life's work was to be in teaching, and I didn't see why this should be changed by the country having gone to war. I couldn't be persuaded that I should give up my life's work to take up arms. This was why, when the time came, I asked for complete exemption. I hadn't become a Quaker, but I knew that the Quakers believed in 'that of God in all men'. I accepted this, and felt that on no account would it be right for me to kill another human being. So it was a religious and ethical stand that I was prepared to make.

As I started my studies I had no idea when I should be called to register. Eventually I was informed that I should register. I then had to work out the sort of statement that I would present to the tribunal. After registering as a CO, again the waiting began. This was one of the most difficult aspects of what I was doing, that I never knew what was going to happen when. Then I was summoned to appear before the Leeds tribunal. Now a friend in Sheffield had asked me if I would like him to write a letter on my behalf. I said, 'No thank you, I want to state my own case.' But when I appeared at the tribunal, it wasn't long before I was being asked questions I didn't quite understand, about a letter the chairman had received. I thought perhaps my friend had written after all, but the chairman was talking about a letter that had been sent by Sheffield Young Friends. The letter asked that he should treat COs with sympathy and understanding and whether this was the sort of treatment I was getting. I had to tell him that I knew little about the letter, that it certainly wasn't written on my behalf, and the Young Friends hadn't known when I was to appear. The upshot was, I was accused of lying. I was told that here was an example of a man who said, 'I will not serve', and I was struck off the register. I was then liable to be called up.

I knew the next step would be imprisonment, but I had no idea when. I then received a call to go for a medical exam. I informed the Ministry of Labour why I was not prepared to be examined. I received repeated requests to turn up for the medical, but I continued with my studies. Then at the end of the Easter term Sheffield was raided, and quite serious damage was done close to where I was living. Most of the students went off home, but I stayed on, as a friend had offered me accommodation. A school was used to take in those who had been bombed out, and I assisted with feeding and looking after people in the shelters when the air-raid sirens went.

There was only one other CO at the university as far as I was aware, a very good friend of mine who later went to prison. Some of the other students knew of my beliefs, but I didn't experience a lot of hostility from them. Some of them grew a little cool towards me, but there was never any real nastiness. I wasn't a member of the university branch of the Peace Pledge Union, but there was some resistance I remember to them holding meetings on university premises; they weren't allowed to hold them there.

The warden of the hall of residence came to me and said that he assumed that it would mean imprisonment if I persisted in this course, and did I really think this was the right thing to be doing? He could understand that I wouldn't want to take up arms, but couldn't I do hospital work, or non-combatant work, even with the Army? I said, 'No, I'm sorry but I can't, I don't want to be involved in any way with the military forces.' So he said, 'But have you realized this action is probably going to rebound on the university? That if you appear before the magistrate and are sentenced to imprisonment, then the reputation of the university is at stake?' And I said, 'Well, that hasn't occurred to me, but if what you are suggesting is that I should resign, I'm quite happy to consider that.' He'd already been in touch with my parents, and I was a bit annoyed about this. Fortunately they knew quite well what I was up to, and they supported what I was doing, and why; later my mother became a Friend.

Anyway, he said he thought I ought to have a talk with the Vice-Chancellor. By this time I had decided that if this seemed the best thing, I would resign from the university. I talked to the Vice-Chancellor, who concluded by saying, 'Well, I don't think the university's reputation would be at stake. Anyone reading in the local paper that you had been sent to prison would simply say, "Well, there's bound to be one young fool in the university." I don't think you need to resign. If you really want to, all right, but don't think we are saying you should.' So I said, 'All right, I won't.' And I didn't.

My summons came towards the end of the spring session in 1941. I had to appear in court. It was a very short hearing. I admitted I didn't want to register, and so I was sentenced to twenty-eight days' imprisonment or a £5 fine, which I was given a certain period in which to pay. I didn't pay it. Then one day I had a visitor. He had come from the police station. He said,

'Where's the money?' I said, 'I'm not going to pay it.' So he said, 'You better come along with me.' Just like that. So I said, 'Can I have my lunch?' And he said, 'No, there'll be lunch provided down there for you.' So I said, 'Can I let somebody know what's happening, and lock up my things in my study?' 'Yes, okay,' he said, 'but be as quick as you can.' I did this, and then we walked to the police station. He chatted with me and was quite friendly, but he couldn't understand 'you blokes who do these things. Who tells you what to do?' I explained that we made up our own minds.

I was carried off to Strangeways Prison in Manchester. I had known long in advance what I would be in for, but I hadn't known what the conditions would be like. There were no other COs there, I was just with ordinary prisoners. Eventually I was placed in a wing where those in the cells were all young folk on remand; I was the only real prisoner. At first I worked in the mailbag shop, and then it was decided that I should become the landing cleaner. This involved wiping the stone slabs all round the wing of the prison on the third floor, dusting and cleaning, and so on. It was a futile sort of business. I also accompanied the prison officer on his round when he took the meals to the cells. He wasn't a bad sort of chap, because sometimes a remand prisoner had left, and the cell was empty, and he hadn't been informed, so there was an extra meal, and he would say, 'In you go, and take this as well.' I was very grateful for this, because I was always hungry.

The weather was cold, the cells were cold, and silence was the rule. Even on recreation we were not allowed to talk. We went round and round the courtyard in threes, with an officer standing on a pedestal. If we approached the three in front of us too closely, he would stop us and hold us back until they had gone on further. There was no talking in the workshop, and of course as a landing cleaner I was entirely on my own. We were locked up at about four o'clock, and remained on our own in the cell until six o'clock in the morning, when we slopped out, and then went back and cleaned our cell, and breakfast was brought to us.

The most disturbing time there was when Manchester was raided. The air-raid sirens went at night, so we were locked in, and all the lights turned off. I could hear the prison officer going round from cell to cell, looking through the spy-hole to make sure we were all there. Then there was absolute silence until the all-clear went. They had gone to their shelter, and we were all left in our cells, entirely on our own, wondering what would happen next. We could hear the planes come over and the bombs fall, and this happened five nights running, although while I was there the prison was not damaged.

When I came out I decided not to return to university for my final year. After one spell in prison, I knew that before long I would be getting a call-up notice, so I didn't want to be just training for something, I wanted to be doing something. I felt that I ought to be doing something that was useful, and so I got a job on the land, though not for very long. I then became a Quaker, and had a short time at Spiceland Training Centre, which was a Quaker centre set up to train conscientious objectors who were to be involved in Quaker relief work. I then got into hospital work at a TB sanatorium in Gloucestershire.

Here I found there were those who were prepared to exploit COs. I'd gone because they were short of staff, I assumed because of the call-up. But in the main it was because of the general treatment of staff. The lowest grades were badly paid and expected to work all hours. Both men and women were objecting to this, and going off to war work where conditions were better. When I made some criticisms to the superintendent, he said, 'I had the feeling that COs were in the market to be bought and sold, to be used as we felt inclined to use them, and I see no reason why they shouldn't be treated in this way.' I decided I would look for a more deserving employer.

I eventually went to a Roman Catholic-run institution for incurable ex-servicemen in Ealing in west London, where there were already two or three COs. Here there was a much better spirit, although there was some opposition to COs on the part of patients, ex-Army men who didn't much like having to be looked after by 'conchies', as they called us. But as time went on we overcame this feeling. I think the service we gave was so good that they began to be more appreciative – they benefited from what we did for them, and this overruled personal feelings they had about 'conchies'.

It was while working there that I appeared before an appeal tribunal, which gave me conditional exemption if I did medical work with the forces. I decided I couldn't accept this condition, which meant that I would be again receiving requests to attend for medicals, to appear before a court, and face imprisonment. Each of the tribunal members asked me one question only, then talked quietly among themselves, and pronounced judgement. This time I was sentenced to twelve months' imprisonment, which was normal for a second offence. As a result I was sent to Wandsworth Prison.

My experience there was really quite unpleasant. I was in a cell on the ground floor, which was very dark; it looked out on to a high wall. Not only that, there was a hanging due to take place, and indeed it did take place while I was there. Although there was little opportunity to talk to the other prisoners, I sensed the feeling they had about the hanging, there was an atmosphere about the place. But I was only there for a short time. I was transferred to Wormwood Scrubs, which was a first offenders' prison – it had been agreed that COs, however many times they went to prison, should always be considered as first offenders.

Wormwood Scrubs was very different from Wandsworth. There were lots and lots of COs, and talking was allowed in the workshop. The officers in charge were more understanding, and there was a good deal more freedom of movement; on exercise you could chat with other prisoners. I remember there were a number of Jehovah's Witnesses there, and a couple of them used to make a practice of getting on each side of a CO and trying to convert him to their way of thinking.

But after only a few weeks there I was asked to appear before an appeal tribunal. I think it was known that I had been doing hospital work. Anyway, they offered me a conditional exemption if I would do hospital or social relief work. I was already doing hospital work voluntarily, and had every intention of returning to it once I was released. So I saw no reason why I couldn't accept this condition. It really didn't make any difference to me, except it meant I was released after nine weeks rather than twelve months.

As a CO I didn't come up against a tremendous lot of antagonism. I knew that York City Corporation sacked their employees who were COs, and there were other local authorities that took exception to them. But I personally didn't come up against opposition of that kind, and in prison I got the same treatment as any other prisoner. In general I didn't mix with other COs to any great extent. I found that life for me was difficult enough as it was just to carry on from day to day, without going out of my way to inform other people that I was a CO. If anyone asked me why I wasn't in the Army, I would tell them, but certainly it wasn't in my mind to convert others to my way of thinking.

When it came to my prison sentence, I really did wonder whether I should go ahead with it. All the time I was thinking hard, trying to analyse the reasons for the stand I was making, questioning whether this was the right thing to do. But I've never regretted the steps I took.

I had gone to prison quite prepared for whatever that meant, and so I never felt bitter about it. I'd brought it upon myself, so no one was to blame. I can only say I'm thankful for the experience. I probably had to think rather more deeply whether what I had thought to be my life's work, teaching, really was the right thing for me, and whether there was anything more important at that particular time, and in those circumstances. I also had to think more deeply about the significance of life at that age than I would normally have had to do. I'm quite certain that I couldn't really have taken any other course.

Letter from 21-year-old Alex Bryan to his parents from Wormwood Scrubs

8 May 1942

Dear Mother and Dad,
As I write this, I wonder if I am mistaken in the value I put on life. It is strange that I should be so and yet many things have come home to me during the past week as never before – truths that have not been encouraging – and I have tried to discover whether my reasons for regarding human life as the most precious thing on earth are really logical. Unfortunately, I see no clear way out of my perplexity at the moment. . . . It is difficult to write interestingly or even to say much about myself. Each day is the same to me, and as I was yesterday, so I am today, and so I shall be tomorrow. Under normal circumstances – last week was an exception for me because of my anxiety about you during the bombing – my mood remains fairly constant. It is one of resignation to things as I find them. In my cell I lose myself in my library books or in the Shakespeare I have; in the workshop my work, my own thoughts and the things taking place about me occupy my attention fairly fully, and generally speaking not unpleasantly. I refrain from dwelling on certain subjects as much as I can, for the simple reason that they tend to make me feel discontented. Many a time I have looked back on the past year and many things have I learnt from the contemplation of it – things I had tended to skip over hastily or ignore altogether. The recognition of them will be an asset to me in the future. And so the days go by – not wasted, though not utilized to the full and perhaps not even as fully as they might be. Living in here where things go on the same from day to day tends to give one the impression that all is well with the world. Here it is the simplest thing possible to take no thought for the morrow. . . . With much love to you all and many thanks for all you have done since my departure from Ealing.

Alex

Community Spirit

We were in a mess, so people put aside a lot of their personal greeds and differences to fight the common enemy.

DONCASTER MAN

I didn't attract as much hostility as some of my civil servant women colleagues. Because of their habit of wearing corduroy slacks, some of them were referred to in the village as VABs – Velveteen-Arsed Bastards.

LONDON WOMAN

My mother never got on with her neighbours. But the day war broke out, I remember her passing a cucumber over the fence, and then we went round to have tea with them. I thought, 'If this is war, it can't be that bad.'

KENT GIRL

We went into a shop with our ration books, and the lady said, 'Oh, you come from London, we haven't got any rations for you London folks.' My mother was incensed.

LONDON GIRL

The black market was widely indulged in. Certain people did it systematically, and made a fortune out of it. But most ordinary people participated marginally.

LEICESTERSHIRE MAN

The nights in the shelter brought a comradeship I have never experienced since. I don't think anyone who didn't live then can know the spirit that prevailed.

HULL GIRL

We had three or four refugees. One boy who made friends with them had his arm twisted, because they were Jewish. I remember someone at school dinner saying to him in a condemning way, 'You Jew'. There was no opposition from anyone to this remark.

KENT BOY

The war, it is often claimed, produced an intense camaraderie between people that has never been emulated in peacetime. Just as the railings surrounding many parks and squares were taken down for salvage, so social barriers were also removed as the nation united in a common cause. The British, so the argument runs, threw off their traditional reserve, their class antagonisms, their selfishness. Instead they were to be found talking to total strangers, helping and sharing with their neighbours, invariably putting their country's needs before their own.

There is no doubt at all that such behaviour was a marked feature of the war period. But this new-found community spirit certainly didn't infect all of the people all of the time. It varied in nature and scale, for instance, in city and village. Nor did it seem to be more than a temporary infection in most cases, brought on by necessity. There was inevitably a much greater mixing of the classes. But social divisions certainly didn't disappear as a result.

It was of course most dramatically visible during the Blitz periods. Throughout the months of air raids on the major cities, ordinary men and women performed countless small acts of quiet heroism and individual selflessness. People provided shelter for those made homeless by the bombs; they helped the Civil Defence services to deal with casualties; they shared their rations of food and clothing with their destitute neighbours; they helped to run a wide range of voluntary services or street activities designed to give practical help and support on the Home Front. At such a time, when survival was the preoccupation of everyone, material values held considerably less sway than normal, and kindness and cooperation became commonplace.

At other times, however, and especially during the middle and later years of the war, there was a different story to be told. Though there was, for example, widespread acceptance of the equity of the rationing system, almost all sections of society seem at some time to have illegally obtained scarce goods on the black market. On a small scale this was generally accepted, and the authorities mostly turned a blind eye to what was going on. But there were also spectacular examples of organized racketeering, of the wholesale disappearance of ration books, and of profiteering in scarce goods, with unscrupulous individuals cornering the market and forcing people to pay extortionate prices.

Money remained a divisive element in many areas of life. Until public protests forced the government to legislate, the wealthier classes were able to eat in lavish style at the more expensive hotels and restaurants, at a time when the bombs were falling, and the ordinary householder was hard pressed to maintain even a basic diet. Those with substantial incomes also found it easier to get round the food and clothing ration system or – in the case of the relatively small number who owned a car – to get petrol under the counter. The middle and upper classes were also more mobile in another sense. Some 2 million of them made their own evacuation arrangements, many leaving the country altogether, sometimes for the duration. Their departure left many decent-sized houses in town and country unoccupied, with gardens that could have been turned over to cultivation left unused. This caused great resentment among the less-well-off, particularly when they themselves were having to accept evacuees in their own, much smaller homes. Meanwhile, the government evacuation scheme also prompted some unfortunate reactions. People of all classes suddenly found a new use for their spare room, or a distant relative that needed housing. In this manner many successfully kept the billeting officer at bay.

Nor was all harmony and cooperation on the industrial front. Though special wartime legislation effected something of a truce between unions and management, there were still plenty of examples of disputes, restrictive practices, poor management, malpractice and profiteering. The battle for equal pay was fought, and in the main lost, with considerable bitterness on both sides. There were many strikes, mostly in the essential industries such as coal-mining, engineering, road transport and the docks, and on the whole about pay. Even within such bodies as the Civil Defence force there was sometimes conflict between different categories of workers, the bad feeling between the regulars and the volunteers in the Auxiliary Fire Service being a particular example.

Britain of course played host to many foreigners during the war years, notably troops from America and other countries, members of governments-in-exile such as the Free French, Jewish refugees from Austria and Germany, and, later, Italian and German prisoners of war. While many of these were given a warm and friendly welcome, and settled easily among the local people, others received a more mixed reception, especially in places where outsiders were a rarity. Some of the American soldiers were famously resented, for their comparative wealth, their sharp uniform and their sexual conquests of many British women. In the latter case, the resentment was often both understandable and justified. The reaction to some Jewish refugees was a different matter. Anti-Semitism, though often suppressed, remained a feature of British society at all levels, from the government downwards. There were both advantages and disadvantages in being an island race.

The Doctor's Wife

We greatly resented the grand evacuees, who came and took very expensive houses and brought a lot of servants with them. They were always saying to us, 'Of course, you don't know there's a war on.'

Joyce Dennys

In the country we were very much despised, you know, because we weren't having bombs dropped on us every night. We had a few, and that was quite enough. I was stuck down in a little place in Devon, Budleigh Salterton. We were all engaged in war things, and some of them really were funny. And so one day I sat down and wrote an article about our doings, and drew three pictures, and sent it up to the *Sketch*. I hadn't done any writing before really, though I had done quite a lot of illustrations in books. The *Sketch* always used to have drawings, and I'd done some for the editor Bruce Ingram before I sent him the pieces. Anyway, he wrote back and said, 'Do another.' So I did another, and then he wrote and said, 'Do another.' So I did another. Then he said, 'Go on, you can do six.' So I did six, and ended up doing them for four years.

They were done in the form of letters addressed to someone who had gone into the Army, and I called them 'Please Forward'. At the beginning of the war you had to send your letters to some extraordinary place in England, and mark them Please Forward. Later it was changed, and you could use the actual address. That was where I got the title from. It fell rather flat when people stopped using the phrase, but by then it was too late to change the title.

I wrote them for fun, but also because I felt sorry for the local people being told they weren't really in the war. So I used to stick up for them. I could point out that food was rationed in the same way, and that the bombs also dropped, and that there were air-raid warnings nearly every night – we used to hear the planes going over to Plymouth.

At first they were published every week. Every Monday I used to say, 'What shall I write about?' My husband used to call it Black Monday. But I found that if I sat with a bit of foolscap in front of me, something would come suddenly. It was quite up to me what I wrote: nobody ever suggested a topic and no one ever turned one down. I was never late with the piece. Usually I would post it, and it would get there all right; the post worked perfectly smoothly throughout the war, which was remarkable when you consider the chaos there was. But if it was a bit tight, or I'd missed the post, we had a train in those days that went right through to Waterloo, and I'd run up to the station early on Friday morning with my copy and shove it on the train, and they would meet it the other end.

I don't think the local people were very interested, it was more people outside the town. The *Sketch* and the *Tatler* were the two society papers, the grand weddings and that sort of thing were put in there. I don't think the *Sketch* was read very much in Budleigh Salterton: it was quite expensive, and people weren't very rich, they were rather poor. But people from outside used to write; all the ladies liked to think they were Lady B, and sometimes they signed their letters Lady B. She was a character I was very fond of. She had had a Grand Past, you know, in embassies and things, and now she lived in a very small cottage in the country. She was very, very kind and broad-minded, and people used to tell her their troubles. She was always stopping people quarrelling and taking the broad view of things.

I had letters about the pieces from soldiers from all over the world, who used to say that it reminded them of their own small towns in England. When I eventually gave up doing them, I had several letters of regretfulness from soldiers. But I never had anyone objecting to them: I was very careful not to tread on people's toes.

My husband Tom was the only doctor in the town. One doctor went to bed for two years, one died, and one went away, so he was all alone, having to look after 7,000 people's health. It was obviously important that he should be kept well, so my job was to look after him. People used to say,

'What do *you* do?', they wouldn't believe it was war work at all. But I hated being a doctor's wife. You got talked about, you were rather a public figure, and I wasn't a very sociable person. I didn't play bridge, I was more interested in the arts than anything else. I think they thought I was a very bad doctor's wife, in fact I'm damn sure they did.

I had to try and protect Tom from people who really didn't need him. In fact he got jolly ill, and they had to send him away for a bit to recover. You see, he sometimes had to get up in the middle of the night to be with the Home Guard, as he was also their doctor, and this was really too hard. He belonged very unwillingly, he said his job was to be a doctor, and not to play at soldiers – although he was quite a good soldier, he'd fought with the Australians at Gallipoli and got the DSO. The Home Guard was very active. There was a tremendously big camp of marines quite near, and the Home Guard would have field days with them, and they all caught colds. The boots they had were terrible. My husband had rather delicate feet, and he used to get the most terrible blisters when he put them on. I always remember one procession – they were always having processions in Budleigh Salterton. It began with the Brownies and then the Girl Guides, and then the Boy Scouts, and then the WVS and then the Red Cross, and finally the Home Guard, and there, right at the end, limping and out of step, came my husband. After that he refused to walk in any procession. He used to drive very grandly along in his car, the only one who wasn't walking, with a stretcher on the top to show who he was. It made him very angry, and he didn't see why he should walk.

Tom said the Home Guard was supposed to delay the Germans for ten minutes, while the marines came down to the front from their camp up on the common. But of course they would have all been slaughtered. People were expecting the Germans to arrive on the beach, and they put rows and rows of barbed wire all along the front – as if that would stop them! Once my little dog got into the middle of the barbed wire. It was a terrible scene. I went in after it and got stuck on the wire. It was altogether a very shaming affair.

The women were awfully keen to do war work. People who really weren't fit and couldn't give up the time, they all joined things. There was a sewing bee, they used to make nightshirts and bandages, and they all got themselves up in white nursing caps and aprons and white overalls. There was a great deal of activity. There was a Women's Voluntary Service, the WVS, who had a rather nice uniform, which was supposed to be designed by one of the top dressmakers. They looked quite nice in it. Then there was the Red Cross, and nearly all the old men were air-raid wardens, if they were well enough to stand up. We used to get up pantomimes and things, you know, all to get money for the poorer folk. People were very good, and we always had very full houses. I think we thought we were running the war.

Of course we got an awful lot of evacuees, the place was absolutely full of them, there wasn't a bed to be had. People had evacuee children dumped on them, and very difficult they were, some of them. They were away from their parents, and they were very naughty, they thought they could do just what they liked. Of course, it was always difficult feeding them, because they were hungry, and ate a great deal, and the rations weren't very grand. There was a billeting officer who went round to people's houses and said, 'How many bedrooms have you got?' and they would just be thrust on people, whether they liked it or not. The officer had a horrible job, because everybody hated him, and was very horrid to him. But he used to try and get the big boys into a place where there would be a man to look after them, and the old ladies to get somebody easier – a little girl, perhaps. People used to be very angry though, especially the old, rather ill ones. Some of them really weren't fit, and Tom used to have to sign things to show this. Some of them could only just keep going themselves.

Tom and I had exemption, because they said he was there to look after sick people. We lived in a fairly big house, but I got so conscience-stricken that we finally had a family stay with us, a father and mother and two little boys from London, who we rather liked, we got on rather well with them. I remember one of the evacuee women was heard to say, 'I 'ates the 'orrid 'ush.' They couldn't bear the quiet, which terrified them at night, except when we had air-raid warnings, when it wasn't quiet at all. These were very frequent. I remember I was a fire-watcher, and we had a big flat roof, and I used to get out of our bedroom and just stand there with a tin hat on. I didn't do anything, I never had to do anything, but I always went there. Down below the air-raid warden, who was a friend, used to shout up and say, 'Is Old Faithful there?'

The people who chose to come to Budleigh Salterton took expensive houses and stayed in the hotels. They considered themselves very superior to the local people. We had a hall, and the local builder flung it open for people to send their armchairs and tables and things safely out of London. Then it had a direct hit, and the locals were very amused. That was terribly funny. We also had soldiers billeted on us, and we used to give parties for them. They were always a great failure, but we used to try. I don't think they wanted to be entertained. I'm afraid we hadn't got enough pretty girls, they were all away in the WRENs and things.

We greatly resented the grand evacuees, in fact we resented *all* the evacuees, because they did really upset us rather badly, and the grand ones, who took expensive houses and brought a lot of servants, we resented them very much, because they were always saying, 'Of course, *you* don't know there's a war on.' Actually I'm not sure if they did have servants, but they gave you the impression of having them; they were always very smart.

I think the war changed people's attitude to women working. When the war came our daughter had just left school, and we said, 'Now you'll have to do some war work, what do you want to do?' And to our astonishment she said, 'I'd like to learn nursing.' Her father was delighted, and so was I really. In fact she ought to have trained as a doctor, but it never entered our heads then that she might do that. It was only after the war, when she had done so well as a nurse, that we thought that. There were *some* women doctors, but they were rather rare.

I think the social barriers came down a certain amount, but they're much stronger down in the west, you know, much. The place is about twenty years behind the rest of England. It's a very conservative part of the world, very, and they've been like that for goodness knows how many hundreds of years. But during the war that was forgotten, more or less.

Minutes of a Birmingham street fire-watching committee, February 1941

Minutes of meeting called by Mr Hubbard and held at Mr Hubbard's, No. 5 Dalston Road. Present: Hubbard, Jenks, Lewis, Hancox, Mole, Wells, Roberts, Lockwood, Bartham.

After considerable discussion, and after various arrangements that might be adopted had been discussed, it was proposed and carried that 2 volunteers should be on duty each night to share a duty period of 8 hours – from 10 p.m. to 6 a.m., the duty period to be split into two periods of 4 hours for each volunteer. When doing his 4 hours' duty the watcher must remain fully dressed, so that if sirens go and danger threatens it will be possible to warn his co-watcher without delay. . . . and if necessary at the watcher's discretion to call up neighbours in the road. The man finishing his duty at 2 a.m. must make contact with his next on duty at 2 a.m. in order to ensure continuity for watching from 2 a.m. to 6 a.m. Mr Hubbard offered to canvass all householders with a view to getting more volunteers, so that 7 nights a week could be covered.

It was decided that Mr Bartham should be excluded from an immediate rota because of his 2 full nights' duty at his works, and also that special arrangement of duties would have to be made for Mr Lewis and Mr Hancox and possibly for others who are also on duty at their places of work. Mr Lewis and Mr Mole offered to do duties on Sat. March 1st – a rota to cover at least 4 nights to be drawn up.

The Mill Girl

Everybody knew everybody else, and everybody helped one another if you had any trouble. The war didn't make people more friendly here, because we had it already.

Nellie Town

I was a weaver in Lancashire during the war, a cotton weaver. It was dirty, mill life. All this fluff from the cotton, you see. It got into your hair and all around you.

One Monday morning I went to the mill and they'd been whitewashing the roof, which they did in summertime. And all the dirt from the top was on the warp and the bit you were weaving. This was 1941 in Todmorden, and my husband had been in the war a couple of years then. So I came home and I said to my father, 'I'm fed up with all the dirt there.' And he said, 'Well, they're setting women on at James Henry Sutcliffe' – which was a furniture shop – 'and the ladies are working on de Havilland Moth aircraft.' These were trainer craft, and they came back pretty badly messed up, you see. They were eight-wheelers, tremendous things, and they used to come with these wings of good Irish linen, beautiful stuff. There were bags, and you'd to pull them on these wings, they were terribly tight, and blanket stitch them on, all across one end. They went then to the men that had been polishers before the war, and they were on dope – they call it dope, it was highly inflammable stuff, and they spread it with this stuff, and the planes went out as new, you see.

With my father working there I had a good chance of being taken on, so I gave my notice in down here, which they accepted, because if your husband was in the war you could do most things. During this time cotton came into its own, and I'd lost about one pound a week from going from the mill to the aircraft, but that didn't matter, because it was the first time I'd had money in my hand. We'd always had piece-work, but there, if you sat down all day you still got your money at the weekend, and it was lovely.

There came a time a bit later when cotton was wanted more than ever before, and they came to this place, James Henry's, and all those in cotton had to go back. Well, me and another young woman said, 'We're not going back at any price.' So we fought it, although we didn't do much, it was the boss that fought for us. So we kept there till 1944. Now by this time all these boys had learnt to fly properly. They were no longer crashing the de Havilland Moths, they were on the big stuff. And so that finished. I remember round about D-Day when I was still there I went back to my mother and father – I was staying with them while my husband was away – and I said, 'This is terrible, it's going to happen all over again.' And my father said, 'Oh no, we'll finish him this time,' which I didn't believe. On top of that these planes were finishing, so where did I go from here? I thought, I don't want to go back in the mill again, I've seen the nicer side of life.

Anyway, the boss came to us one day, and he said, 'If you can do aeroplanes and precision work like that, you can make furniture.' Eee, well, nobody had ever made any furniture. 'Oh,' he said, 'you'll be all right.' So on one side of the main road here we were on planes, and on the other side we came on to furniture. All the pieces of furniture were made up, and all you had to do was put things together: we made dressing tables, sideboards, wardrobes, tables, the lot. It was all utility furniture. The only thing we didn't make were chairs, but I must have pressed thousands of bases of utility wardrobes, day in and day out. But you could sing all day long, you could talk all day long, it were quiet. All sorts of funny things could happen there that couldn't happen in a weaving shed, because there you can't hear.

Before the war a lot of women worked at the mill, 'cos your wages didn't keep you at home. Nearly always your child was looked after by grandparents or something like that. All the friends I knew, their mothers worked. Mine didn't, mine used to make stockings on a stocking machine at home, but mostly they went out to work. My father, he was against the war, though not in a nasty way, but in a thoughtful way. He had been in the First World War, and he thought they were absolutely mad to go to war again. Absolutely mad. He never got over the First War. He wasn't military at all, he felt there shouldn't be wars. He had two friends that would go down to the Cenotaph between the wars, every year. My father wouldn't have gone to the street end. Not that he wouldn't do for his country, he just thought they were crazy to even *think* about military things again. He said, 'Yes, remember, certainly, but not all this visiting' – he wouldn't go to the Todmorden memorial, never mind London. In the First World War he'd been left out in no-man's land for twenty-four hours, and he was never the same again. He was always bitter, and he hated Froggies – he said he'd rather have a German, you knew what they were thinking.

The only time you knew there was a war on was when you got to big places, like Bradford or Manchester, for instance – but not Burnley or Rochdale or Halifax, it had to be where a lot of Army people were. We didn't see much at all. Aeroplanes were a very unusual sight – you went out to look at them, because you so seldom heard a plane. We didn't get any bombs. We once had a doodlebug over, and we once were bombed top end of Burnley. And in the beginning in 1940 we could hear it when the Blitz was on Manchester. Apart from that, you didn't know there was a war on really, apart from the fact that everybody had somebody away, that sort of thing.

It was much drabber being at home than in the forces, you were living the same life as before, doing the same thing that you'd done for years, but without your husband. So you thought more about the war, it was more of a terrible affair than it was to them. It took you a long time to adapt to going about with others, it was an awful thing really. We used to do a lot of hiking, because there were no buses. Sometimes buses came, sometimes they didn't. There were six of us and we went all over, walking. Your life was different altogether.

We were pretty well off for entertainment, we were. We had two picture houses then in Todmorden, the Olympia and the Hippodrome. Entertainment at the Hippodrome was a lot of variety shows for various funds for each of the forces. We had some jolly good shows here. We had all the big names that were round about, a lot of them had been evacuated from London. At Burnley we had the Old Vic and Sadler's Wells, they were stationed there. So we used to go there: we saw all the operas, the ballet, the big plays. I remember we took father to *Macbeth*, he thought it were awful. They kept coming on with this bit of scenery and putting it down. You know, it was done like it would be in Shakespeare's day, but he said, 'I reckon nowt to this.'

I can't ever remember being short of food, but we'd only one egg a week, and a right tiny bit of butter and lard, and you'd go down to the shop and there'd be a jelly or funny things like starch – you had funny things like that, they didn't go together at all. The butcher at the bottom used to find us all sorts of extra meat for our son, and up to quite recently he used to say, 'Well, he grew up to be a big lad' – because he'd always find him a bit more of this and that.

There was a funny incident once about the black market. When my husband came home on leave, we used to go to Morecambe. He'd get out of his uniform and into his civvies and off we'd go. And we'd take a bit of this and that with us, a bit of sugar and a bit of lard. When we got there, I remember this lady said, 'Ah well, I'll find your ration' – because we had ration books, you see. 'And I'll use them some time else, but thank you very much.' While we were staying there we met a couple who lived in Leeds. Now the woman's father had a big grocery shop. So one day we arrived down at Leeds and when we got into Leeds there was a strike on, with the trams. And we were going to a place called Meanwood, which is on the outskirts of Leeds, and there were two RAF men and my husband. My husband used to drive a tram, so he asked them, 'Have you ever driven a tram?' 'No, don't drive a car, never mind a tram.' 'Well, we're going to drive this thing whatever happens.' So we were in the centre of Leeds and we got on this tram and a lot more people got on, and we got to a place called Cardigan Square. 'Which way are you going?' 'We're going to Meanwood.' 'Oh, we're going to Roundhay and places like that.' Well, Meanwood won. So they got out and changed the tram wires, and off we set to Meanwood. We picked people up and we dropped them – I don't think we collected any fares. And when we arrived at Meanwood we left this tram, and off we went.

When we got there the woman who we came to see, Kathleen, her father was a butcher, and he said, 'I've had a right rotten experience this week, I shall never give anybody any extra rations again, because they've split on me, and it's all but done me for my business.' He'd found them bacon and ham and butter and margarine and all the things that were rationed. And someone must have been jealous of Mrs So-and-so having this and her not. Anyway, he said to us, 'Whatever you want, you can take.' So we filled this attaché case that we had brought with us, and it was full with butter and margarine, with lovely strawberry jam that we hadn't seen for years, and bacon – you mention it, we had it.

There were no trams back, and there were no buses running, so we bundled into a contractor's wagon – I was four months pregnant at the time. We got landed down at Leeds station. There were thousands of these redcaps going up and down, and us with this little attaché case. My husband said, 'What if we get stopped, what if they look in this case?' Anyway, we arrived in Todmorden safe and sound. When my father saw what we had in this case he nearly had a fit. He said, 'You came through Leeds like this?' 'Don't mention it,' I said, 'we've driven a tram, we've been in a contractor's lorry, but we've arrived home safe and sound.'

But the blackout was the worst thing, definitely. If you had any meetings, you went when the moon shone. There were no drawn curtains, every window was black. And when you got up in the morning it were all pitch black, like being in a coal-mine. Ooh it was horrible, it was no joke. There were no lights anywhere, and even in the buses and the trains there were just these right little blue things. I remember on VE Day all the blackout curtains came off; I remember this blaze of light.

You used to listen to the radio a lot, that was all right. You had some good music on, especially on the Light Programme. It was light music, none of this pop. They were right good tunes that are going yet. But listening to Churchill's speeches, I used to think, he's a good man, but he used to get me down sometimes. It was all blood, sweat and tears, and you've had enough after six years, you're getting a bit fed up. When I look back, I don't know how we survived. You see, it was your young days that were going, you were wasting your time. There was nothing new, no new designs in furniture, nothing. Your clothes were utility, it was all utility. It was a waste, actually. We'd only been married just over twelve months when the war began, and I always feel that those six years were just wasted. It's a lot out of your life, really.

The war didn't make people more friendly here in Todmorden, because we had it already. I mean, we knew everybody on this street – now I mean everybody, on all three blocks – that's six sides. My husband had an aunt who lived in Maidstone, and they had a big air-raid shelter, and they didn't know their next-door neighbours till the war started, and they joined this shelter. There was nothing like that round here, everybody knew everybody else, and everybody helped one another if you had any trouble. Like a mining community used to be, this was then.

Letter to a friend from a major in the War Office

1 May 1942

Dear David,

I received your letter of 19th February yesterday, and I was very glad to get it too. You describe perfectly the feeling I have had for so long now that it is becoming almost intolerable. It is the haunting loneliness which comes from living alone as a member of the Army among the civilian population. I was certainly not born to be a soldier, but still less to be a civilian. As you say, the comradeship that comes with a shared mode of existence, however uncomfortable or unwanted, is a compensation which makes up for a great deal and makes such a life not only possible but at times enjoyable.

As a civilian in uniform, though, I am neither in the Army properly, because I live in digs and go to work like an ordinary civilian, nor am I really a civilian, since I wear all the time the clothes and badges of an Army officer. I am accepted neither in one society nor the other, and am therefore uncomfortable in both. How much longer I can stand it remains to be seen. What I want to do, as you know, is to get into a combatant arm of the service, or preferably to transfer to the RAF. But at the present time I am not allowed to do that, so I try to lose myself in my work, which is of such a volume that I am usually able to do so.

As you rightly say, this appalling loneliness has the effect of decreasing vitality. I have never in all my life suffered from such acute and overwhelming fits of deep depression as during this last winter. I have, therefore, I am afraid, very little to offer you in this letter except sympathy for the similar state in which you apparently find yourself now.

You can perhaps understand how it was that I said I could never hope to live up to the example Spencer has set us all and be worthy of having had his friendship. There is scarcely a spark of vitality or enthusiasm left in me and I feel a helpless traitor to his cause.

I agree with you about the sacredness of human life and perhaps my letter about Dennis sounded callous. If I had not shared your convictions about life I should not have come through this winter. It is after all our only real heritage, and of all the sacrifices one can make, the sacrifice of one's life for others is surely the noblest. It is no less true now than it always has been. Conversely, the basest act a man can stoop to is to take his own life in his own interest. That is why one has no sympathy with the criminal who shoots himself when he knows he is certain to be caught and hanged.

The more I observe the more I am convinced that everyone is naturally grossly selfish; and that normal life in peacetime gives material advantages to those who put their selfish aspirations first. The greatness of war is the greatness of death and danger; it presents overriding circumstances which remove altogether for the time being the motives of selfish people – the immediate prospect of advantage over others. These people realize at once that in the face of death we are all equal, and only then do they let the false pretences drop and become real, ideal human beings. What a pity it lasts for so short a time – not war, but the change of heart that it brings. By war I mean danger, death and destruction, not a game of chess in which most of the time is spent in waiting for the other man to move.

The Small-town Boy

When the invasion scare happened, I can remember my aunt having some ladies to tea. They were playing cards, and one said, 'I hear he may come any time', and the other said, 'So I've heard.' They didn't realize what the invasion would mean.

John Dossett-Davies

I was an only child, and I was a bit below par when war broke out, my parents' divorce had had an effect on me. When their marriage broke up my mother and I went to live in Witney with my grandfather and her unmarried sister. We stayed there throughout the war.

I went to the local mixed grammar school, though I hadn't won a scholarship, I was one of the ones that was paid for. The impact of the war on my education was considerable. Of course the better teachers tended to get called up into the forces, leaving just the older ones, and then they imported people who I suspect were not real teachers. For example, we had a Latin master who was the vicar of one of the villages near by. He was quite unable to keep control of the children, so there was a great deal of rumpus in his classes. There was another woman who was obviously a refugee from Austria. She was supposed to teach us French, but she couldn't really speak English.

There was a shortage of paper, I remember that, and we had these wartime pencils which were just plain cedar, they were not red or green but

just the colour of the wood, and they were very thin and they kept
breaking. We also at the start only went to school in the mornings, because
Ashford Grammar School in Kent was evacuated to Witney, and they had
the buildings in the afternoons. There was a lot of rivalry between the two
schools, a lot of fighting between the boys. I remember they wore a much
smarter uniform than we did, so there was that.

We had two invasions of children. I remember the massive evacuation
from London just as war began, and a huge crocodile coming down from
the station and winding across the park near where we lived and into the
school. They were predominantly from the East End of London, from
Silvertown, East Ham and around there. When the Ashford boys came
later, it was a rather more middle-class group of children. Two of the boys
lived with us as evacuees. They were slightly older than I was, but I quite
welcomed them, being an only child. But there was quite a general feeling
of rivalry.

I remember as the Germans broke through in 1940, first Belgium and
then Holland and so on, at assembly we had these dramatic meetings with
the headmaster, saying that another diabolical thing had happened, and
then we all had to sing 'There'll Always Be An England'. I remember him
saying, 'I never realized the Germans had reached such infamy.' As they got
nearer and nearer, and Dunkirk happened, and all France fell, and then the
Channel ports, I remember it as quite dramatic.

We had an avenue of elm trees that went from the school into the town.
After Dunkirk there was an Army vehicle under each of these, camouflaged,
I suppose. We had soldiers in the actual school, not defending us, but I
suppose in preparation for the invasion. And of course they did things to
the town: they built tank huts at the entrances to the town, they put up pill-
boxes and sandbags. It was very exciting for me as a boy. I can remember
going and talking to the soldiers, and they'd let us have a go on their
wireless. They also built temporary buildings on the green, and took over
any sort of halls that were available.

When the invasion scare happened, I can remember my aunt having some
ladies to tea. They were playing cards, and one said, 'I hear he may come
any time', and the other said, 'So I've heard.' They didn't realize what the
invasion would mean. Around this time there was a great scare about spies,
there was a general atmosphere of the fifth column, and stories of German
soldiers parachuting into Holland dressed as nuns. One or two outsiders
had come to live in Witney, one being a Polish man, very elderly, who wore
knickerbockers and other unusual clothing. The children thought he was a

spy, and told him so, and he was followed by different children, who wondered what he was up to.

Around Christmas 1940 I was very aware of the huge number of children in the town. It was a 'safe' area, so not only had Ashford School come, but children from other areas. There were hordes of children all over the place, it was teeming. There were fights and gangs, and the boys from London were much tougher than we were. Although they were smaller they seemed to be stronger and more aggressive. We also had some Jewish refugee children from Germany and Austria. One of them was rather a bumptious boy who was rather unpopular, but I don't think it was anything to do with him being foreign.

Once a week we were given half a day off from school, so that we could dig up potatoes on a local farm. This was in 1941 or 1942 when food was getting scarcer. Different forms used to go out to this particular farm on the outskirts of Witney to help with the potato harvest. Occasionally we used to work alongside Italian prisoners of war; the authorities seemed to have a very relaxed attitude to them. We also sometimes took part in War Weapons weeks to raise national savings. They would try to persuade us to buy savings stamps, or to help in some way with the Wings for Victory week.

We did have two bombs in Witney, in the autumn of 1940. I think it was a plane turning and going home which just dropped its bombs. They only killed one person, but the school had to be closed for a time, so we had to make do with going to the town hall, which was brought into operation. It was a bit hazardous. Also one or two planes crashed in the town. I remember a glider, and one that knocked the church steeple off, and people were killed. There were quite a few accidental deaths in the blackout. I remember some nights it was *so* dark, you really couldn't see anything. Later they painted the edges of the pavement white, so you could follow the white line.

From our attic window in Witney we could see when Coventry and Birmingham were being bombed, you could see the glow in the sky. The bombers came over our house. I remember the German plane had a particular kind of engine which was different from the British one, it made a rising and falling noise. We all became experts, my friends and I; we used to have outline silhouettes of planes. I once saw a Dornier flying over the park, having just bombed Brize Norton – it was called the Flying Pencil. I was the only person in the park, and when I saw it I couldn't believe it was a German plane. There were no sirens, it just appeared.

There was a good spirit in the town. I can remember national days of prayer, which they had periodically when things looked particularly bad.

I remember for Wings for Victory week they brought in part of a German plane that had crashed and displayed that in the market square. They put up a platform with flags on it, and they had various free entertainments there. Then there'd be an auction of things that people gave for sale, and the money went into War Savings. They had a huge barometer to show how much had been saved. I remember one of the items was a signed photograph of Churchill when he was younger.

We used to have celebrity meetings in the corn exchange, which was the civic centre. Myra Hess came once, and I remember Freddie Grisewood gave a talk. We also had concerts, sometimes put on by the local forces to entertain civilians. And we put plays and concerts on at the youth centre. Later, when the Americans came, they provided concerts too. I remember going to hear Cab Calloway play. They had a huge tent, and I remember getting underneath to hear his band.

The King came to Witney. He spent the day with the troops and inspected the guard of honour, and the people broke ranks and crowded round him. I remember a friend of mine saying, 'I touched him!' After that he was known as The Boy Who Touched the King. I remember also that Queen Mary came to take tea with the local blanket manufacturer. She lived in Badminton, and she used to take forays out to keep herself entertained. I remember seeing her in her Daimler.

As the war progressed you became very aware of the food shortage. My aunt was in charge of the catering arrangements, and it must have been a great burden for her. My grandfather had been a wholesale grocer in another part of Oxfordshire, so he did get a bit of black market food, brought in by a friend. It was just some tea and sugar and butter and biscuits, but the way it had to be brought in from the car in a suitcase, the sense of apprehension was amazing. I was made to keep out of the way while this chap came. I knew it was going on, but I was sworn to secrecy. What sex is today food was in wartime: there was a sort of aura about it, illicit almost. I remember a friend's father had a sweet shop, which was completely bare except for these cardboard replicas of cigarettes. He used to wait until there was nobody in the shop, and then I used to be able to buy some sweets – truly under the counter. There wasn't much to buy in the shops at all. I couldn't buy sweets, I couldn't buy clothes because that meant coupons. I remember having ten shillings for my birthday, quite a lot of money in those days, and having literally nothing to buy.

I remember when the American troops came, how differently they marched from ours, and what a better uniform they had. And then of course there was the first time we saw a black American. The Americans were quite an influence on the town and the area generally. In Oxfordshire there was a youth camp where we used to go for weekends. I remember we had an American week when we ate American food. They gave us some talks and taught us how to play baseball; I think it was to indoctrinate us. We had a Russian week too: there was no Russian food, but we had a film on Russia.

It was a very extraordinary experience to be a child in the war, because of all these happenings. There was such a tremendous proportion of the population in uniform, men and women, and so many different ones from the various countries. We had a fairly large house, so after the evacuees went we had other people to stay. We had a sergeant in the Intelligence Corps billeted on us and then we also had three other sergeants, and tragically two of them were killed on a motorbike.

A friend of mine and I used to go fishing on the outskirts of town. One day we were going across the fields and we came across an American officer and a lady in a compromising position. And we were so startled by this that we stopped and looked at them. She, of course, instead of doing what she should have done, which was to cover her face, covered herself where we wouldn't recognize her. Anyway, we pushed on and talked about this. We were shocked and excited and alarmed all at the same time: we knew her husband was with the Eighth Army in the Western Desert. Two or three days later we saw her in the town, and we spoke to her. She looked very startled. We continued to speak to her whenever we met her, and we forced her to speak to us if she crossed the road when she saw us coming along. We gave her knowing looks, we called out, 'How are you?' and she became more and more embarrassed. Later I left Witney, but I've been back since, and even today, if ever I see her when she's not with her husband, she speaks to me, but if she's with him, she doesn't. It's reached the stage where *she* speaks to *me* if I don't notice her. It had that kind of effect on her. There was certainly a very strong feeling against girls who went with Americans.

People couldn't go on holidays, so you had holidays at home or you went to relatives. The council used to organize sports and other things; I remember they had a big baseball match in the local park. Cinema was a great thing. We went once a week. There was only one cinema in Witney, but it was always very crowded. The programme would change twice a week.

At one point I had to go into hospital for three weeks, as I had some skin trouble, psoriasis. I was in a male ward in the Radcliffe in Oxford, and there were some soldiers in there as well, so I got to hear their view of things. Up to that time I had been rather protected living with my grandfather, and I got the full blast of male attitudes to girls and so on, and all the excitement with the nurses. I remember I was there when Pearl Harbour was attacked, and I remember the soldiers saying, 'He's lost now, he won't win against America.' It was very dramatic to hear that on the radio.

I left school in 1943. I didn't take the school certificate, my education was sadly lacking. It was only in the forces later that I was able to retrieve the situation. It was then that I joined the ARP, first as a messenger, and then as what was called 'report and control'. I had to sleep one night a fortnight in the council offices and man a telephone with someone else. I remember we had cocoa and biscuits.

I also went to work in the de Havilland aircraft factory. It was a complete social mix, because there were a lot of people working in factories seeking to avoid going into the forces, so you got all sorts. Not everybody was doing that, of course, but it was often a factor. So you got very incongruous situations. We had a bookie, an Indian who had been a salesman before the war, someone who had been a tea-taster, and a girl who had been a debutante and been presented at Buckingham Palace. We also had a physiotherapist and a woman who had flown planes before the war. There were some conscientious objectors there. They weren't treated too badly, they were pointed at by other people, but I can't remember any particular harassment. I just remember people saying, 'Did you know he was a conchie?'

When I was seventeen I became an aircraft inspector, which seems incredible now. I was in the repair unit, where they had Spitfires and Hurricanes, which either had crashed or had to be stripped down and gone over after 240 hours of flying time. My job was in a place called Survey. They brought the planes in, they took the wings off the tailplane, and took the engine out, and then a team of six of us had to inspect the different parts. I was responsible for doing the report on the electrical installation. On the basis of this report the factory repaired it. And I got this job by just learning it working alongside somebody for eight or nine months.

The war period has been described as the last time we were all happy. I think it was a very innocent time, but there really was a feeling of community. For myself, the war has left two permanent marks. The first is that I can't let a day go by without hearing the news. The second is that I eat too much bread.

The Miner's Daughter

People who were travelling round the country often dropped in at our house and asked for refreshment, complete strangers. We met people who we would never have met normally.

Pat Palmer

I was six and a half when the war started. I can remember the declaration clearly: it was a nice day and we were in the garden, and suddenly everyone went indoors and clustered around the radio. My first impression was of utter fear. We were a very quiet community; I was brought up about 2 miles outside a colliery town, Coalville, in the Midlands. I was relatively shy, I suppose, and brought up away from the main community, and war meant to me lots of people and extreme fear.

My next memory is of going to school, and having to try the gas masks on. Even now I can remember the smell and the claustrophobic feeling, very frightening indeed. I didn't dare express my feelings about it. When the teacher said, 'Put your gas mask on', you had to steel yourself. I had a younger sister who was backward, and I was terrified she wouldn't get her gas mask on in time. One of my childhood fears was daring to race out of my classroom and race into hers, and help her on with the gas mask. The other thing was, being from rather a poor family, there was a tremendous stigma attached to carrying the standard gas mask case. The posh middle-class people had specially made leather cases, but we carried ours in the standard square box with a canvas case over it. So when you walked to school people could tell what kind of family you came from.

My mother had to go and register to show she wasn't eligible for the forces, and as a joke she came back and said she'd been told she had to join the WAAF. She didn't realize how much this added to our fear and apprehension. I remember controlling myself very carefully, and telling my sister that we *mustn't* let my mother know that we were scared of her going into the forces, because it was the war and the war effort. One caught it even at that early age, that one had got to be enormously brave. It was a tremendous relief when I found out it was a joke. But for what seemed an age I thought my mother was going to have to leave us.

We used to hear the bombers go over, you'd wake up in the night. We went into my mother's bedroom and we all huddled there listening to it. I remember the night Coventry was bombed, we could see the sky lit up with all the fires, which was frightening. Being in the country we weren't immediately threatened, so our fear was of the unknown. It was a different experience from that of the children in the cities, who were suffering directly.

One of the local families had five sons, and three were in the RAF. One of them was stationed nearby, and when he went on a raid he would circle round above his house, and he'd do the same when he got back, to let his mother know he was safe. It was quite a local event. In fact she lost three sons in action, so it was very sad.

I went to a modern primary school, in a spanking new building. But the claustrophobia came in again, because it had a lot of glass in the design, French windows and so on. Many of them were bricked up, and those that weren't had the sticky netting stuff put over the top. This claustrophobic feeling is quite a potent memory. But the main problem in school was the shortage of materials. I remember my first painting lesson in the junior school. We had a long introduction on how to do it, because having this one piece of paper each was a great thrill. With sewing and all the crafts we were told we had to be very careful with all the materials. And I remember the terrible, *terrible* squeak of the chalk on the slates, which we used for some of the time.

My father was in a reserved occupation; he was a miner. But he was unfortunate because, though he was tough, he developed stomach ulcers, and he had to leave the pit face, just as the money was building up. He'd been in the pit in the 1930s when there had been considerable unemployment; he'd started at the age of thirteen. So it was terribly galling for him, and the differential between the underground and surface workers was considerable then. It took many years before the union campaigned to close the differential, and by that time my father had died of cancer of the lung.

He was a male chauvinist in some respects, except he was such a kind character, and he liked cooking so he didn't mind being seen in the kitchen, which was unusual then, particularly for miners. He didn't agree with make-up or women drinking beer or things like that. He was very radical in other ways. During the war we had two very grand houses, in each of which there lived a rich couple. I remember him saying that they should commandeer those houses and put the evacuees in there, instead of putting them in with the poor, who were already overcrowded. He said as usual it was the poor helping the poor, while the rich still got off all right.

In fact my mother was more radical than my father, and joined the Labour Party before he did; he was originally a Liberal. When he became ill during the war, she had to get a job, as there was no money. She'd been in domestic service before she married, and that was the only thing she could do. So she went to the colliery canteen and became an assistant cook, cooking these huge meals for the colliers.

My parents were very generous. We had a lot of friends and relatives in uniform who would come to the house, and it was our job to give them a good time, because we were supposedly the lucky ones. Strange things happened. Because there weren't so many cafés, people who were travelling round the country – cyclists and walkers and people who got about under their own steam – often dropped in at our house and asked for refreshment, complete strangers. My mother would offer them eggs because we had extra, and home-made cake. We met people who we would never have met normally. We met a couple of business people from Nottingham, who were completely out of our class, but they became firm family friends – I remember them helping me with my homework.

We had relatives in London, and we used to send them food parcels, as we had a big garden and were relatively self-sufficient. We kept animals like most people did – rabbits and hens and pigs – and my father used to pack up eggs and chicken and fresh green vegetables and fruit. The post must have been very good, because they always got them all right, even though there was tremendous disruption in London. But we got very few of the shortage foods like biscuits and oranges and the fruit from overseas. We lived about a mile and a half from the nearest shop, and if my father came back and said he had heard there were oranges around, one of us would hurtle down to the shop on our bike. By the time we got there they had usually gone. But the bottling and preserving were a tremendous help, and again my parents would give a lot away to those who were less fortunate. There was a lot of sharing. We weren't involved in the black market, but there was a lot of bartering and recycling. We weren't sweet-toothed, but a lot of people desperately missed sugar, so we often traded sugar for, say, butter.

In theory my father was anti-Semitic – the Jews were responsible for everything, he thought they'd helped cause all this chaos. But when a conscientious objector who was a Jew came to work at the mine with my father, he responded with an ordinary human reaction to this desperately lonely man, who wasn't very highly regarded by other people. He was invited regularly to the house, and because he was a little bit more cultured and cultivated, as it were, he took me to music concerts, which affected my musical education. Later in the war he took me to see Eileen Joyce perform and we had to cycle 15 miles to the concert and 15 miles back. I was only eleven then. My parents would never take me to anything like that. This man also encouraged me to write: I remember him bringing me a big exercise book in which I was to write, because he felt I could.

In informal education there were all sorts of opportunities, because it was make your own enjoyment and pleasure, and anyone with gifts and talents was hugely valued. I started piano-playing when I was seven, and my first teacher was a Land Army girl; she couldn't give lessons during harvest time of course. As soon as I could possibly play I was expected to perform, and when people came home on leave they brought the latest sheet music, and I was supposed to entertain them. At the church too we made our own entertainment, and had a lot of concerts. It was odd really how ordinary people became familiar with classical music who might not otherwise have done.

We didn't travel much, we didn't have any 'away' holiday. My father didn't risk going to the seaside, as many people didn't. I went once when I was four before the war, and didn't go again until I was about twelve, and I was *desperately* longing to see the sea. But by then I was too old for buckets and spades.

What impressed me, even as a child and thinking about it since, was that although we were patriotic, it wasn't naïvely so. When later in the war we saw the German and Italian prisoners of war working in the fields, my father would invite them in for a cup of tea. He would say, 'That poor bloke's been working out there all day.' We had one in to a meal, I remember. They were just human beings. The independence of my parents was very strong, they weren't easily conditioned into thinking this was right because this was England. I didn't feel a savage hate, this wasn't encouraged in my family.

Towards the end of the war, at the grammar school, we had one Jewish boy, and he was terribly, *terribly*, victimized. We had a teacher who taught German, and he was very right-wing indeed, and particularly vicious. This boy was treated very badly, he was very much ostracized. There was a terrible attitude, that the Jews almost got what they deserved. There was a very mixed feeling about things like this. The war spirit was negative as well as positive. Some people are very easily conditioned or persuaded to support the country or the state or the party. I think people are usually looking for a scapegoat, and that's where the poor Jews were suffering.

I remember the tone of voice in the newsreels when my parents took me to the cinema, and the cheering that was whipped up when the commentator talked about 'our lads' having done something. I can't recall that I was caught up in that sort of feeling. I feel very strongly that things like nationalism and patriotism don't need to be taught or encouraged, because people's natural fear when an emergency arises will make them come together. If I had to encourage anything it would be to strengthen individual choice and thought, because strong individuals don't feel threatened anyway. I think this feeling comes from my parents, who were humble working-class people, but who had strong views and were not easily persuadable.

I remember that everything was going to be all right After the War. I waited for this After the War, and of course it didn't happen, it was a letdown when it finished. I remember the huge celebrations on VE Night, and winning five pounds in a talent competition – there were a lot of competitions and parties then, and we had the time of our lives. But immediately afterwards I felt I had lost my childhood, that there was a lot of fun I hadn't had.

Extracts from the diary of a ten-year-old Essex schoolgirl, May 1944 to May 1945

2 May. Dad was in bed when I woke up at eight o'clock.

3 May. The soldiers came and put their guns in our field.

5 May. Played with the soldiers.

6 May. Played with the soldiers and gave them some tea about 3 o'clock.

7 May. Dad went on guard all night.

11 May. Dad got up at 9.30 a.m. after being on guard all night. Went and heard the bagpipers play.

19 May. Played with the soldiers at Hot Rice; Dad went on guard all night.

21 May. The soldiers went at nine o'clock.

6 June. Invasion started in France at dawn. Did fractions – got on all right.

7 June. Went to Brownies; had my bike out; went to bed at eight o'clock; got a 12-mile beach head.

12 June. Mr Churchill went over to France with a lot more people; mum not very well; did biking.

19 June. Went to bed under the table; the warning did not go. Can get off my bike properly.

22 June. Went to bed under the table. Eight warnings in the night.

17 July. Went to school – had new people from London start.

19 July. Went to school; warning went; did not have my poetry.

27 April. Linked up with the Russians. Had netball.

8 May. War over. Victory. Had a flag up. Had a bonfire.

9 May. Three days holiday from school. Went to church. Saw a VE party.

12 May. Victory party in Louvaine Avenue.

Out of Step

*Dissent was tolerated as long as it didn't become serious opposition.
I got quite a reputation for going round and trying to persuade people
of the wrongness of war. At least one person was told officially not to
encourage me by arguing politics, because I'd argue with anyone. But
I didn't succeed with anyone.*

LONDON MAN

*It always seemed to me strange that our church leaders would be
saying it's a just war, and the church leaders on the other side would
be saying the same. It seemed illogical to me.*

DONCASTER MAN

*Most people undoubtedly saw Churchill as the great war leader.
I didn't respond to him at all, but that was a small minority view.*

HULL MAN

'In this country no person should be penalized for the mere holding of an opinion, however unpopular that opinion may be to the majority.' This assertion of the right to freedom of speech was made in July 1940 by Herbert Morrison, the Home Secretary. It was expressed at a moment when invasion by Germany was expected daily, and the need for national unity never greater. Yet the government's attitude towards dissent and criticism of its actions and policies was not always as tolerant as Morrison's words would suggest. Many who stepped out of line, privately or publicly, found themselves in difficulties, and sometimes prison.

The need for a balance between free expression and national security is never an easy one to get right. In order to discourage treasonous and subversive acts, the government passed a Treachery Act and various defence regulations. One of these gave the Home Secretary the power to imprison anyone who seemed likely to him to threaten the safety of the realm. In the spring of 1940 the media-inspired 'fifth column' scare, which suggested Britain was overrun by spies and Germans disguised as nuns, panicked the government into action. Using its emergency powers, it indiscriminately interned and deported thousands of 'enemy aliens', many of them Jewish refugees whom Hitler had forced out of Germany. It was a gross over-reaction, a classic example of rumour triumphing over fact. It brought unnecessary misery and suffering to thousands of innocent men and women.

More absurdly, the government introduced a regulation which made it an offence to 'circulate any report or statement' about the war which was 'likely to cause alarm and despondency'. People were exhorted to 'Join Britain's Silent Column – the great body of sensible men and women who have pledged themselves not to talk rumour and gossip and to stop others doing it.' This inept campaign to try to control what people could say produced several successful prosecutions for 'defeatist' talk before it was quietly dropped.

There was in any case plenty for the ordinary civilian to be alarmed and despondent about at different moments of the war. There was the frustrating inaction of the early months, when Chamberlain's government seemed both sluggish and out of touch with the popular mood. When the Blitz became a feature of daily life in the cities, the government came in for criticism on a number of counts – notably on the shelter issue – as did many local authority officials for their bureaucratic ineptitude. Later, military reverses in North Africa and the Far East brought both civilian and service morale to a new low, and even prompted a vote of no confidence in Churchill's leadership in the House of Commons. While this was roundly defeated, an increasing number of people were talking about the need for social reforms, and for something more constructive than their leader's war aim of 'victory at all costs'.

Dissidents and critics were inevitably hampered by the electoral truce agreed by the coalition government set up in May 1940 under Churchill's leadership. The three main parties had agreed not to put up candidates against each other at by-elections, so leaving the party in power with an enormous in-built advantage. However, candidates from the smaller parties, as well as some independent candidates, attracted substantial support from disaffected supporters of the main parties. The pacifist-inclined Independent Labour Party, which in December 1940 had introduced a motion to Parliament for a 'negotiated peace', polled 20–30 per cent of the vote in some Conservative-held constituencies. The new Common Wealth Party actually achieved some by-election successes. Its policies, centring on changes in the ownership of industry and land, a greater democratization of the electoral system, and an improvement in the morality of public life, appealed to many in all parties who were beginning to turn their minds to postwar reconstruction and reform.

While the Peace Pledge Union, the Fellowship of Reconciliation and the Society of Friends mounted moral and pacifist critiques of the war, the main political and ideological opposition came from the Communist Party and its various sympathizers. While the party often captured and exploited popular anti-government or anti-capitalist feelings, its frequent changes of stance caused by its direction from Moscow alienated much of its potential support. The government, however, was taking no chances. Following the first assembly of the party's People's Convention, where a number of fiery speeches advocating a 'people's government' produced a positive response from the 2,000-plus audience, it banned the party's newspaper the *Daily Worker*, and kept the ban in force for eighteen months, so stifling much of the opposition.

This was not the only conflict between the government and the press. The *Daily Mirror*, and especially its noted columnist Cassandra, was a persistent and outspoken critic of many government actions, and became a genuine 'voice of the people'. Churchill tried to suppress the paper, and was only restrained by more moderate colleagues. In similar fashion, the campaigning magazine *Picture Post* came under pressure for supposedly undermining morale with articles attacking the conduct of the war. When the editor stood firm, the government withdrew the subsidy which allowed the magazine to be sent to British troops overseas. The outspoken anarchist magazine *War Commentary*, published by Freedom Press, had its offices raided, its workers charged with disaffection of the forces. The sentences of those involved were only kept to a minimum through the energetic work of a special defence committee set up to fight the issue, which gained the support of, among others, Nye Bevan, Michael Foot, Herbert Read and George Orwell. In Orwell's view, if the war was about anything at all, it was a war in favour of freedom of thought.

The High School Teacher

I realized that the document was the thin end of the wedge, and that it's very, very easy, even inside a democracy, for something like that to be whipped up, and for people to lose all judgement and sense of values.

Elaine Robson-Scott

Just before the war, when I was a young woman in my twenties, I had been a postgraduate student in Germany. Because of this I had very strong feelings and compassion for the German people, and close friends in Germany. I had hoped to visit one girlfriend who lived in the Rhineland during August 1939, but the signing of the non-aggression pact between Russia and Germany put a stop to that. The day after the declaration of war I had my last letter from this girl. She lived near the Dutch border, and as Holland was still free, she had cycled over the border to post it to me. In this letter she said: 'I hope now England will not yield as she did last year over Czechoslovakia. That is a triumph I would not like to experience.'

I went to teach German in a large girls' high school in south Wales. I particularly enjoyed the teaching of the sixth form. Naturally we read the literature, and that led one to talking about Germany and the Germans. I told them quite openly that nearly all the Germans I knew held the kind of sentiments that had been expressed by my friend in her letter, and that for them patriotism and morality did not coincide. In this country we have been fortunate that in most instances they *have* coincided.

In the school there was never any difficulty in teaching German; on the contrary. From 1933 onwards, the great influx of refugees to this country made people able to distinguish between the Germans and the Nazis. It was not the same as the First World War – orchestras did go on playing German music, thank goodness.

One day, shortly after the fall of France in May 1940, the headmistress came into the common room where the teachers were assembled, and said that the local authority had given her a document for each of us, which she then distributed, and asked us to read. I thought I had never read anything so crazy in all my life. The document consisted of three questions. The first was, 'Are you a member of the Peace Pledge Union?' The second was, 'Are you likely to be a member of the fifth column?' And the third was, 'Are you in favour of the successful prosecution of the war?' I thought to myself, 'Well, if one *is* a member of the Peace Pledge Union, they will have a list of members somewhere,' so there would be no point in disguising the fact. If one was a member of a fifth column, the *last* thing one would do would be to say, 'Yes, I am a member of the fifth column.' And of course everyone there was anxious that the war should be brought to a successful end.

So, in the quiet of my place in that common room, I decided that I would refuse to sign. We were all given time to look at the document, and the headmistress asked us to bring them signed to her study at the end of the afternoon. She went out of the room. There was a long silence, and then I said to the woman sitting next to me, who I suspected might have feelings similar to mine, 'I'm not going to sign it.' I didn't give any explanation, I just said, 'It seems to me the most ridiculous document I've been presented with in my life.' And then, out of a staff of about forty, five of us refused to sign. One *was* a member of the Peace Pledge Union, but the others were not, and they all had varying reasons for refusing. I felt that we should offer no explanation for our refusal, but there was one very intelligent woman, who taught history and who had studied in America, and who was very articulate. She said that we ought to sum up our reasons, and say that one of the reasons why we were refusing to sign was that this kind of investigation of the political and religious views of any member of a teaching staff in Britain had been finished long ago. So we did that. Against my will, we did draw up some small statement of that kind, and the five of us took our unsigned documents to the headmistress.

Though I had never thought of her as very liberal, she was in sympathy with us. She didn't reveal whether she was presented with the same document herself, but she accepted our unsigned ones, and said that she would notify the local authority that she had five members of staff who were not going to sign. And I think the five of us who refused to sign were her most valued members of staff, and this must have struck her, so she was in greater sympathy that I had expected. She did inform the local authority, and the one woman who did belong to the Peace Pledge Union was suspended, I think on full pay, for about two months, while they sorted out the position. There were, I should say, ten or twelve men and women in the town who belonged to the Peace Pledge Union, and they were all suspended. We never knew whether it had anything to do with the fact that five of us had refused to sign, but after a couple of months we were informed that the local authority had seen that it had taken a very foolish step, and that it was not pressing these investigations any further. Whether the decision came from the ministry or not I don't know. It may have been just one councillor behind it, one fanatic. What he thought he could achieve I can't imagine: what did he think he was going to do with us all?

I refused because I had been in Germany in 1934 at the time of the death of Hindenberg. There was an election, and the family where I was staying had shown me the sort of thing on which they had to vote Yes for Hitler. And the questions were so absurd: 'Do you want a good, strong, unified Germany?' Of course everybody said yes. Then I was also in Vienna in 1938 when the *Anschluss* took place, and this too was followed by a plebiscite, also asking: 'Do you want Austria to remain strong and united?' and of course everybody said yes.

So I realized that the document was the thin end of the wedge, and that it's very, very easy, even inside a democracy, for something like that to be whipped up, and people to lose all judgement and sense of values. That is why I refused. I think the others refused for the same reason. None of them had had my experience of living in a totalitarian state, so they were not as aware as I was that this was something very similar to the sort of questions that were always circulated among Germans. They were never asked, 'Are you for an anti-Semitic, anti-Christian, pro-war Germany?' They were always asked, 'Are you for a good, strong, united Germany with everybody happy?'

The members of the Peace Pledge Union were eventually all reinstated. One single woman came back to our staff after a break of a few weeks, and was never penalized in any way. But the incident did cause problems among the staff. I think the people who were refusing to sign thought that the others thought we were giving ourselves airs, making ourselves morally superior, which was not the case at all. It just was a matter of firm conviction. None of us could afford to lose our jobs; I certainly couldn't have done.

At the time I heard that there was a woman staying in the town who had been principal of one of the Cambridge colleges. I knew that she was a woman of strong conviction, and I rang up her hostess, whom I didn't know, and asked if I might come round to talk to this elderly lady. She was immensely encouraging, and said, 'I think you are absolutely right, this is the kind of questionnaire one *must* refuse to answer – firstly because it is so futile, and secondly because it is morally wrong that these kind of investigations should be made at such a time.' It was a panic measure on the part of the local authority. I would say it was an isolated incident, something that came out of the collapse of France.

The head teacher was a very reserved woman, and kept her own counsel about all this. But she made the non-signing much easier than any of us had anticipated. We were all enormously gratified that she took it as well as she did. She said, 'I respect your judgement.' We never got any apology from the local authority, we just jogged on in our jobs, unmolested. When nothing happened to us the whole excitement soon died down. But I always remember among the staff who had gone which way – and I can tell you to this day.

There was quite a lot of heavy bombing in the area, and this did make the pupils physically tired. But nothing else; there was never any hysteria or indeed depression. On the contrary, I think young people in the sixth form today must be far more depressed than they were then. There was a kind of exhilaration and a feeling of community. Also I do remember when you met people in the town who had lost their home, they had sorted out their values and priorities. I remember one widow, who had lost her husband some years before, saying to me, 'What does it matter? Of course, I've lost my flat and all my furniture, but my daughter and I are alive, that's all that matters.' People did get that kind of view of things.

To me Churchill was the embodiment of how fallacious is the Marxist doctrine that personalities don't matter, and that it is economic forces that determine history. Had it not been for Churchill, I think we would have succumbed, we would have made some kind of peace with Hitler. The personality, the voice . . . I don't think anybody who didn't go through the war will quite realize what that voice was like to us. Now one knows that he didn't always tell the whole truth, but he told a very great deal of the truth about casualties, and when things were not going so well, so that one did feel one was getting an honest account.

I think in 1945 that a lot of people were very determined that what had happened after 1918 was *not* to happen again, that there really *were* to be homes fit for heroes this time. This is what really determined people to vote Labour, myself included. Much as I admired Churchill as a war leader, I knew that for the first vote of my life I was going to vote Labour. We wanted a different kind of society, there was a very strong feeling about that. Among other things, it was the evacuation of children from the big cities to small towns that had revealed the kind of conditions of life that many of them lived in. We had some evacuees from Liverpool and one saw what a divided society we had been. There was a determination on the part of many young people that this was to end, that things were going to be better.

I don't think people help one another now in the way they did during those years of crisis. So much has gone. It was very marked, the readiness to share, to give hospitality, it did bring out the generous side of people. I don't think one is putting a rosy glow on it all. People talked to each other in the neighbourhood, as you do in a time of crisis. During the bombing people were very kind, and took you in if you were passing, you'd just knock on the door and dash in. And then people came out the next morning and went to work. I think adversity does bring out the good qualities in people.

I think what people found hardest in London were the flying bombs, they really broke the nerve of people who had gone through the Blitz. That was certainly the case with my husband, he always said that was the straw that broke the camel's back, and I think *many* people felt that. What was interesting was that when my husband and I went out to Germany after the war, we found that no Germans believed there had been any flying bombs. They said that Goebbels had told them so many lies like this, that when it was the truth it was not accepted at all, that there were these wonder weapons. They just thought it was another piece of propaganda.

The Party Member

The policeman said, 'You said yesterday – and I quote – "I would like to see Hitler in Buckingham Palace, the king shot, and the Nazis take over the country."' So I said, 'You must be mad.' With that he slapped me in the face.

Frank Mayes

I was perhaps more interested than most people in the overall struggle, the politics and strategy of the war. My family were Anglo-Irish Catholic, and I was brought up on the inequity of Ireland, very much so; my father was a member of Sinn Fein, although he was an Englishman. I suppose that was the paramount thing, but there was also pacifism. My father had been in the Army in the First World War, and he had a burning hatred for war. I suppose that rubbed off on me, because I began as a pacifist.

Just prior to the war, when I was fourteen, I went to work as a printer in London, and soon became involved in the class struggle. I worked extremely hard with very low wages, and I became influenced by the shop steward, which in our trade is called the father of the chapel. He was a member of the Labour Party and a pacifist. He used to get the boys together and try to inculcate his ideas into them, and he succeeded with me. We talked about the coming war, which was obvious to anyone who thought about things in those days, and he said, 'It doesn't matter if your employer's name is Schmidt or Smith', and I believed that, 100 per cent. The manager of this firm was a colonel in the Army, and he was busily recruiting lads – this was in Stamford Street, a huge printer's. He managed to persuade quite a lot of these boys to join the Territorials. I, of course, refused.

The print shop was bombed out. I went to the Labour Exchange and said I was a printer, and they said, 'Forget it'. So I got a job in a light engineering factory in Peckham in south London, making tin boxes for tanks. I was about seventeen then. While I thought the print shop was hard, I couldn't believe my eyes when I got to this place. We used to have to put our hands up to go to the lavatory. We were timed, and the job consisted of pulling a handle with a big ball swinging on the end of it, the most monotonous thing you could ever imagine. It so happened that while I was there I met a young fellow in the same circumstances as myself. He had worked at the print shop too, and we commiserated with each other at the state we were in. Between us we said, 'Let's form a union.' We had been in the union at the print shop, but this was a Transport and General Workers' Union thing. Nobody was in the union, and everyone was disgruntled. So we said we'd call a meeting in the lunch break. I remember standing up on a bench and saying that this was a dreadful place, and that we ought to do something about it, and did we want to join the union? About three-quarters of them said they did – some of these were middle-aged men, and I was just a youth.

The next day I went over to Transport House and explained the situation, and they gave me 100 union cards to dish out. When I came in to work the next day the foreman, who was a typical bully type, said, 'You're wanted downstairs in the office', and the other fellow I knew, and two others. When we got down there the place was full of police. And they sat me in a chair, and they said, 'You know what we're here for, don't you?' They always say that, even when you don't. They kept saying this, and I said, 'I suppose somebody's bike's been pinched.' And he said, 'No, it's not that.' He was a high-ranking, three-pip fellow, and he said: 'You said yesterday – and I quote – "I would like to see Hitler in Buckingham Palace, the King shot, and the Nazis take over the country."' So I said, 'You must be mad.' With that he slapped me in the face. 'Don't talk to me like that,' he said. Then he said, 'Right, you get out now', and he had the others in and frightened the life out of us. He said, 'You'll be charged tomorrow.' They were what was known as Cooper's Snoopers: Duff Cooper had brought in a law whereby anybody talking in a pub, saying, 'This war doesn't look too good, looks as if we're going to lose', could be arrested. The law had been brought in a couple of days before this happened, I think, and the police were quick to jump in. It was obvious that this foreman fellow had rung the police and got them in. His angle was he didn't want the place unionized, so the powers that be saw a good way of getting rid of us by having us arrested under this new law.

Anyway, my mother went up and created hell at the firm, and she went to the police station and said, 'Isn't this what we're supposed to be fighting against?' They had us in the next day and told us to shove off; we all got the sack, but we weren't charged under this law. I think it was thrown out quite soon afterwards, it was too much for Parliament. I don't think they really wanted to hang anybody for saying they thought we would lose the war. Of course all that hardened my left-wing convictions.

The unions made great strides during the war, with the women going into the factories. But the TUC was 100 per cent behind the war, and they did relax many conditions that the trade union movement had held to, such as boys not working at night. I later got a job like that, it was quite illegal, but the union turned a blind eye. I think the emergency regulations did away with all the existing Factory Acts, but the union acquiesced in that sort of thing, and so did the people in general. Although we knew it was illegal we didn't complain, because at that time everybody was in favour of the war effort.

Then came the moment when I had to decide what to do when I was called up. All the young men were wanting to go into this or that, but I'd made up my mind that I wasn't going into anything. My father supported me 100 per cent – in fact when the time came he urged me to go and live in Ireland. Another lad there who was a bit older than me was called up, but he refused to go, and ended up in prison. And I was prepared to do the same thing. By this time I had joined the Labour League of Youth.

Of course what happened then was the invasion of the Soviet Union, which threw us all into a turmoil. After it happened I became the most enthusiastic warmonger of them all. I threw everything overboard, all the pacifism. I didn't even wait to be called up, I volunteered for the Navy, I left the Labour Party to join the Communist Party. This became a very popular thing to do, people were joining all over the place. In Portsmouth we had a Communist Party branch of the Navy.

We saw the Soviet Union as being in danger, and we wished to come to its assistance. I suppose you could say that while we were fighting in the war we were fighting for the Soviet Union. We were still opposed to the set-up in Britain – for instance the class-ridden Royal Navy – but they were on our side. Everybody talked about this sort of thing, but there was no altering the brass in the Navy. The mess deck was going further left all the time, culminating in the 1945 election, which swept Churchill from power. I suppose the lower-deck vote for the Labour Party must have been about 99 per cent.

The immediate struggle was to defeat fascism. After the invasion of the Soviet Union the Communist Party acquiesced like the unions in support of Churchill. The big issue they did take a stand on was that of air-raid shelters. The party conducted a campaign for deep, bomb-proof shelters, which didn't succeed. But it started an agitation for the tubes to be open, and this was successful. I've just read in my diary that my mother used to sleep in the tube; I'd forgotten that. According to my diary I went down there when I was on leave, and saw 'ten thousand people at the Elephant and Castle tube station, indescribable squalor and dirt; how I hate those bastard capitalists'.

Other than that, the government was merely urging people to work harder and win the war, be patriotic and everybody together. The country was united, mostly for the obvious reasons, King and Country – except for the Mosleyites. There was a debate in the House of Commons when Churchill's leadership was severely criticized, but I don't think the mass of the people thought too much about that; I think they probably saw it as a few oddballs criticizing the great man.

There was a great deal of camaraderie under pressure; it was probably the only good thing that came out of the war, the fact that people genuinely helped each other. There was feeling for each other. I suppose we thought it was some sort of socialism at the time, but it was probably the fact that we were all in the same boat, and the only sensible thing to do was help each other. Unlike a lot of the things people say, that was a fact of the war, the camaraderie. If you were bombed out, people would come immediately, help you to remove what furniture could be salvaged, and offer to put you up. When we were bombed out I slept in people's homes and we didn't know them from Adam.

I got a lot of leave in 1944. I was stationed in Portsmouth, and we used to hitch up to London when the flying bombs were on. I hadn't realized until I looked at my diary what a dreadful thing it was. My father was in the London Ambulance Association, and was at the sharp end of all this. He was dragging people out, or rather bits of people. He was probably the last man who should have done that job, he was very squeamish and fastidious. I'm afraid it had its effect on him, he had what used to be called shell shock. His voice went funny, he started stuttering, things like that.

Had it gone on much longer he would have become a casualty along with the people he had been rescuing.

I ended the war working as a printer on a Navy newspaper in Sydney in Australia. The night the election result came in, we had one of those old-fashioned ticker-tape things. There were two or three officers there and a crowd of ratings, and the tape said, 'It's now obvious that it's a Labour landslide', and a great cheer went up. And one of the officers said, 'Well, that's it, I'm not going back to England.' And a rating said to him, 'Well, we won't bloody well miss you.' It's the only time I heard a private speak to an officer like that. It was a sign of the euphoria of the times. We all thought the brave new world was going to come about. Of course it didn't, and we were very soon disillusioned.

Whether my change of heart over pacifism was an honourable thing, I don't know. Looked at from a bourgeois point of view, it would be quite dishonourable, I suppose. Those people who supported the war all along could criticize people like myself and say, 'You don't care about England, you only supported the war because the Soviet Union was involved.' People did say that, but at the time they seemed wrong. I had said I wouldn't go in 1939 despite the fact that we knew what the Nazis had done in Spain, we knew they were the enemy, we knew they were anti-Semitic and anti-union. I don't know, the horror of war was such. . . . It's so obvious now, but I saw it then as a re-make of 1914, probably the silliest war in history, which I certainly would never have supported. But it wasn't like that, and I suppose you could say we made a colossal error in thinking it was. There were those who supported the war in 1939 and those who didn't, and I was one of those who didn't. I think we were wrong, completely wrong.

Extract from Frank Mayes's diary, 1944

Dad looked wonderful, I haven't seen him look so good for years. Mother then let me into the secret. It appears that on the day after D-Day he broke down and confessed that he had made himself ill worrying about me and the Second Front. He too had visions of a bloodbath, and feared greatly for my safety. So they had both been this way. How I hate myself for being the cause of so much suffering, for making my dear father so unhappy. This was the real reason for his being so irritable, so hard to get along with. My God, the people that are responsible for this war!

The Organizing Secretary

*People frequently strongly disagreed with me, but usually
took the line that this was something I clearly couldn't help,
poor soul.*

Doris Nicholls

I think it was the work of people like Fenner Brockway, who went to
prison in the First World War for their pacifist beliefs, that was the main
reason for the more sensible attitude that people had in the Second, in at
least recognizing that there were people who conscientiously could not
take part in war. And I think it was a wonderful thing that they did
recognize that.

I was a professional pacifist well before the war started. I'd had my
pacifist convictions from quite a young age: I'd always felt like that about
war. My parents were marvellous people and lovely Christians, but I think
the idea of pacifism wouldn't have occurred to them. When I was fourteen I
resigned from what was called the Junior League of Nations, because I
could *not* believe in the morality of armed force. But it wasn't until I was
about twenty that I first heard of the Fellowship of Reconciliation, and
started to go to meetings and get more and more interested, ending up
running a local group. In 1938 I was asked to take over the organizing of
the Fellowship of Reconciliation in London. After two years I was asked if I
would be organizing secretary for the whole country. The fellowship was
started in the First World War. By the time the Second broke out, there were

about ninety groups in London alone, many of them very small, and all attached to church groups. It was recognized that a lot of Christians who hadn't really considered whether or not they were pacifists would probably find that they were, and would then need support.

Once war was declared, we found that many of the people being hauled up before tribunals needed help. We would sit and talk with them. I personally felt very strongly – and this was the position of the fellowship – that no man should opt to be a pacifist in wartime until he was absolutely certain that this was the only option open to him. So the first part of my job when I met somebody was to challenge them as to whether this was really necessary. In fact I frequently said, 'If you *can* go and fight in this war against an evil like Hitler, then you ought to do it.' I'm certain that, having been really challenged, they were able to consider whether they were being sentimental or frightened, or had some other reason other than conscience.

If they decided to go ahead with their stand, I then had to try and help them to present a reasonable case to the tribunal. These were eighteen-year-olds, who had never in their lives had to justify anything on moral grounds, except perhaps in a Bible study group or something of that sort, and who were now going to have to present a case before a group of men who were not inclined to be sympathetic.

I attended hundreds of tribunals. You could have someone there to speak for you, though there was no guarantee that they would be called. You could be represented, and occasionally people would take a solicitor or someone of that sort along to put their case. But usually it was felt that this wasn't a very good idea. I can remember one occasion when I went with a young man who was so utterly terrified that he literally lost the power of speech. He got a few words out, and then dried up, and then a few more. He was sweating, and was in a very bad state. I felt he was very brave, because it was quite obvious he was never going to be called up anyway, since he had bad asthma. But at that stage this wasn't necessarily taken into consideration, and he felt that he had got to make his stand. But when it came to it, he just couldn't utter. I remember that the chairman asked if there was anybody with him, and when I indicated that I was, he called me up and said, 'Can you please explain to us what it is that this young man wants to tell us.' So I did, and in fact he got an unconditional exemption. But I'm sure this was chiefly because they saw he was never going to be taken by the Army anyway. I think it probably also made their numbers up a bit.

I felt that the tribunals did as good a job as could possibly be done by men doing the impossible job of trying to test someone else's conscience. But there were some instances who I would have staked my life were what they said they were, who didn't get the kind of exemption they demanded. Many of them were prepared to go into non-combatant services or do ambulance work or go on the land, the number who weren't was very small. But the tribunals couldn't accept what they had to say about themselves as being adequate, and a number of friends and people who I interviewed finished up in prison. One such friend came out of prison the morning I got married, and we had a telegram saying, 'Congratulations from all your friends in Wormwood Scrubs.'

Only a few women went to prison. I think it's not generally known that there were women conscientious objectors as well as men during the war. Many of them had been called up into the services. One woman I remember was called out of our office to go into the War Office. She refused, and was called to a tribunal, which gave her a six-month sentence for continuing to say no. I myself received notice that I was due to be redirected, but it just never happened. I think after a time they probably felt it simply wasn't worth the hassle of directing people like me doing that kind of job.

In my job I had to go all over the country, wherever I was invited, and talk to people about why I was a Christian pacifist. I can't remember ever having had a really bad experience with other people because of my own stance. I found that they frequently strongly disagreed with me, but usually took the line that this was something I clearly couldn't help, poor soul, and so they wouldn't be angry about it.

I had one very amusing experience when I went down to Canterbury. The clergyman who was going to speak had been warned that the police were going to be there, and that it might lead to difficulties for him afterwards. At that time his wife was very ill, and he came to me and said, 'Look, this is going to be really difficult, I don't think I have the right to jeopardize her life by getting picked up at this moment.' So I went instead. It was a good meeting, with a couple of hundred people, and I stood up to say my piece, which was simply why I was a Christian pacifist. Just before the meeting started one of the locals came in and whispered to me that he thought I might like to know that the police were there, but not in uniform. I thanked him and got on with what I had to say. Afterwards the chairman called up the small group of policemen, thinking it was better for us to take the initiative. We waited on the platform, and they came up, and the chairman said, 'We just wondered if there was anything you wanted to ask our speaker?' And the police spokesman said, 'No, but we were very interested in what the young woman was saying.' People generally *were* interested, and were rarely really horrid about it.

I was also asked to speak once to a women's cooperative guild in East London, somewhere near Aldgate. I was told by the person who had invited me that I really must keep off the Christian stuff, because these women were not Christians, and it was no good my going on about it. So I had as straight a talk as I could without bringing Christianity in. But when it came to the time for questions, I had to say after a couple, 'Look, this is where I stand, and so the answer is this . . .' I smiled at them and said, 'I have to tell you that my reason for being a pacifist is that I am a Christian, so I can only answer questions if I'm really honest with you.' This went down extremely well: they all nodded, so I wasn't going to hurt anyone's feelings. But right at the end one of the ladies said, 'All I can say is, if more Christians was pacifists, there'd be more people like us who were Christians.'

I can also remember a very big meeting in Liverpool, which was just for men of call-up age, which the local churches had organized; it was felt that the men should at least know what the Christian pacifist position was. They clearly didn't all agree with everything I said, and there were a lot of questions, but they were never antagonistic. The number of public meetings was relatively small; most that I went to were either in churches or private houses, there were house meetings all over the place. I never had any idea what proportion of the audience was pacifist, but I was constantly amazed and thrilled that there was so little antagonism. I think because the organization was called the Fellowship of Reconciliation, normally those of us who were talking publicly or privately would have wanted to reconcile rather than annoy. For me, pacifism is a vocation, and maybe that helps other people not to feel threatened. There were some in the fellowship who were more politically minded, but I think the majority were in it because of their Christian understanding. The Peace Pledge Union had a more aggressive stance, it was more geared to politics, but I don't think I could ever have been a member of that.

I like to think that those who went through the last war as pacifists will have helped any future government to recognize that there has to be a place in a democracy for people who can't accept what the majority feel is right, and that they can't just be thrown in prison.

POEM WRITTEN BY A YOUNG MOTHER IN THE WINTER OF 1941

How far, how far has this war eaten
Into the minds of men?
Not meaning who will be beaten
Or who will win,
But how will the hating stop, the loving begin?
And the wishing to be loved, when will it come again?

How deep, how deep are we drowned in sorrow?
Will the tears ever cease?
Will men stop killing tomorrow
Who kill today?
For years the guns and the aeroplanes have their way
And how will their way turn into the way of peace?

The Office Girl

I never listened to Churchill's speeches, for me they represented the insanity of war. But mostly you didn't argue with people.

Irene Gillon

I was almost seventeen when war broke out. We were picking up a bit financially. Mother was just beginning to relax after years of hardship. Even when my father was working, we still had a job to manage, because he was a seaman and the pay was only so much. I was just beginning to enjoy myself, meeting people, talking, discussing. I was interested politically. And being young I didn't realize how near we were to war. When it broke out the reaction of my friends was, 'This is exciting, this is it, we're really fighting fascism.' My reaction was more selfish. I just thought, 'This is my life finished again. I've had a rotten beginning, I've just seen my family get on their feet, and now this is it.'

My mother had fought in the Cooperative Movement and the Labour Party for peace, so the war was a very bitter pill for her. She had gone through the First World War and brought up three children during all those shortages, when my father was in the Merchant Navy. She lost one child with rickets just after the war, which affected her very badly. She had to struggle to feed us, and she became more and more bitter as time went on.

My father had been blacklisted for trade union activities; he was a member of the Communist Party. He tried to organize a seamen's union, got it going, was sacked on some pretext, and then found out he was blacklisted from one end of the country to the other, not just his local area. So he was out of work, we were on the means test, and unemployment was rife in Liverpool. It didn't pick up until about a year or so before the war, when my father got a job, and things started to improve for us.

I remember when the means test fellow came along I used to shake, and my father used to say, 'You're not coming in' – as soon as he put his foot inside the doorway father was there. Although he had nothing in the house, he wouldn't have him in, it was just the idea of him going round and seeing if there was anything we could sell. But there was absolutely nothing, we had nothing. We were down to if you had jam on your bread you couldn't have margarine, and vice versa. It was as basic as that.

When the means test man put his foot in the door, my mother would run up and down this little hall, jumping up and down and screaming over her shoulder, 'Get rid of the bastard, get rid of him' – and she never usually swore. I used to be quaking. The spectre of the means test man was always there. But they'd already reduced you to the basics, so I suppose my father was in the right, because he wasn't hiding anything. In Liverpool we had a Tory council, and they were very hard on the UAB – the Unemployed Assistance Board. You used to have to go before them to plead your case. It was a matter of principle with my father. You were left with no self-respect anyway. He used to smoke Woodies, and he used to get me to slip out and get five. He had no prestige left, nothing. But one thing he could do was keep this fellow out of the house. I remember my mother having to go in front of the UAB because she had pyorrhoea and needed false teeth. There are lots of memories of this sort of degradation and humiliation.

Because my family were political, I was bound to take in quite a bit of the politics. When I was twelve or thirteen during the Spanish war, people used to come and discuss things at our house. I took it all very seriously. I saw films of ordinary people running against the bombing, and the bombers were very low, you could see that. You didn't have to be very astute to realize they were helpless. I understood that the British government were not getting involved, while Italy and Germany were. It seemed tremendously unfair, I was very passionate about it. My emotions were very highly pitched. I knew one or two of the young chaps who went to Spain, they came to our house. They weren't extreme left-wing, they were unemployed, they were Labour Party men, and I think it was more a sense of adventure than real conviction. They knew Spain was going through it, but I don't think they really understood all the implications. But they went, and one of them was killed. It's quite vivid in my memory, I was the only one in when his girlfriend came to the house to tell us he was killed. That to me was a terrible thing to happen.

So when the war came, all these things influenced me, plus the fact that it was the same government, the same system that had declared war, and I didn't trust them. On top of that, somewhere inside me was this instinctive dislike of indiscriminate slaughter for ideological beliefs. I didn't work it out then, but it was there I think, submerged, a very strong idea. I knew chaps who were volunteering, who said, 'Hitler's gone as far as he can go, and we're going to push him back.' That was a very good, straightforward argument, and it should have convinced me. But I was seventeen, and you don't look at both sides, you only look at your own point of view, and you're self-centred and single-minded enough to say, that's it. I realize now I was far from right. I remember arguing with people who argued against the Communist Party line in Spain, and I thought they were really traitors. I realized later they were correct, but the discussions then were very heated, very emotional.

When war came I did toy with the idea of volunteering for the Land Army, but my mother was in such a state of tension, and I was the only one at home, I decided not to. I went and became a typist in Vernons, who were doing mail order, people's clothes and so on. Once I was trained they put me in the pool. One day I got up to go at half past five, but no one else did. Miss Prince, a big battleship of a woman, sailed down the room and said, 'Where do you think you're going?' So I said, 'I'm going home.' 'You can't go home until all that correspondence is finished.' I said, 'I came to work for *these* hours, and if you want me to work longer you should give me notice of working late' – that was an established thing in my previous job – 'because I've got other arrangements.' 'Oh', she said, 'I'll have to see about that.' And she got her boss along. The other girls were tugging at me, saying, 'Sit down, sit down.' He said, 'What's all this?' So I told him what I had said, and he said, 'Don't you know there's a war on?' And he gave me a week's notice.

That caused quite a to-do. They got a round robin going; apparently they were all fed up, but no one had ever done anything. That week I had to get up at half-five and walk out every night. It was a round robin because they were so scared. I was probably contemptuous of them, because all they had to do was get up and walk out with me, but they all sat there. And yet they expected me to go in and see the general manager with this round robin.

I knew there was quite a lot of intimidation going on, so I said I would. But they still hadn't fixed an interview when the end of the week came, and I told them that as my week's notice had finished, they'd have to sort it out without me. I was cocky enough to think I could just walk out and get another job. No one could get through to me that there was a war on, because I just wasn't interested. Possibly these girls had been got at from the patriotic point of view, and that had paralysed them. But their sympathy was definitely with me.

I left and went to the Co-op, and was soon in trouble there. In the office most of them were right behind Churchill. I never listened to Churchill's speeches, for me they represented the insanity of war. But mostly you didn't argue with people. There was one girl working there, she was of Irish extraction, and naturally rebellious and socialist; her family were rather that way. We used to talk between ourselves, but we were overheard – we didn't make any big secret of it. We were talking about the lack of air support – my brother-in-law's ship had gone down in about half an hour in Crete. We were known not to be very sympathetic, though it was a very difficult position – there were people with husbands, boyfriends and sons. You tended to say nothing, though somehow or other people know, you don't have to spell it out. So we were reported, and my friend was threatened with the police. She told me the next morning, and she said, 'I'm going to see the boss, will you come with me?' I said, 'OK'.

Actually she forced her way in, bringing this Jewish girl with her. She was Zionist, so we had a rather rip-roaring argument, as you can imagine: she used to say that the Jews were persecuted in Russia, and we didn't believe her. She agreed to come along. She wouldn't have had anything to do with you if you were against the Jews. So we managed to get into the manager's office. Anna said, 'If I can't face the people who accuse me, I'm going to call a quarterly meeting.' The boss said, 'You can't', and she said, 'Yes I can, if I get a quorum of twelve.' So he gave up. The girls came in, and they were very sheepish. All they'd said was that we'd been talking about lack of air support, and that was apparently considered to be a crime. So it was all dropped. But the comical thing was, when we came in to work the following morning, they had these old-fashioned screens, and they put them round our desks, so we were isolated for three months. People used to pop their heads over the top – it was really comical. In the end we came in one morning and they'd gone.

I remember once one of the girls asked me, 'Now that there's been that attack on Hitler's life, do you think the war will really come to an end?' She must have been aware that I had my own point of view. All she was really saying was, 'I'm bloody fed up', but it was unpatriotic to say anything like that. I gave an answer which tried to point out the difficulties, to give another view, and I think at times people were looking for this, for the war dragged on much longer than they thought it would. Despite the fact that they were trying to be happy about it, it did get very dreary.

When the threat of invasion came, it seemed inevitable. I was very pessimistic, I just thought, 'It's quite possible that me and my family will just be cut off, or shot.' There was a lot of panic on then, people were panicking mentally. They were all going to work, doing their bit, but underneath you sensed there was a panic. If I had said anything a bit over the top, I'm sure I'd have had my eyes scratched out. The only reason I didn't panic was because I thought of it on such a huge scale. Why should we think ourselves so different? France had been invaded, Spain's democratically elected government had been smashed, Abyssinia had been smashed, what was so different about Britain? Being young, you tend to get this heroic outlook on it, and you can then detach yourself and say, 'So what?'

I was mixing with girls who lived a very sheltered existence, who had very easy soft jobs in the Co-op, and who were on the whole Tory or very establishment. Their lives had not really been disrupted in any way. Those few that did go into the forces went into the WRENs and were in the Liver Buildings, or went into the Army, and were mainly clerks. So they didn't change their lifestyle. They used to come into the office and chatter, but I never talked to them, because I found the uniform repulsive. Again that was emotional, but I always felt they glamourized their positions; really they were just clerks with uniforms, that was all.

I can't remember much community spirit, I didn't come into contact with that. We lived in West Derby Road at the beginning of the war. When the raids started we used to go to St George's Hall. But then it got so crowded and smelly, so we used to go in the cellar during the raids. But you used to get a bit blasé after a bit: I went to the pictures when the raids were on. After a bit it was just a question of getting through the war, and trying to better the rationing system if you could.

Rationing wasn't easy. There was always a black market in coupons if you had the money. My sister worked in an office in Liverpool, and she said there were comings and goings, eggs and so on, but the police ignored it, it was too small-scale and widespread, and to be expected really. Women who were at home had all the queuing, travelling around trying to get to shops that did stock the food you wanted. My mother used to queue, but she wasn't strong, and I think the war wore her out completely. She used to worry about my two brothers. She had wanted them to be conscientious objectors on political grounds, but they weren't motivated that way. The one in the Merchant Navy had a bad accident on a ship. In those days if anything happened, all that you knew was that your money was stopped. You went to the office, and all they could say was, 'Your money's been stopped.' So that left you in a very anxious state, and you'd only gradually hear what it was.

It isn't the sweeping headlines I remember, or the heroics. It's the little heartbreaks, the trivial things of our daily lives. I know many people showed great courage and made sacrifices, but I didn't. For me it was just a time of standing still.

Extract from a letter to a twelve-year-old Wiltshire girl from her mother, 9 May 1945

Last Saturday six of the German prisoners came. They were very interesting, and had six different occupations in civilian life. One was in his father's factory, which made household aluminium goods; Two was going to university when war broke out, and had to go into the Army; Three was a painter; Four was a clerk in the big chemical works; Five was a clerk but wanting to do electrical engineering in the future; and Six was a professional pianist. He played to us for a bit, and was thrilled to have a good piano and good atmosphere. The others said he wouldn't play much in camp because they had three terrible pianos and the atmosphere wasn't right. They all enjoyed themselves, and Klaus, the university one, wrote me a charming letter on behalf of them all. We hope in a very small way we may help towards a better understanding of the two countries.

An art student's recollection of VE Day in London, written after the war

On VE Day there was a mood of manic excitement in London. It was a beautifully hot day. Locally a vast bonfire had been prepared, and there was to be dancing and singing in the evening. Ann, a friend, was staying with us, and she and my mother Lucille were very busy preparing to go, dressed from head to toe in red and white.

I felt very flat. I certainly felt relief that the war was over, relief that I was still alive, relief that I wouldn't live each day in dread and fear. But also unbelief that it was all over. It just didn't seem real, and I certainly didn't feel like dressing up and dancing. I felt completely cut off, and obviously irritated my mother and Ann.

Ken, my boyfriend from art school, came round. He was a mildly cocky boy, blond, thick-set, and fond of slinky jersey shirts undone to display his hairy chest. He wasn't very talented, but he was kindly. He proposed that he and I should go to central London to see what was going on. So after tea we left the family to their suburban junketing and headed for Trafalgar Square. We headed for the National Gallery like the good little art students we were. The Nat Gal was home; 'Meet you at the Nat Gal at the top of the stairs' was one's usual arrangement. So up to the top of the steps we went, to watch the cavortings. Not to take part; we were the cool observers of idiotic mankind.

There were crowds of people charging about, singing, shouting and dancing in their own little circles. A vast, snake-like procession was coming down Charing Cross Road, young girls and American soldiers, and among them, carried shoulder high, a naked man crowned with silver leaves waving a chamber pot. It was all very happy, very noisy and no violence.

Ken and I moved down to sit on the little grassy plot below the parapet. Neat and polite we sat, holding hands and comparing light and shade. Next to us was a couple, copulating. I was fascinated that for the occasion they had both taken off their shoes, and *only* their shoes, and placed them neatly side by side on the grass, just as though they were in a hotel, and had put their shoes out for polishing. Copulation was certainly the order of the day – or night – but not for Ken or me. Oh no, we were serious art students, observers of the scene, and anyhow we hadn't got further than kissing, and I didn't really fancy that very much.

After midnight we decided to walk home. There was no transport. It was the best part of the day. All through north London we walked, via Euston and Camden Town and Hampstead, and in the little side roads there were parties, the houses and streets were hung with bunting, and tables and chairs were out in the road, large fat mums were kicking up their heels, while dirty children were dropping off to sleep among the remains of celebratory meals. We stopped at one or two places and had a drink and a chat, and then walked on. It was a lovely warm night and we were now happy and peaceful.

A Brave New World?

I was working as a hospital porter when the results of the general election came through. We had a sense of revolution, of something going right down to the roots.

LONDON MAN

The only thing that really changed was that instead of saying, 'Don't you know there's a war on?' you said, 'Don't you know there's a peace on?'

HAMPSHIRE WOMAN

We thought for a while that the war had altered class structures. But it soon righted itself, did capitalism. The boss was going to be the boss, and the other bloke the underling.

LANCASHIRE MAN

I think the war made women much more equal to men, but people still went back to square one when it was over.

DEVON WOMAN

War is the greatest abomination, but at the end of it the reaction is so great that out of it can come great progress.

LONDON MAN

The war showed people that anybody can get anything if they try hard enough, and that class is really nothing more than an accident.

LONDON WOMAN

As soon as the war ended party politics returned to something like normality. In July 1945 a general election was held. The main issue was undoubtedly postwar reconstruction, a topic that had been occupying many people's minds for the previous two or three years.

The war had exposed many ugly inequalities to view. To those without money or power, these conditions were part of their lives; to others more privileged, they came as a revelation. Increasingly, the public mood was one of support for fundamental change. To some extent this was already under way in certain spheres. The Beveridge Report on welfare, for example, had been published as far back as December 1942. Despite the attempts of certain Conservative members of the government, it had received considerable publicity, and attracted widespread support, even acclaim. In similar fashion, proposals for a radical restructuring of the education system had gained all-party backing, and had resulted in a major piece of legislation, the 1944 Education Act. Work had also been done on future possibilities for housing, land, transport, the countryside and other issues.

Since both parties were committed to social reform, the election campaign was in part as much about style and past record as about the rival manifestos. Though the opinion polls, then in their infancy, predicted a Labour victory, the press and the political establishment assumed that the people would want Churchill to, in the words of one of his election posters, 'finish the job'. But the job now was very different from the one that needed to be done in wartime. The widespread desire for change also worked against Churchill, as did his campaign warning that if Labour tried to implement their socialist programme 'they would have to fall back on some form of Gestapo'. On the contrary, Labour's modest nationalization programme echoed a majority view among the electorate at the time. Churchill had misjudged the popular mood. The result gave Labour a huge parliamentary majority, with 393 seats compared to the Conservative total of 213, the other 31 seats being distributed between the Liberals, the Independent Labour Party, the Communists and a few Independents. Clement Attlee was now in charge of the first Labour government to have a clear majority over all other parties, and to many the result seemed to herald a new socialist dawn.

In fact, for many ordinary men and women, life in the immediate postwar period seemed little better than it had been during the war years. Rationing continued, in the case of some commodities for many years, and the climate remained one of austerity. The freezing winter of 1946/7 produced much hardship, coal shortages, power cuts and unemployment to the tune of 800,000. Housing plans did not work out as hoped for, and many of the areas of the cities worst affected by the bombs remained desolate and unreconstructed for several years.

Yet there were important differences from the immediate pre-war years, some a direct result of the war. The Beveridge proposals eventually led in July 1948 to the introduction of the National Health Service. The emergency hospital service set up at the beginning of the war had shown the pre-war system to be antiquated, inefficient and discriminatory against the poor. The family doctor service was equally deficient. In contrast, the NHS aimed to give everyone the opportunity to benefit from the best medical service available, and to make personal income irrelevant by providing both hospital and doctor services free of charge. The National Insurance scheme of 1946 similarly provided proper coverage for millions who had not been able to afford it before.

The changes to the education system brought about by the 1944 Education Act were equally fundamental. Under the old system, most children had to go to the second-class, overcrowded elementary schools, while only an élite minority received a full secondary education at the grammar schools, which in any case were a matter for the discretion of the local authority. The new act compelled the authority to provide secondary education for all, in grammar, technical or modern schools. Children were selected for the appropriate school on the basis of their performance in the new eleven-plus examination. Few people perceived at the time the divisive nature of this system.

For women, the onset of peace brought many difficulties apart from those brought on by the continuing austerity. Many who had enjoyed the independence of working outside the home now found their jobs at an end, or taken back by men returning from the services. There was pressure for women to return to their traditional home-making role, and this was reinforced by the closure of many of the crèches, day nurseries and nursery schools specially set up in wartime. For some the new situation meant a welcome return to family life, for others it was a very regrettable restriction of opportunity. Yet during the war women had clearly demonstrated that they could tackle a wide range of jobs, many of them physically demanding, which had previously been thought beyond their capabilities. They had also disproved the pre-war notion that married women were not suited to certain jobs.

As for social class, the vision of a permanent erosion of differences quickly proved an illusion. The working class certainly benefited from the major postwar reforms. In the emergency climate of wartime people had undoubtedly been prepared to downgrade the differences in income, attitude and behaviour of the classes. But once the threat of defeat receded, most people went back to the old ways of living. Not even six years of war could undermine a structure as powerful as the British class system.

Further Reading

GENERAL

Blythe, Ronald (ed.), *Components of the Scene: An Anthology of the Prose and Poetry of the Second World War* (Penguin, 1966). A view of the war and the individual's place in it, as seen by some of the major poets, novelists, short-story writers and essayists.

Briggs, Susan, *Keep Smiling Through: The Home Front 1939–1945* (Weidenfeld & Nicolson, 1975, Fontana, 1976). A lively and original description of home-front life, which skilfully uses popular song themes of the period to explore moods and behaviour.

Brown, Mike and Harris, Carol, *The Wartime House: Home Life in Wartime Britain 1939–1945* (Sutton, 2001). A wonderfully detailed, heavily illustrated portrait of the middle-class suburban home in wartime.

Calder, Angus, *The People's War: Britain 1939–1945* (Cape, 1969, Granada, 1971). The classic social history on the war: comprehensive, challenging, scholarly, an immensely readable and radical critique of many received views about the changes brought about by the war.

Calder, Angus and Sheridan, Dorothy, *Speak for Yourself: A Mass Observation Anthology 1937–1949* (Cape, 1984). An absorbing selection of material from the invaluable Mass Observation surveys of the time, with first-hand accounts of women's lives, the Blitz, and some key wartime political events.

Costello, John, *Love, Sex and War: Changing Values 1939–1945* (Collins, 1985, Pan, 1986). A thoroughly researched and entertaining account of changing sexual attitudes and behaviour on both sides of the Atlantic caused by the upheavals of war.

Fitzgibbon, Constantine, *The Blitz* (Macdonald, 1957). One of the first postwar books to use eye-witness accounts of the Blitz. A skilful weaving together of conventional documents and the experiences of individual Londoners, complemented by some of Henry Moore's famous sketches of men and women under fire.

Gillman, Peter and Leni, *Collar the Lot! How Britain Interned and Expelled its Wartime Refugees* (Quartet, 1980). An absorbing and very revealing narrative of one of the more shameful episodes of the war, from which few politicians emerge with their reputations untarnished.

Harrison, Tom, *Living through the Blitz* (Collins, 1976, Penguin, 1978). A brilliant, provocative and myth-breaking book, written by one of the founders and the wartime director of Mass Observation. Makes extensive use of diaries and reports compiled by MO's observers at the time.

Hayes, Denis, *The Challenge of Conscience: The CO's Story 1939–1949* (Allen & Unwin, 1949). For many years the standard work on the position of conscientious objectors in the war, with a useful foreword by one of the central characters, Fenner Brockway.

Hewison, Robert, *Under Siege: Literary Life in London 1939–1945* (Weidenfeld & Nicolson, 1978). An analysis of the impact of the war on cultural life in the capital, which examines the way writers, poets and artists adapted to the changing circumstances.

Hopkinson, Tom (ed.), *Picture Post 1938–1950* (Allen Lane, Penguin Press/Penguin, 1970). A selection from the pioneering magazine of hard-hitting photo-journalism, which includes many of the celebrated political and social features of the war period.

Hurd, Geoff (ed.), *National Fictions: World War Two in British Films and Television* (BFI Books, 1984). A provocative collection of essays which looks at how our current view of the war has been shaped by film and television images.

Jackson, Carlton, *Who Will Take Our Children? The Story of the Evacuation of Britain* (Methuen, 1985). A useful and wide-ranging look at the problems thrown up by the evacuation, providing many new details on a well-known feature of the war.

Journeys into the Past: Life on the Home Front (Reader's Digest, 1996). An impressively comprehensive collection of wartime illustrations and photographs.

Kee, Robert and Smith, Joanna, *We'll Meet Again: Photographs of Daily Life in Britain during World War Two* (Dent, 1984). A marvellous collection of photographs, many of them now classics of the period, drawn from the John Topham Picture Library and the archive of Planet News/UPI.

Kendall, Alan, *Their Finest Hour: An Evocative Memoir of the British People in Wartime 1939–1945* (Wayland, 1972). A general account of the wartime life of ordinary people, with an interesting selection of photographs.

Lewis, Peter, *A People's War* (Channel Four/Methuen, 1986). A detailed and balanced picture of wartime life viewed from the bottom up, and based on the excellent Channel Four series of the same name (which itself drew on Angus Calder's seminal book).

Longmate, Norman, *How We Lived Then* (Hutchinson, 1971). A fascinating and exhaustive survey of daily life in wartime, based on a vast number of written recollections submitted to the author from all over the country.

Marwick, Arthur, *The Home Front; The British and the Second World War* (Thames & Hudson, 1976). A book that used contemporary photographs, many of them censored at the time, to explore the reality of people's dislocated lives. Balanced, authoritative, visually striking.

Minns, Raynes, *Bombers and Mash: The Domestic Front 1939–1945* (Virago, 1980). A well-researched and wonderfully detailed account of how women coped with the sundry deprivations of wartime life. Includes many offbeat illustrations, little-known facts, as well as recipes of the time.

Moorhead, Caroline, *Troublesome People: Enemies of War 1916–1986* (Hamish Hamilton, 1987). A book which contains substantial new material on the experience of conscientious objectors during two world wars, and attitudes towards them. Based on interviews with many survivors.

Mosley, Leonard, *Backs to the Wall: London under Fire 1940–1945* (Weidenfeld & Nicolson, 1971, reprinted as *London under Fire*, Pan, 1974). A kaleidoscopic picture of wartime London, which draws on a wide range of experiences of both national figures and ordinary citizens, and puts them into a narrative form.

Panter-Downes, Mollie, *London War Notes 1939–1945* (Farrar, Straus & Giroux, 1971). An affectionate view of life in London during the war, full of immediacy and interesting perceptions, and based on the dispatches the author filed every fortnight to the *New Yorker*.

Taylor, A.J.P., *English History 1914–1945* (OUP, 1965, Penguin, 1970). This masterly synthesis of the period contains four substantial chapters which offer a characteristically individualistic view of wartime politics, and an examination of the way politicians' behaviour affected the lives of the civilian population.

Thomas, Donald, *An Underworld at War: Spivs, Deserters, Racketeers and Civilians in the Second World War* (John Murray, 2003). A startling, original, brilliantly researched account of the criminal underbelly that flourished during the war years.

AUTOBIOGRAPHY

Beardmore, George, *Civilians at War: Journals 1938–1946* (John Murray, 1984, OUP, 1986). A vivid account by a lively and engaging young clerk of what life was like for ordinary Londoners, based on his own spirited diaries.

Blishen, Edward, *A Cack-Handed War* (Thames & Hudson, 1972, Hamish Hamilton, 1983). A marvellously poetic, moving and also funny description of the life of a conscientious objector working on the land, and the people he encountered there.

Brittain, Vera, *England's House: An Autobiography 1939–1941* (Macmillan, 1941, Futura, 1981). A collection of snapshots of the first two years of the war, seen through the eyes of a leading and idealistic pacifist, who was able to move around the country and observe how people were coping in these crisis months.

Broad, Richard and Fleming, Suzie (eds), *Nella Last's War: A Mother's Diary 1939–1945* (Falling Wall Press, 1981). The edited diary of one of Mass Observation's volunteer observers, this intimate description of private and public life in Barrow-in-Furness wonderfully catches the trials of everyday working-class existence, and the difficulty of sustaining personal relationships.

Church-Bliss, Kathleen and Whiteman, Edith, *Working for Victory: A Diary of Life in a Second World War Factory* (Sutton, 2002). A revealing account of the harsh realities of life in a factory, written by two Surrey women who had previously enjoyed a comfortable life.

Donnelly, Peter (ed.), *Mrs Milburn's Diaries: An Englishwoman's Day-to-Day Reflections 1939–1945* (Harrap, 1979, Fontana, 1980). An authentic and delightful view from 'Middle England' of the progress of the war, based on the diary of a middle-class woman living near Coventry, and concerned both with small domestic matters and the wider political and military issues.

Dunn, Kate (ed.), *Always and Always: Wartime Letters of Hugh and Margaret Williams* (John Murray, 1995). A touching correspondence between two people in love and separated by war, the actor Hugh Williams and his actress wife Margaret Vyner.

Hannam, Charles, *Almost an Englishman* (André Deutsch, 1979). A fascinating account of how one adolescent Jewish refugee tried to find acceptance in wartime England. Idiosyncratic, outspoken and humorous.

Mayhew, Patrick (ed.), *One Family's War* (Hutchinson, 1985, Futura, 1987). A strikingly original book which draws on the various experiences of the scattered Mayhew family, both in Britain and abroad, as reported in the letters they regularly sent home to Norfolk.

ORAL HISTORY

Grafton, Pete, *You, You and You!: The People Out of Step with World War Two* (Pluto Press, 1981). An anthology of reminiscences based on taped interviews with both civilians and members of the armed forces who were critical of certain aspects of the war. Absorbing material, slightly marred by poor organization and the anonymity of the interviewees.

Lummis, Trevor, *Listening to History* (Hutchinson Education, 1987). A valuable up-to-date survey of the theoretical and practical issues involved in the use of oral evidence, especially that of authenticity. Useful for practising historians of all kinds.

Terkel, Studs, *'The Good War': An Oral History of World War Two* (Hamish Hamilton, 1985, Penguin, 1986). America's most celebrated oral historian includes a small number of British subjects among his sample of 120 interviewees drawn from many countries.

Thompson, Paul, *The Voice of the Past: Oral History* (OUP, 1978; 2nd edn 1988). The standard work for anyone interested in the subject. It looks at the historical development of oral history, at its radical aims and potential, and at how it can best be used in conjunction with traditional sources. Essential and stimulating reading.

Westall, Robert, *Children of the Blitz* (Penguin, 1986). An original and diverting collection of children's reminiscences of wartime life, assembled by a children's book writer whose own boyhood coincided with the war. Excellently illustrated.

LOCAL HISTORY

In recent years there has been an explosion in local or community publishing, much of it dealing with the history of a locality or one or more individuals within it. Many of the books and pamphlets that have resulted from the setting up of community presses, reminiscence projects and similar ventures have made use of oral evidence to explore ordinary people's experiences of the Second World War. The publications are too numerous to list here, but many of them are stocked by local libraries, local history archives or the projects that initiated them.